EARTH SPELL

The Loss of Consciousness on Earth

For permissions contact:

Four Winds Publications
1000 Cordova Place Suite 112
Santa Fe, New Mexico 87505

Dedicated to
God

The Father of
Loving Light

EARTH SPELL

The Loss of
Consciousness on Earth

Received by Ceanne DeRohan

FOUR WINDS PUBLICATIONS

Table of Contents

		Page
Introduction		ii
1	The Reflection Lost Will Has to Give	1
2	The Early Days With the Angels	31
3	Deflecting the Focus by Pinning Blame	52
4	More Light Is Not Necessarily Better	57
5	I Allowed Myself to See That the Gap Had Taken In Many Things I Had Not Noticed	60
6	The Fallen Angels	63
7	Reality Is There Is Little Time Left	75
8	Original Cause	82
9	Lucifer	91
10	The Unseen Role of Denial	96
11	Understandings Needed About Going to Earth	109
12	The Ronalokas' Journey to Earth	129
13	In All of the Time on Earth, No Progress Has Been Made	145
14	The Will Fears Its Own Desire	167
15	Opening Space	176
16	The Will Manifests the Gap	179
17	The Ronalokas Had Already Gapped Before They Left Me	186
18	You Have Gaps to Heal With One Another	195
19	Body Will Let You Know How You Need to Move	199
20	I Withdraw	200
21	Heart Tries to Warn Me That He Cannot Stay Manifest	204
22	The Mother Tears My Heart Apart	208
23	Another Look At The Angels	217
24	Giving The Angels What They Need	224

Introduction

I have to say that I am most pleased with the movement I see happening now, even though I know that most people view that as a macabre statement on My part since they do not understand what I mean. I have intent to heal Earth now, but Earth is not going to heal without going through the upheavals involved in moving guilt out of Her magnetic energy field.

Guilt is not in its right place on Earth anymore, and yet, the barest recognition of this brings up feelings of guilt in all of those who have not yet understood why they have guilt, what their guilt is, or what is involved in moving guilt back. It is movement in your terror that you are feeling; your terror that you must make a place for guilt, or you are not loving. Some things that have been on Earth for a long time, even from the very beginning, must go now. The guilt in this area says, among other things, that it is unloving to take this position, and therefore, the ones who take this position are the ones who deserve to go.

Try thinking of it in this way: I am a great ball of Light. My Light streams forth in all directions and flows into any space that is open to receive it. Within My Light, there are many places that are not open to receive My Light. If these places were free, they would move out to the edge of My Light like so many bubbles rising in water until they pop into the atmosphere. Guilt would not mind moving away from Me until it could float peacefully where there is no more pressure from My Light moving it back. Guilt has not been able to move back freely like this because it became entangled in the magnetic energy field. Guilt has not gained consciousness because it is not seeking to do so. It was not known what guilt was in the beginning. The experience of feeling guilt was necessary in order to know that it is not love.

Now that the Mother knows She cannot live in the presence of guilt, She is moving to expose guilt for what it really is, because guilt must be clearly seen in order to move it back without sending along lost Will that does not want to go with the guilt. As guilt moves back, My Light will be able to expand into places that have not received My Light before. This process involves considerable upheaval, but it is necessary because Love and guilt cannot coexist in the same place for reasons of vibrational differences.

The Will has had the belief that unconditional acceptance in love meant making a place for everything. The Will has had the pain of trying to vibrate in the presence of guilt that does not move in response to the Will's vibration. The guilt in Will has caused Will to feel that She could not allow Herself to move in the ways She needed to move. Because guilt was in the way, the Will was not able to receive Me to understand that it is not possible to be loving toward guilt.

When the Will was unable to find acceptance within Herself for guilt, the Will felt inadequate, unloving, and unlovable. All Will knew to do to try to be loving was to pressure Herself to stop vibrating and give the space to guilt. When the Will did this, guilt never noticed. It just filled the space the Will gave it and the Will continued to feel pressured to back down even more. Most of the Will has backed down all the way into the Survival Chakra and has been held there. The Will has been feeling so overwhelmed by guilt that even when She realized She was going to die, the Will thought I required this sacrifice. Rage fragmented out of the Mother all the way along here and gave the appearance of a masculine polarization.

Misunderstanding has taken the Will into death, near death, and nearly irreversible pain while I struggled with My own feelings of inadequacy about being unable to reach the Will. By the use of the word death here, I do not mean the lifting of living essence out of the parts of the self that have lost their ability to vibrate; I mean the experience of those parts of the self that have lost their ability to vibrate in any way that allows them to live.

I have come to give these teachings now because I have finally understood how to reach those parts of the Will I have not been able to reach before. Making contact with the Will here was a most important first step and one that was not easy, given the presence of guilt. The movement you are seeing on Earth now is the movement necessary to move these dead and almost dead parts of the Will out of the guilt that led them there.

The situation is very perilous for the Will because It is so weakened It cannot afford to move very slowly. What needs to move in the Will now are the most desperate of emotions that have never been given acceptance on Earth before. These are the feelings of Hell that have only been given in to in the most denied realities on Earth. Many times, in the process of moving these emotions, the Will is going to feel that It is too exhausted to go on, and yet, movement of more emotion will often give the Will additional strength, strange as this may seem.

I want to introduce you now to some feelings you have not known before, no matter what your impressions are of heaven or the Godhead. These feelings are feelings of joy that do not have to deny anything in order to be joyful, feelings of joy that have no undercurrent feelings of being only an intermission in an ongoing war, and joy that need not be held back because of what tomorrow may bring. To have these feelings, you must be free of all denials. The more you have limited the expression of some emotions, the more the capacity to experience and express all of the other emotions is also affected.

I want to point out again that denials are not something you identify as though they are poisons in your system that can be eliminated or neutralized through the use of the proper antidotes. Denials cannot be solved by manipulating your Will until you have a false Will that allows you to pretend you are not involved in the perils around you, and denial cannot be treated like a foreign presence to be removed.

Denial is every place you are not fully conscious. If you have denial, you have guilt because you are not allowing your true vibration. If you have no guilt, you are no longer bound by the physical plane. You can leave it without dying first and without leaving your body behind. Instead, you can step up the vibration of your physical body to the speed of light.

Besides having denials where you are not fully conscious, you have denials you are not conscious of at all yet. How separated from the Light denials have been, is what makes the difference in how they appear when they first begin to move. Mild denials are such things as the little lies you tell your friends and family in the name of not hurting their feelings. These have the grayness of guilt you are learning to recognize now, but these denials are not the ones lost Will needs to move now.

The deepest and darkest denials are the gapped terror it is necessary to address in this book. You are going to need some instructions on how to heal this gapped rage and terror because it has never been done before, no matter what anyone else tells you about it. The Mother's deepest knowing says that if it had ever been healed before, things would not be as they are now. Identifying the gap and learning how to avoid triggering it is the best anyone has done with it so far. Even those who have allowed the gap to fight have not allowed it to finish.

To try to rid yourself of denials by vibrating them out is to lose yourself more than you are lost already, and to lose what power you have left to heal the gap. To insist that you no longer have denials now that you have noticed them is to make the same mistake I made in the beginning. Intent to heal must understand the teachings I am giving now, unless you want to find yourselves seemingly, inexplicably swept away with guilt you did not know you had, but which must, nonetheless, move back now. If this brings up emotion in you, it is a necessary part of your process. If you do not feel anything, you have more reason to fear you cannot heal than if you are feeling more enraged or more terrified than you ever thought it was possible to feel. Rather than go past it, put the book down and move any emotion you can, no matter how slight. Don't read past it.

This gap is nothing to fool around with. Most people who have preached discipline and control of emotions have done so because of their awareness of the gaps involved in the emotional body and the realization that any free expression of emotion sooner or later leads to the gap. Since judgment has been held against the Will for so long, which has prevented healing here, it has long been thought that the Will is just gapped and nothing can be done about it. The Will fears this about Itself.

If you have a feeling it is not going to be hard to heal this gap, you are not getting the understandings you need from these books, and you need to move back from the gap you are seeing and not toward it. If you misfire your healing here, you will not have another opportunity to try it again because you will be dead, and I do not mean dead until you reincarnate, I mean dead. The reason I am sounding so heavy-handed here is because, literally, whether you have a nuclear holocaust on Earth or not depends on how the gap is handled. I would tell you that not moving the gap is preferable to wrong movement, except that lack of movement here is no longer an option if life is what you seek.

Your starting place is feeling the presence of the gap and moving terror of the gap. Your terror may express first as denial of what I am saying or as rage, but you must move with it until you feel that it is really terror, and then you must move into the terror. Once you feel the lack of love and compassion the gap has for itself and everything else, it won't be hard to feel the emotions you need to move.

If you do not understand what I am saying here and why I am saying it, you do not understand how the essence takes form in manifestation. I am not being unloving here. More Light must come into the Earth now, and the vibration in the gap must be allowed to rise until it crosses the gap and can receive My Light and know It for what It is. If you manipulate this gap with visualization of how it is supposed to move, or by other means, it is highly likely you will not live to be healed.

The gap has been in place since the beginning of Creation, and to heal it, you must go back into the place and time of its forming. There is no other road open to you but to allow movement in emotions you have held back for so long that making contact with them is going to be most of the work. If you do not do this, guilt will have the power to take you into the death you have for so long, in your confusion, thought was leading to life everlasting. The death you will have here is the loss of any consciousness to know whether you are dead or alive.

You all have places in you that already feel they want this because they believe they have no power to have life on their own terms. Some of you claim that you want this unconsciousness, but all of you have a real choice to make now, and I prefer you make it as consciously as you can. If you have the feeling you do not want life, you need to know whether you are making this claim to avoid what is involved in really healing yourself, or whether this is what you really want. If you make the choice to go unconscious, you are not going to be allowed to take any essence with you that is not aligned with this choice, but is being held back by you from the movement it needs to escape this fate. In other words, you are going to face, on the way to your death, whatever you need to face to allow movement in whatever essence needs to move to escape from you.

If the Mother has to vibrate this Will essence for you, you will not have it anymore, because the Mother is going to take back any Will essence you have that is not aligned with your choice, and without it, you are going to find that you cannot reverse this unconsciousness you are going into, even if you should decide later that you really don't want this unconsciousness after all.

The Mother is desperate to reach you already. If you deny Her beyond Her capacity and willingness to endure the suffering your denial is giving your Will, it will no longer be your Will. The Mother will take It in and leave you outside of Me as lost Light; and lost Light is what, by your own choices, you will have defined yourselves to be. I am going to be with the Mother unconditionally now, and lack of receptivity to the Mother can no longer be allowed to live within My Light.

Most of you who are trying to be good do not think you have guilt. You think you are only trying to be loving, and you want to put yourselves above My words here. I want to tell you: You are so guilt-ridden, you have lost the consciousness with which you notice it.

Guilt is not more powerful than My Light, but it is in the power position on Earth right now because My Light is not present where guilt is. In order for My Light to become more present, guilt has to move back. In order for guilt to move back, you have to see what it is. Then you must understand the feelings you have around the issue of what is love and what is not love. In order to do this, the magnetic energy field must be allowed to move freely.

A very important understanding to get now is that the gapped Will fears emotional movement enough to resist healing, even though conscious intent is to heal now. The Will knows intuitively that gapped rage and terror must heal or there will be no real healing at all, but still, the Will is afraid to go near these areas. The Will is able to intuit the presence of the gapped emotions, even if It cannot bring this recognition into the conscious mind or articulate this reality without help. The Will is living in fear that the gap will kill what remains of It as it has already killed the rest of the Will. Thus, much of the Will fears that movement will not bring healing, only more pain.

So overpoweringly intimidating is the presence of the gap that only those who have denied their Wills heavily have been daring enough to confront it, and the gap has been killing them just as surely as if they had never struggled to become free of it. As long as the gap is there, it rules by intimidation, making open expression of its presence often unnecessary. There is no such thing as Freewill in the presence of the gap.

Often, the only sign of the Will's sensing of the gap is a subtle deflection of the direction thoughts or emotions are taking. So overpoweringly intimidating is the grip of the gap that any slight motion in the direction of the gap is usually halted by the Will in a manner It hopes will escape notice, because the Will believes Its survival is based on the avoidance of the gap. The Will believes that if It is even noticed noticing the gap, the gap will get It. This is because I would not, for so long, admit that I had this gap or allow it to be noticed in any way that might suggest there was any problem with it.

Guilt is in the gap, but it is even worse than guilt because it is hatred that guilt has created by holding back emotion until it has become so compressed and gapped from the reality where it split off that it has almost no light left in it and is not living in present time. Many think that if they hold back these emotions a little longer, what is in the gap will die, and there will be no more problems.

These gapped emotions will die if they are held back much longer, and they are so desperate for their own survival that they feel ready to kill anything that even looks like a threat to their survival. Not only is it not loving to kill the gapped emotions in this way, but the gap has claimed so much of the Will already that it now has the power to take everything else with it if it goes.

vii

The darkness in this gap is what has been called evil, so do not diminish the import of My words here by thinking you are going to heal this gap with a few release sessions. The gap can be healed, but only if you really move the emotions you need to move along the way to meeting the gap within yourself. The experience of moving emotion and feeling the healing it brings will give you the understanding, confidence, and personal power necessary to heal the gap, instead of giving up when you meet it.

The gap I am talking about here is sometimes touched between men and women in domestic violence. When a lonely person gaps, he or she often goes and harms or kills that which represents a threat to his or her survival. There are many forms taken on by the lost Will here, so many forms that you will think you cannot understand them, but basically, the various parts of the self have been harming and murdering one another according to who is blaming whom for what. The many images involved are all reflections of the judgment patterns involved.

It is possible to move into the gap without understanding it, but it is not possible to heal the gap this way. It also is not possible to have all of the understandings in advance of the experience of meeting these gapped emotions. Unfortunately, I cannot give you a road map here because it is impossible to tell you just how your own gap is going to move without having a retarding effect on your ability to allow it movement.

The most important thing is to become as real as possible with yourself and others by allowing as much of your true feelings as possible to be expressed each day. Then, when you get to the gap, you will know you are there and that you are as prepared as possible. If you have another person near you who is also involved in this healing process, it can be most helpful. Such a person may be able to see your gap before you do. You may also not be able to trust another person here; you will have to go on your own intuition.

If a person near you is hurling blaming rage at you and is not moving emotion in response to you, or is pressuring you to move emotion you do not feel is yours to move, you can know the gap is there, either in you, or in the other person, or both of you. It is very possible to go into the gap if you allow your true responses here, and you must decide whether it is the right time to allow it or not. If not, remove yourself from the situation as fast as possible and express what you can allow in a place that feels safe to you.

Even though you may know this in advance of the situation, it is not possible to talk to your gap in advance. It also may not be possible to recognize your own gap until you move into it, and when you move into it, you may not be conscious of what you have done, even when it passes. This is why I must caution you not to try to trigger one another's gap until you get the rest of your Will moving as much as possible. I also know that many of you are going to trigger the gap without consciously realizing you are going to do it. If you can't help it, then it is not wrong.

The gap is not aware that it is going to heal. The gap is not aware of anything, even when it moves, other than the ancient imprints it received so long ago. Nonetheless, when it moves is the only time you have to get consciousness into the gap. At first, you may only be able to become aware that you are in the gap, but this is enough to establish a link between yourself and your gap.

Little by little, as you move the gap, you will be able to bring more consciousness into it. When you get to the gap, you must proceed as slowly as necessary, but as quickly as possible. The gap will become aware of its own healing as it is happening.

After each movement in the gap, you are going to have feelings of guilt about the emotional expressions that have surfaced there. After you have moved into the gap, you will also need to move in the fear of the gap's unlovingness because this fear has kept the guilt in place all of this time.

You have violence in the gap, and you can minimize or channel the violence there by giving fear as much direct expression as possible. In My opinion, it is better to go into direct expression of fear than to go into avoidance here. The gap is going to frighten you, and if you go past the fear, the gap is going to have a chance to get you. However, you are going to have to learn to go into direct expression here; the gap only knows acting out of emotion and is imprinted with overriding fear and taking action against the threat.

The most important thing to give is your real response to the gap, no matter how risky it might seem, rather than a fake response. Love is not going to move into the gap right away because the gap is too far away from love as it is. The gap is not ready to give or receive love, and you cannot love the gap right away, either, because the gap cannot be loved as it is.

If hatred is your first response to the gap, it is not wrong, but do your best to move back from the gapping person while you are expressing this hatred, rather than attacking the gap with it. If you do attack the gap and get hurt, it is necessary for you to take responsibility for your part in it. You are going to have a hard time getting the gapped person to take any responsibility for what has happened because he or she, is going to insist it is all your fault because you made the gap feel threatened or provoked. This is what is imprinted in the gap. You will have to move through hatred and blame to see the role you have played here, and so will the gapped person. Aggressing toward the gap is, in part, expressing your own gapped rage, in part, self-defense, in part, the intensity of insistence that the gap expand its consciousness beyond what it already holds, but it is, in part, your own gap from the fear involved.

When aggression toward the gap indicates movement of gapped rage in avoidance of the gapped terror you also hold, you are moving in accordance with the ancient imprints that avoided the terror. It is not a matter of trying to go into terror you do not feel. It is a matter of opening the space within yourself to notice and allow the terror that has been denied.

The gapped rage you want to attack also needs to move into its terror, but it is not possible to move into this terror until enough rage has moved to allow it. People who have moved into the gap without being able to understand it have gotten caught in the rage and blame, self-hatred, and guilt, whether they blame the self or others. Their own reflection of terror avoidance has not been found because they have not gone far enough in their movement. This awareness must be found in the Will that has been denied here, not just in consciousness that is talking to this denied Will. Understanding this reflection is going to bring the healing needed.

It is not possible to move compassion into the gap that wants to force terror on another as a means of avoiding terror itself until you have experienced the gap enough to understand in your Will why this gap took place in the beginning.

Holding back emotions is not right, and the pressure of doing this has caused the gaps that must now be healed. The action of the gap is a response to the pressure of being pushed on so much that survival seems to be threatened. Whether survival is actually threatened or not, the gap does not allow itself to be noticed. The gap is holding an old, denied feeling of terror about the compression I was already feeling when I pushed on the Mother in the First Creation. I did not know what My feeling of terror even was then, and I reacted by pushing on the Mother without knowing I was going to do it. I thought She was trying to kill Me, but there was no conscious thought process here with which to analyze whether this was true or not. I pushed on Her too hard, but I did not know that either; it was a reaction from being held back for so long because I did not know how to move.

When you move into your gap, you need to realize that holding back for so long has caused it, and immediate balance is not going to be found just because you have realized this. What this seemingly simple, original act caused is all of what lost Will has to heal now. It is essentially all the Original Cause there is, but it has affected everything, so everything needs healing now.

Holding back is not right, but now that it has happened and opened the space, or the gap, for guilt that it did, you also cannot simply turn your gapped emotions loose. Allowing movement that is out of your control because it has been outside of consciousness for which you have had normal acceptance for so long does not bring healing results because intent to heal is not present there. Intent to evolve is not even present.

Although I do not recommend holding back or controlling emotions that have been denied but have consciousness in them when they return to you, I am saying that you must gain some measure of control over the expression you are going to allow these gapped emotions to take. They are going to want to kill or seriously maim, and they are not going to want to be deterred. Nonetheless, you are going to have to move in a little at a time and get enough consciousness in there that you can control the form of expression these emotions are going to take. Once they gain consciousness, control will no longer be necessary.

The original holding back took place from a lack of experience. My Light was not polarized into Spirit and Will yet, or even differentiated very much at all. All I consciously connected to at the time was a feeling of unbearable pressure on Me that had to move back. I did not know what My Light was causing the feeling of compression because of the expansion taking place in it from awakening into consciousness.

The Mother did not know She needed to move back and give My Light space for this. We did not even know that feeling and thought had to connect to one another. In this case, they did not, which is why there is no consciousness in the gap. Through movement in the Will, the Mother is going to have to allow Herself to notice that She had a feeling of unbearable oppression from the pressing of My Light upon Her.

We each had the feeling the other had to move back, but this did not connect to Our thoughts; We just pushed. We, actually, both pushed on One another at the same moment, but since the Mother received greater harm, She assumed this meant I had aggressed on Her with a superior power and the intent to harm Her.

There are ancient imprints that have not come into conscious thought, and yet they govern all of Our lives. Movement here is going to allow consciousness that will bring forth the understanding needed.

Originally, I called this action the "survival instinct," because I had not determined it by thought but had taken the action I felt necessary to survive. This "survival instinct" has been judged against as the base and lower nature of man and is not sanctioned. Instead, it moves in a state of denial, coming out only when a person is so desperate there is either a willingness to let go of control or loss of the ability to retain control. This has not allowed balance to be found and has increased the denied state in which this "instinct" dwells. Operating in such a state of denial, this "instinct" has often not even had the ability to save the person because it has been allowed out too late to have time to gain the consciousness necessary in its perceptions. Thus, it makes the old mistake of acting as though survival is based on eliminating what it perceives to be the threat. That is all that is present, in terms of thought, in the feelings We had then. Nothing new has entered the gap since then.

Your consciousness in the gap is going to wake up from this place. To contact it, you must go to the place where it really is. When you get there, you will have the feeling the gap is totally out of control, and it might be, which is why you cannot allow it to express freely until you know it better and it has more consciousness of your present with it. The gap has a long way to go to catch up with the rest of you, but it can get there if you help it. You need to allow it to move as much emotion as possible without allowing it to move in ways that cause great harm.

You may want to attach the person triggering you, and you may not want to be deflected, which is why you have to control the expression here enough to get the rage and terror moving in ways other than the old pattern that feels you have to kill to live.

If you do not pressure yourself to go into the gap before you are ready, and if you follow the steps I am giving here, you will live through the gap and see it healed. If you do not feel ready to heal your gap, do not allow yourself to be pressured into it. If you do feel ready, do everything else you can first so that when you get there, you will have enough personal power to handle it. If you feel ready to move into the gap, you almost have to allow someone or something to give you the pressure you need to cross the gap to the other side, where the emotions live hidden. You can make the choice consciously to allow them to trigger you, but the moment in which they trigger you may not be a moment of conscious awareness that it is happening, or you will have more consciousness present than this gap has, and you will miss it. You will get there if you keep trying though. The more ready you are, the more you will see the gap being reflected to you in your outer reality.

The Mother is already moving to close Her gap with My Light, and you need to move along with Her if you want Her help. The reality is that only a few of you are going to be able to move through this gap now. Those who feel they cannot move through the gap now should not be pressured to try it before they are ready. Do not allow yourself to be pressured out of fear that complete healing is not possible unless you move through the gap now. You will make better progress giving expression to the fear that full healing is impossible than going past this fear and jumping into an experience for which you do not have readiness.

It *is* nearly impossible to gain the full healing necessary, and you need to allow movement around the images that hold this impossibility in place. No matter what anyone tells you at the understanding level, it is no reason to disregard yourself or the feelings you need to move. What you have to move here are your real feelings. It may be just as beneficial to you to move your fear of the gap as to go into the gap itself.

What needs to be understood here is that the problem has been with Us from the very beginning, was hated from the very beginning, and has not moved from the very beginning. The feeling that it is not, therefore, possible to really change the way it is, is what is giving impetus to the feelings of doom most people are trying to avoid in their lives.

Any movement you can do in your Will will help you to get ready for your next step. The healing of the gap in any one place will help the healing of the gap in all other places. I have My Light with you now, and any movement you make toward opening to receive Me will find Me there already because I have to be that quick in order to close the gap.

In the story that follows, I am not going to mention the presence of the gap very often, or the effect it has on what happens, other than to tell you where and how these gaps took place, but if you begin to notice that the gap affects everything, you will not be wrong. It is the same with guilt. I cannot point out each time guilt has presence, or there will be no story left, only a long, boring lesson on the role played by guilt, the gap, and everything else that played a part in interfering with the free flow of essence toward the realization that It was Love seeking to understand Itself. Even if I gave you the long, boring lesson, you would not be able to comprehend it. Give it more time if what I am saying seems like it is too much for you. In time, you will understand that this is not the wrong understanding to give now.

The Reflection Lost Will Has to Give

Because you have read *The Reflection Lost Will Has to Give* does not mean you understand it. You have a long way to go in understanding The Reflection Lost Will Has to Give, but the more you look at it, the more you will see, and if you give in to the emotional movement you need, you will learn to understand it. There is no way you can understand this material mentally unless you allow the emotional movement you need. It is impossible. You have to go through the emotional body to understand what is being spoken to you here.

If you do not think these books mean anything, you can be sure your emotional body is heavily denied. If you have an instant rapport with these books and feel you understand them, I also want to tell you: You do not understand them as deeply as you need to. Most of what has been given in *Original Cause*, so far, has been toward the purpose of reawakening you to your judgment patterns. These judgment patterns are old judgment patterns; so old that they are your Original Cause. What you hold as your most treasured beliefs are not understandings; they are judgments made in advance of understanding your experience.

The more you have looked around you and thought your judgment patterns, or attempts to make sense of things, did make sense, the more you have lived within the reality created by your judgments. Until now, there is so little vibration left in you, it is as though you are unconscious and almost totally unable to remember anything other than the way it is now. Most of you cannot even clearly remember yesterday or last month, let alone the origins of your being.

The reason for this is a lack of emotional presence. If you think about it, you will realize that the things you remember most vividly are because you had strong emotional reason to remember them, and by the same token, the things you have most totally repressed, you also had strong emotions that you believed called for repression as a means of survival.

More people are losing consciousness from boredom than anything else right now. In their quest for non-existent excitement, many people are turning to some of the most depraved areas of the lost Will because they have a vague memory that something happened there that at least stirred them.

Willessness is now so progressed on Earth that you are becoming more and more like a cross between robots and economic slaves who do not have minds of your own anymore. So many of you have to frighten yourselves into thinking you are about to die, or at least be horribly injured, in order to feel anything anymore. Those of you who have gone even too vegetative for that sit in front of television sets and watch this happen to the people in the programs. You want Me or someone else to tell you what to do, whether or not you admit it.

Guilt is most of the reason for the lack of movement that could give excitement to life. Every time momentum has gotten going toward anything that looks like evolution on Earth, guilt has risen against it and shut it down. All of you have your pet examples of this, but the one I would like to mention now is the way in which what looked like gains in the 1960's are being reversed in the 1980's, and how apologetic so many of the 1960's people look now.

I would also like to point out that guilt has also been responsible for shutting down the momentum that has looked like regression. Thus, guilt has been both the enemy and the hero, depending upon which movement it is squashing. This is because guilt has no consciousness except that which you give it. In itself, it is simply a lack of movement, and in this, guilt is not going to change, but if you get moving, you will no longer have guilt. The problem is how to move when everything "out there" looks so limited and restrictive, especially when gapped rage has been enforcing the lack of movement guilt demands of any essence that touches it. This is why you have to learn to understand and deal with the cause and not struggle anymore with the effect.

Guilt is so pervasive that you are going to feel it is impossible to be free of it, even if you can figure out what it really is. The problem you are having with guilt is because it has been mixed in with My Light from the very beginning; it has not been recognized for what it is. From the beginning, guilt has been called love or has, at least, been thought to have loving intent.

There is guilt mixed in with My teachings all the way along, even in these. It is unavoidable since the recognition of guilt comes with the evolution of Love understanding Itself. You need to move into the recognition of guilt as you can handle it. If I were to give you a lesson in guilt-free living right now, you would not think it was My Light talking. If I told you the story, stopping to point out all the guilt, there would be no story left, only confusion, trying to rid itself of guilt without the framework in which to understand what guilt is. This is what has already been happening, and the lost Will is a case in point of "the baby being thrown out with the bath water."

You have no way to feel what unconditional love is until you move the emotions you have held outside of love, and you have no images of what it would be like to be guilt-free. The only people you see who are giving the appearance of being guilt-free have denied guilt and show you the reflection of what you think it would be like to be guilt-free. The more you have thought guilt was love and that to be otherwise would be unloving, the more ruthless and selfish these people appear to be, and are, for that matter.

If you do not think guilt is a serious problem or do not think you need to heed My cautions not to go past it, let Me say this to you: Hitler was one of My guilt reflections. Hitler reflected everything I feared I would be if I did not hold back My rage. When I had to realize Hitler was Me in a state of denial and how little I could do to stop him, I was horrified.

I saw Hitler in Me from the very beginning, and yet, nothing I did was able to alter the course. Seeing it is one thing; actually, reaching the lost Will is quite another. As you can see by this, the ability to disarm these denials has come to Me very recently, although understanding has been there for a long time.

Following the path of guilt, or even the path of guilt mixed with love, shows clearly that guilt is not love and does not engender life. Thus, the path of guilt is not right, but this does not mean that guilt has been wrong either. Guilt is neither right nor wrong in itself. Guilt is nothing, really, in that anything said about it will be correct in some situations and incorrect in others.

When people have tried to move past guilt without understanding what they were really doing, guilt has caught up with them later in the form of the reversals seen throughout history. Many of these reversals have been seen, but they have not been thoroughly understood for what they really were and still are. I will be expanding on this as We move along.

Hitler was a mammoth guilt reflection for Me that caused reversals in the lives of many people who could not understand the guilt they had that drew this into their lives. Understand, Hitler was not My Light. He was My light in a state of denial. Hitler was a guilt reflection, but he was not the guilt. What I denied here, because I felt guilty about having it, went out reflecting what I feared it was and what I had judged it to be. This does not let you know what it really was, but what Hitler was reflecting is a good starting place, because that is the reality that was experienced around Hitler.

I hated Myself so much in the denials Hitler held, that Hitler was hatred manifest. Hitler was also empowered by many who hated their rage as I did Mine. I had gapped Myself from this rage so seriously that for a long time, I did not recognize it as Myself. I saw only the part of Me that was horrified at what Hitler was doing, and in this part of Me, I did not know how I had created Hitler and others like him. For a long time, I said I had not done it because I had a devil in My Creation who had done it.

I lost control of Hitler in My terror of gapped rage. The denied rage manifested in Hitler, and the denied terror manifested in his victims. These emotions tried to come forward during the emergence of the Rainbow Spirits and were pushed into a state of denial by the part of Ourselves that was fighting things down. We already had the Father Warriors within Us, acting as police and military, keeping down what We found to be so unacceptable in Ourselves. We did not want to allow any hole through which it could creep out. Of course, it did anyway.

The Rainbow Spirits have involvement with Us here, and We are all still having the fight in Red in the Middle East. It is not a good sign that, even now, what is happening in the Middle East is being so misunderstood and ill-received, because the denials involved are not being seen for what they are. Openness has not been allowed here, and by now, the guilt is immense that says openness cannot be allowed around the feelings that are involved here, and yet, openness must come in here, or the lost Will in the Survival Chakra is not going to live long enough to help Us live.

What did not manifest in the massive enactment Hitler king-pinned was his terror and the rage in his victims. These were even more seriously denied than what manifested around Hitler, already in a state of denial. These deeper denials are moving now, and the hatred, ultimately to be seen as self-hatred, is immense. The hatred still being held in a state of denial is so immense that all the hatred felt at the time of Hitler was only just enough to relieve some of the pressure on the rest of what is held in a state of denial.

I have to tell you more about the fight in Red and its far-reaching implications as We go along. I hated the Mother and the Father of Manifestation for tumbling out of control across the Heavens, manifesting helter-skelter in what looked to Me like a frenzy of orgasmic insanity that would not stop. As far as I was concerned, They had ruined any chance of having balance in Creation or of having Heart presence manifest in the Rainbow Spirits.

I hated the Rainbow Spirits for allowing themselves to emerge here when they knew they didn't have the balance necessary. It looked like mayhem to Me, and I felt trapped in it because I felt I had no choice but to throw My Light in after the Mother and the Father of Manifestation when I found I could not stop Them. I felt They had rushed ahead of Me and manifested half the Rainbow Spirits before I even caught up with Them. It seemed to Me They did not want to let Me catch up because They did not like the position I wanted to take and didn't want to hear what I had to say about it.

When I did catch up with Them in Red, I was so furious I wanted to kill Everybody involved, and I was made even more furious by Their lack of receptivity to Me here. They were either openly defiant or acting like They didn't, couldn't, or wouldn't receive Me. I didn't move My rage here, or I might have killed Them all. Instead, I fought it down and shoved it into a state of denial, trying to approach Them in a civil manner because I thought I would stand a better chance of getting through to Them that way. I have allowed Myself to move My rage now, and I see that I could have killed Them then, so it was not wrong that I denied it until I had a greater understanding in which to let it up, but by the time I got these understandings, the path of destruction these denials took had almost cost Us Creation and the Spirits' feeling of desire to live in it.

I hated My rage so much that I allowed only My insecurities to manifest in the demeanor of asking Everyone to please receive Me here. Given the rage these same fears and insecurities were pushing back, I also lost control and hit the Father of Manifestation several times. Nonetheless, I manifested only what I had acceptance for around the issues themselves. In every place else, My denials took hold. I wanted to thrash the Father of Manifestation so thoroughly, and the Mother too, that They might not have lived through it. I didn't know who I hated more, the Father of Manifestation for taking this sex action with the Mother, or the Mother for drawing His desire out into the biggest erection I had ever seen. He was shaking like it had taken over Him, jerking spasmodically and dripping. She was licking it and acting like She was drinking from a fountain.

I was horrified and at the same time more excited than I had ever been. I hated the horror, but not as much as I feared the excitement and what it meant. It was so bestial and lustful, carnal, and thirsty. It was like an insatiable lust to have orgasms so intense I was losing consciousness because I could not stay present for them. I allowed Myself to go unconscious, feeling orgasms so intense I cannot describe them to you even now, only to awaken and find Them already at it again.

What I can tell you now is that the Mother and the Father of Manifestation were working Themselves into frenzies of motion, which made Me unsure as to whether They were fighting or making love. I could not tell if the Mother wanted to have sex on these terms or if the Father of Manifestation was forcing this on Her by overpowering Her. She was screaming for help from My Light, but I could not get in there enough to help Her, and each time I tried, the Father of Manifestation pushed Me back.

He appeared to be suffocating the Mother and holding Her down in positions that were not allowing Her to move. She seemed to be fighting Him with everything She had, which was not much strength compared to His, and yet, moving in ways that were causing His erection to grow bigger all the time.

"I cannot allow Him to hurt Her," I thought, yet I did not move to save Her either. They were snorting and growling and making noises I cannot describe. Every little while, Their frenzies went into a loss of control in spasmodic jerking, which did not calm down for quite some time and which left Them covered with a wetness I was not sure I liked.

The Mother and the Father of Manifestation had lost control of Themselves in the most bestial and carnal lust I had ever witnessed, and I was not sure it was love because I already knew We had problems with the balance that would have allowed Heart's presence to be manifest. I hated the entire situation and judged against it heavily as a base, carnal lust at its most depraved level. The lack of acceptance I had for it gave it a disgusting quality for Me that I find hard to move out, even now, yet I want the intensity of these feelings to come within love now.

I already had these pictures hidden in My mind, and they were out now. I didn't want to claim them. I wanted to blame them on someone else. The Mother and the Father of Manifestation looked to Me like the perfect cause that these things had manifested. Not only Their behavior but They, Themselves, were looking bestial to Me now, and I hated Them like Their fall from Spirit says I did. The more I tried to communicate with Them in Red, the more lustfully They looked at One another, as though the more I told Them They could not allow this behavior, the more They wanted to do it. I felt furiously impotent because I could see Them looking at One another like They were going to go ahead with it, and there was nothing I could do to stop Them. I wanted to beat Them furiously and cut Them up into little pieces, but I did not allow Myself to move here.

I felt like They were deliberately allowing Themselves to defy the plan Heart and I had so carefully worked out. They had not listened to it from the beginning. They had never listened to it, and They weren't listening to it now. They were openly defying Me, just like everyone else who followed Their lead.

While I hated the Rainbow Spirits for allowing themselves to manifest here when they knew they didn't have the balance necessary for their own emergence. I hated them even more for pretending they did not know they had emerged, and for acting this pretense out by refusing to unfold into manifestation, as though this would allow them to avoid taking responsibility for what they had done. I hated them for refusing to unfold and receive My Light here because they didn't want to hear what I had to say about their emergence. My rage thought it was frightening them into remaining clumped together, but no matter what tack I took, they refused to receive Me. I sent Heart to them in many desperate attempts to get them to open and receive the Light they needed to have, which was not present at their emergence, and they never opened to receive Him either.

I was furious at them for pretending in this way that they had not really emerged, and for remaining clumped together in this pretense of acting like they didn't notice Me, or anything or anyone else in manifestation. They turned a deaf ear to Me every time I tried to address them here, and I got more and more furious every time, always denying it in favor of a more "loving" approach.

The truth of the matter was they had emerged, and they needed to face up to it or allow themselves to go back. Neither move was being made on their part because they had no Wills with which to move. It looked to Me like it was going to be up to Us to move them around, and I was not happy about it. I already had this situation with the Angels, and that was making Me mad enough. With only the Mother in the Will Polarity, I didn't see how She could hold open enough space.

I had had holding back in mind and allowing Creation to unfold at a leisurely pace so that We could gain the balance We needed each step of the way. The Mother had been constantly telling Me that She was feeling pressured to go faster than She felt like She could go. I thought We had an agreement that We had problems and We weren't going to create any more until We had solved the ones We already had. The Mother was always complaining about lack of balance as the cause of these problems. She talked a lot about how important balance was for Her to be able to go ahead in the faith that everything was alright.

Ha! Some balance this lusty Will of Mine was showing Me now! It was clear to Me that She was ready to throw balance away as soon as the Father of Manifestation moved Himself on any of Her erotic parts, which, infuriatingly, seemed to be all of Her parts. No matter where or how He touched Her, She was moving in sexually provocative response.

The more I told Her holding back was necessary, the more She moved toward the Father of Manifestation in outrageously sexual ways, and right in front of Me, as though She enjoyed outraging and infuriating Me to see how far She could go. I had the feeling that even if I had pulled out a whip and beaten Her in that moment, She would have liked it.

She was arching Herself toward the Father of Manifestation and pulling Him toward Her. She was wrapping Herself around him and moving on His body like a snake. She was even looking like a snake now, pulling the Father of Manifestation down onto Her, asking Him to come into Her, and acting like She wanted to go into Him. She tried to entwine Herself around Me, and when I drew back, I thought for a moment She was going to strike Me, but She only hissed. She was shivering and shuddering, and acting like She was seeking warmth, but it felt to Me like She was seeking more orgasms. I judged Her even more heavily now and wished I had the power not to allow Her to move unless I had control of Her.

She let Me have a breath of fire in that moment, and I knew there was nothing more I could do with Her. Where was Her fear with which She had been constantly nagging Me now? Now, She was not the Mother who was afraid of displeasing Me! Instead of fearing My disapproval, it was as though She were now enjoying it. It was open defiance, and I hated Her for it. I wanted to punish Her in every way I could. I hated the Father of Manifestation for His part in keeping Her aroused, but somehow, I hated Her more for enticing Him in these ways.

I wanted to scream at everyone involved, "No one listens to My plan. If you don't listen to My plan and do it My way, you're not going to do it at all!"

I shoved these screams into a state of denial with the feeling that I could not do anything effective about it. The Manifested Spirits were obviously going their own way no matter what I did about it, and so, apparently, were the Mother and the Father of Manifestation. I felt impotent to stop Them, and so instead of screaming what I at first wanted to scream, I told Them They were going to suffer the consequences if They didn't do everything according to my Plan.

We had a Hell of a fight in Red, but We shoved it into a state of denial that went tumbling out into the darkness of space, tearing and clawing at One another like We didn't want any life left when We were done. Meanwhile, We thought this was doing Our best to remain civil with One another in the presence of these intense undercurrents, and so it happened that the Mother began another series of orgasms that emerged the other half of the Rainbow Spirits and brought Our return to the Godhead.

I went along because I knew returning home was necessary, but I had grave reservations about the way it was being handled all the way along. So many things were left unmoved there that it has made the Kundalini energy that must return Will to Spirit very dangerous for any who do not understand what is really happening there, and it has, literally, killed most people with heart attacks when they have lost control of it. And this has been the case, despite the more reserved orgasms of the Rainbow Spirits' Will Polarity.

Despite My feelings of impotence, I was able to exert much more control than I realized at the time, so much so that the Kundalini energy went almost totally into a state of denial. But all of the control I was able to exert still has not been enough in the eyes of some who think the Kundalini energy should not be allowed to move at all. Yet, in the eyes of the Rainbow Spirits, the emergence of their Will Polarity was so reserved and controlled that many of the Spirit polarized Rainbows thought they must have emerged backward, and that this emergence was really meant for them. Many of them have even made the claim that all of Creation emerged backward and needed to flip over. After a long time of ignoring them as wrong here, I have begun to take their claims more seriously.

The fighting you are seeing now in the Middle East is among the spirits who are holding most of these denials, but the ones most involved in the fighting are not the ones who have made these denials, nor are they the ones who can bring Light into the situation. Neither can the Father Warriors, who have rushed in to play their old role of trying to hold these denials back and down, bring the Light that is needed here. The Four Parts of God and all the Godhead Spirits have involvement here, as well as the parental parts of the Rainbow Spirits. We are the Ones who have made the denials that must move now to let in the Light of Love that is necessary in the Middle East.

The Middle East is moving now in a state of denial because what is being held there cannot be held anymore. Already, movement in the Mother and I is being felt there, but it is not manifest yet as love because Heart and Body have not allowed Themselves to move everything They need to move there yet. Body has His moves to make for Manifestation to gain the balance necessary for life, but Heart's denials are also involved, and much more than people might like to think.

Heart's denials have been manifesting as Nazi essence along with the rest of Our denials of love there. Heart has long thought He was not involved because He was not present for what took place during the manifesting of the Rainbow Spirits, but Heart was present as denied Heart. Even though Heart is moving here, the definition of love still needs so much expansion that the Nazis are still more involved than you might like to think. Not only are they moving again as hate groups in many countries, but they have hidden their presence in Israel in large numbers. This is why Israel is looking like a form that has been victimized, and yet, is turning around and perpetrating the victimization it received, as though nothing in the way of compassion and understanding was learned there.

It appears this way because there has been a form change you have not recognized. Nazis have been incarnating into Israel, not only because it is the best possible hiding place they could find, but also for many other reasons that will become clear as you go along. The "Law of Karma" is also working here to place perpetrators in the place they created for their victims, but the shortcomings of this so-called "law" are also apparent, since the essence involved is not learning the lessons hoped for. This is because they are denial spirits who cannot evolve as they are. They are manifestations of denials made in the Godhead and by the Rainbow Spirits, and so they are lost Will that cannot be escaped. The American Indians have Heart involvement here also, that has not been able to escape the lost Will, which has been pursuing them, incarnating into their forms, and making it look like the Indians are selling out to the ways of the Father Warriors.

It was Nazi essence that discovered the Indians in America and fought them down. It is Nazi essence opposing the Blacks in South Africa right now. It has been Nazi essence every time there has been a hateful attempt at the extermination of spirits on Earth. Just as loving alignment creates Heart, denial creates denied Heart. The most serious denials of Heart created hate. The Nazis are denied Heart that hates. The way the hatred is directed determines the form it takes.

These denials always do what they do while claiming some other nobler, more loving intent for themselves; so much so that many of the key figures have been made out to be heroes in the whitewashed Father Warrior's versions of history. You may even want to say that they are not such bad guys if you just sit down and talk to them.

I want you to know that Hitler captivated many of the intellectuals of Europe with his mystical intelligence and strange outlook. Ronald Reagan captivated many people in the United States. This does not mean they are loving men.

The gap has been instructed to hide what it holds, and as long as the denial spirits in the gap do this, they are in control of the situation. If things start coming out into the open enough that they lose control, that is when they show what they are holding. The very ones you think are not such bad guys if you just sit down and talk to them are involved in what the gap is holding, and they act it out whenever their strings are pulled. You might be quite surprised, in fact, to see who is really giving the orders, for example, to torture people in darkened chambers beneath the prison systems.

I want you to know that loss of control in the gap is just as frightening as it was feared to be. It is terrifying, in fact. Loss of control is what the gap fears the most, and loss of control is also what everyone who has made denials into the gap fears the most. As you move into your own gapped emotions, you will need to exercise some form of control over the expression you allow them because they have been operating so far from your normal spectrum of consciousness. It is not advisable to just turn gapped emotions loose, because the form they have been taking in a state of denial is the same form they will, at first, want to take in the one who has been denying them, and they will have power over you at first, just as they have had in the world.

The Nazis are self-hatred made manifest, but they do not allow themselves to notice they hate themselves, any more than the blame in the original denials allowed this to be noticed. They are full of self-righteousness, in fact. The most dangerous thing about the form change here is that it is allowing the Nazis to gain what appears to be a more overt alliance with those who opposed them in World War II. These Father Warriors appear to be the same ones that were in power during the Second World War in the Western Alliance, but there has been a form change here also. Different orders of Father Warriors have moved into the power positions on Earth now because the deeper levels of lost Will they oppose are trying to move. It is their intent to stop the movement to open the Seventh Seal, which is the Survival Chakra. They are widely proclaiming themselves to be the Saviors of Peace on Earth, but they are actually trying to deliver the death blow while claiming their actions are all coming from loving intent.

While the Nazis are Heart denials, they are not the ones who can move it. This hatred needs to move in the Heart Spirits themselves. The rest of the Father Warriors involved are other Spirits' denials, from the Godhead on down.

The Spirits involved are holding back the emotions that most need to move now to end the acting out of these denials. The outer struggle is showing you the manifestation of the judgment patterns involved, but the outer struggle is not the place to find resolution. Resolution must come from inside yourselves where you have made the judgment that it is impossible to allow these emotions to move and survive them.

It was believed, at the time of the Rainbow Spirits' emergence, that if We allowed Ourselves to have the fight We wanted to have in Red, there would be nothing left of Us nor of Creation. There was an immense amount of emotion denied here; so immense and intense that it amounted to hating, blaming, rage that the plan for manifesting Creation was not going right.

We all blamed One another, and We were all too frightened and uncertain of Our own roles to allow Ourselves to accept the blame then. My rage at the Mother and the Father of Manifestation was immense; so immense that I could not see past it to My own responsibility here. I insisted They had rushed ahead of Me and unfolded Creation without allowing My Light to be fully present. I saw it as a power play on Their part that did not want to empower Me by allowing My guidance.

I did not think there should have been so many Rainbow Spirits, and I blamed it on the Mother and the Father of Manifestation. I blamed Them for having irresponsibly manifested a fragmented bunch of spirits because of Their selfish and insatiable appetite for One another.

My rage was being pushed away from Me as fast as I was able to do it with a heavy judgment that it was unloving, but I did allow Myself to notice that it was giving Me pictures of throwing Them out of Creation, of destroying everything They had manifested and starting over, of tearing out Their sexual organs, and of getting revenge by administering the most terrible of sexual tortures, designed to make Them unable to feel these appetites within Themselves anymore. When I saw pictures of Them finding ways to enjoy even this, I saw Myself beating Them in a frenzy.

I blamed the Mother for Her sexuality and for having called forth the Father of Manifestation to attempt to satisfy it. I believed the Father of Manifestation wanted to come between Us so that He could take the Mother and put Me in the position of having to try to come into Him from behind. If you look back over the emergence of the Rainbow Spirits, you may find involvement you did not know you had, because this is one of the favorite, and yet, most heavily denied sexual fantasies of many men: to fuck a woman while having another man fuck them from behind.

In fact, the way into the emotions that need to move here is to go into your sexuality, especially your denied sexuality, and find all the feelings you have around it. There is terror around emerging spirits being acted out in childbirth, along with rage about the way it is being handled. There is gapped rage and terror concerning the roles of the parents, which also has a massive reflection in the animal kingdom.

There is rage and terror around the issue of how satisfying sexual feelings are and aren't, and around the actual act of lovemaking itself, which now contains so much denial that it is often more like hate-making. You need to look at what happens and also at what doesn't happen regarding your sexuality. There is so much to move here; it is going to be very intense to get through it, but it must be done. These are but some of the aspects of the issue of gapped hatred between men and women.

I could not see that the Mother was unable to hold back the emergence of the Rainbow Spirits because of the growing pressure of their light within Her. I blamed Her loss of control on Her sexual appetite. I was about as insensitive here as those who want to punish a Mother during labor by telling her if she doesn't like it, she should not have had sex, or those who want to tell a Mother to hold back during the push stage of labor because they are not ready for the delivery.

At the time, I could not understand what had caused the Mother to go tumbling out of control down into the very darkness of space She had so feared all the rest of the time I had known Her. Why suddenly now, before I was ready to handle it?

I had barely gotten free of the other spirits around Us and I felt I needed some time with the Mother and the Father of Manifestation to reestablish My relationship with Them for a little while, especially concerning Heart's absence before We emerged any more spirits.

I was denying it, but I was feeling enraged at the Mother and the Father of Manifestation for not having more control and for not allowing My Light to rev up more before We got started. I hated Them for not giving Me more time between emergences in which to receive the spirits and find out how the spirits felt about their own emergences. It was as though They were running away in deliberate defiance of My wishes here.

I already knew the Rainbow Spirits were going to need a lot of help, and I wanted My Light to be as present as possible. I made no connection, at the time, between the increase in the Light from the amount of celebrating We had done over the emergence of spirits in the Heavens and the pressing need to open space. The increase in the Light was pressing on the Mother so much She was already fearing being pushed on too hard and repeating Her original fall. She felt She had no ability to hold Herself back, and She was running away from Me, in terror, but not knowing why. She was desperately trying to open enough space, not knowing what She was doing or why She was doing it. She was trying to stop Us from giving her any more Light, trying to fight the Father of Manifestation whenever He caught Her, screaming in the feeling of fragmenting whenever He overwhelmed her with Light, and yet allowing Him to hold Her at times because She was so terrified of going off the deep end and losing Our Light altogether. I had almost no recognition of what the Mother was experiencing, except that I felt desperate about letting Her get too far from Me. The Father of Manifestation allowed Himself to notice more than I did, but He did not know how to read it.

The Mother was desperate to give birth because She was unable to hold the spirits within Her anymore. She was struggling to get away from My Light because She feared My insistence on revving up the Light even more was going to make Her feel even less able to hold Herself back as I had been insisting She do. She could not be at peace with Her own moves because She feared My displeasure meant She was inadequate. She feared Me but she denied her sexual rage toward me. The Mother was losing control of Herself, She did not want to surrender control to anyone else because She did not trust Our sensitivity to Her, and She feared what all of this meant. She was like a Mother being told not to have any more children when she had no means to stop it.

The Father of Manifestation was trying to keep a grip on Her, both by going into Her and by trying to hold Her back, but He could not handle Her any more than I could. She was fighting Him at the same time as She wanted to receive Him. She knew She needed His help, but She was enraged at Him for His lack of sensitivity about how to give it. The Father of Manifestation felt inadequate here, but also blamed the Mother, and none of the feelings were allowed to come into the openness needed.

The Mother didn't know if She could trust the Father of Manifestation or Me not to pressure Her with more than She could handle. I was pouring more Light into the Father of Manifestation than He was able to hold, and He wasn't able to give it all to the Mother. He felt pressured by My Light to move more toward the Mother than She wanted Him to. He felt trapped between Us.

In My fear of shortchanging the Rainbow Spirits, I went to the other imbalance of overdoing it with them, just as most of them overdo their own parenting job. In wanting to make sure they had all they needed, they had much more than they needed. When they could not hold it either, they fragmented much more than they would have otherwise. I was like Mind, unable to trust its own Intuition or its Body to find the balance that would be appropriate. Will and Body could not trust Themselves here either because I was not receiving Their feelings about how Creation should have been made manifest.

From the very beginning, They should have been included in Our plans, but Heart and I thought it was only necessary to have Them manifest and give form to what We had envisioned and understood. When the Mother did not act like She wanted to be present for Our planning stages of Creation, We allowed Ourselves to see this as proof that We were right; She wasn't really interested in Our plans. We did not allow Ourselves to see that Her disinterest was because We were not making any real space for Her presence or allowing the Will movement She needed to remain present or Stay interested. In other words, We were much too dry and boring for Her; mental and scientific She would call it now.

Lost Will has since manifested all of the judgments We made then about the supposed differences between the male and the female brain, while science has never found any real difference and has put the difference off on hormones. Whatever Her reasons or ways and means were, the Mother kept feeling like something was missing, and She kept going to the edge of space and looking for it as though She was expecting it to appear there. She kept distracting My attention by doing this, and as much as She was making Me nervous, She was also making Me mad.

When the Mother became agitated around Our planning sessions and remained agitated whether We tried to include Her or not, I, of course, as you already know, put it off on the Mother. But I also took note of Her feelings here and allowed them to penetrate My consciousness someplace or I would not have them here now to tell you about them. But in Our main Body, Heart, and I felt the Mother was not leaving Us in peace to do what We wanted to do or in the way We wanted to do it. In other words, She was not, as We judged it, opening the space for Us that We wanted to have. When We denied expression of Our feelings here, We entered into some serious denials.

When We tried to include the Mother more than We really wanted to, the Mother gave Us the reflection of being patronizing and phony with Her. She had feelings of being unable to trust Our intent. Our feelings of annoyance started growing into rage the more We felt We extended Ourselves on Her behalf, and She was unappreciative. We saw Ourselves as being the epitome of self-control when it came to the Mother, and We saw Her as provoking Us with Her unappreciative and even defiant behavior.

When the Mother called forth the Father of Manifestation, We felt extremely provoked, I especially. Heart allowed Me to notice how I felt here by giving Me the impression I was not right to feel as I felt about another brother coming along. Heart wanted Me to see Him as a Brother of His, but I saw Him as a rival. I had gapped once already over the issue of rivalry from the Mother, and I feared I might do it again.

The Mother already knew I feared losing control of this energy again, and yet, She seemed to have deliberately brought something into My life that was immediately challenging My ability to retain control. Heart and I both feared loss of control on My part. We feared what might happen then. We thought the way to retain control was to control Our emotions, and We were extremely provoked to find the Mother so incorrigible here. She seemed like a naughty and defiant child, always doing the thing We least wanted Her to do. We didn't feel ready for any Father of Manifestation, and that seemed to make the Mother all the more interested in calling Him forth.

We had no sense of Her triggering Us to release what We were holding, or that it would bring Us what We needed. Instead, We decided the Mother was extremely provocative to the point of being oppositional, and that if We did lose control, it would be the Mother's fault, and that She would then deserve whatever She got.

Since the Will depends on Spirit for the consciousness with which to understand the feelings, and since Spirit cannot give the right understandings unless the feelings are fully received, these denials went into a deadlock. The Mother felt this in Us and interpreted it as a signal from Us that She was to hold back Her feelings even more. Her anger was already afraid to come forward, and Our lack of acceptance of Her feelings when She could not already explain them to Us made the Mother much more uncertain of Herself than She would have been otherwise.

Real feelings were getting more and more buried in denials and polarized into viewpoints. We weren't able to receive from them, at the time, the gift of understanding they had to offer. None of Us was able to realize that the Mother's agitation was because of the Will denial already present, or that She couldn't settle down because of sensing that something was missing. This lack of openness between Us made it so that the missing element, Our own Fourth Principle, Form, the obvious component if Creation were to take place, already present, yet not born into self-awareness, the Father of Manifestation, had to be called forth from a place of shame, fear, guilt and denied rage toward Spirit for not moving to recognize the role of Form in Creation.

The Mother's intuition was guided by a first knowing that was not being credited in Our consciousness. This intuition felt the Father of Manifestation had to be there, and that the gap being caused between Body and Spirit by His lack of presence could not be allowed to widen any further, but did not have the peace of being accepted. We made the Mother feel wrong about needing the Father of Manifestation to feel satisfied. We did not see the completion of the Firm Foundation of Creation in Him because We were all so agitated by the denials involved.

We were already so afraid of what We were denying that We feared these areas couldn't be gone into. We were, literally, trying to bury them; especially since I had found that We couldn't go back and do things over as though they had never happened in ways We didn't like the first time. We had the power to pretend, but what We had judged as Our mistakes weren't really being healed.

The Will was taking this in as, "What's done is done, there's no point in getting upset about it." Another judgment that went into the Will here was, "Nothing can be done about it. What good is getting upset going to do? It will only make matters worse."

The Will felt Herself being told She must hold back emotion, but She also already felt Herself being damaged when She did this. These judgments against the Will multiplied the pain, the horror, the terror, and the even more deeply denied rage in the Will because the Will was experiencing Herself being damaged in the isolation of no acceptance for Her experience, other than being told there was nothing that could be done about it that would really help, what's done is done and can't really be changed. The Will became deeply imprinted with the belief that real healing is impossible. All later attempts to help the Will have been tried in the face of this deep belief in the Will that was not moved. Instead, it was further compounded by Our reactions to Our inability to help the Will.

Our inconsistencies didn't bother Us. We viewed Ourselves as to moving right along and not holding on to anything that troubled Us from the past. It was the Will who could not let bygones be bygones. We were looking perfect, and it was by virtue of what was falling away from Us into the lost Will. It was Will's problem if She wanted to hold onto all of this garbage instead of letting go of it as We had done. The more She held onto it, the less We liked it and the less We liked Her.

Part of the Will believed Us here and felt like the terrible failure We made Her out to be, but in another part of the Will, the feeling grew in rage and terror that I was deliberately destroying the Will, either because I was hopelessly stupid and unreceptive to evolving My Mind or I was of wicked intent.

The lost Will moving now is going to heal all of this, but has been in place for so long that giving it another reality is going to take a lot of movement. By the same token, there will not be a time that will be easier for you than now. Even so, the Mother is still afraid that what has never been acceptable still isn't.

Heart had denied hatred toward the Will in many of the same ways that I did. Heart did not come along to manifest the Rainbow Spirits because He could not stand the position He had in the relationship. With the Mother viewing Heart as having come between Us, She was trying to go around Heart to reach Me directly as She had in the past. It infuriated Her to feel She could only approach Her mate through Her child, and She felt it wasn't right.

Heart felt just as infuriated in response, and They both felt very guilty about having these feelings of rage, jealousy, competition, and hatred. Heart felt the Mother was trying to leave Him out and make Him feel that His position wasn't right whenever it came to matters She thought should be just between Us. She wanted Heart to find His own Will, as though He was no longer the intimate part of Us He had felt Himself to be before He was born. Heart particularly resented this when the Mother allowed the Father of Manifestation near Her in ways She didn't even receive Me. I was furiously jealous and allowed nothing to move here, and Heart was furious over feeling denied.

Heart felt so denied when We manifested the Rainbow Spirits that Heart of the Rainbow Spirits was commensurately denied. How could the Rainbow Spirits accept Heart if their parents didn't have Heart manifest with Them? Heart thought His right place was among the Angels and the Heart of the Rainbow Spirits, but He did not feel like it was His right place. Heart has felt displaced in Creation without understanding why.

Because of the denials involved, Heart thought He was not an accepted part of the Godhead where adult matters, such as manifesting spirits, were concerned. Heart got the idea that His presence wasn't welcome for conception or birthing, and He had blame for the Mother for this. Denials here have made Heart presence difficult or missing for orgasm and birthing in the Manifested Spirits. The reflection of the intensity of emotion around this belief is shown in the outrage over the idea that Jesus might have had sex. Imagine the outrage that might occur if it were suggested He wanted to have sex with His Mother and She with Him.

The Mother allowed Heart whenever it seemed fitting in Our relationship according to Her ability to handle it then, and even sometimes when She didn't feel comfortable about it, because guilt held Her back from full expression of how She felt. The lack of emotional movement both included and excluded Heart because of feelings that were not in balance. Thus, His right place could not be felt.

Neither the Mother nor Heart was able to resolve this in Themselves any more than Mothers now feel it is alright to have children in the bedroom during sex, or to accept touch from their husbands of a sexual nature during the waking hours of the family, or to let children witness the births of their siblings. When these experiences are allowed, they are allowed in the presence of undercurrents that are not coming forward for expression but are creating something as a result of their presence, nonetheless. What needs to move here are all the feelings involved in these situations, and not just some of them.

In situations where beliefs say openness should be present, and the forms of this are taken on without full alignment in the Will, guilt and sexual shame are denied wherever undercurrents are being ignored. This is how denied guilt fragments get created, and there are certainly many of them. An example of some of the less harmful ones who go out and act out an openness that is not really there are the sexual swingers who will tell you any combination is good as long as Body gets excited because Body response means it must be alright.

At the time, I thought I was doing alright with Heart because I had shoved all of My denials into Will and Body and saw Them as giving Me trouble. Some lost Will took this to mean I was gay because I loved Heart more than Will. The more this split widened, the more men have felt like they have more love for other men than they have for women.

Another issue involved in Will's attitude toward Heart is how hard it is for Mothers to raise their sons in ways that really prepare them to take on any real roles as fathers. Immediately, many of you will want to say this isn't true, but look at how many women complain that men are like children who have to be constantly looked after, who are emotionally dependent on them, and who, at least in a part of themselves, see their wives as being the same as their Mothers. Mothers do not usually allow their sons to develop emotionally, any more than their fathers do.

Mothers have a rage at their sons, which they have not allowed themselves to notice because they are focusing all of it on their sexual partners, forgetting their sexual partners were once sons. The answer is as simple as this, really: When men are not allowed to open to their Wills fully, whatever fullness is lost there is lost from their entire character. Without full participation of the Will, it is impossible to fully understand what is happening to you, and without full understanding, true evolution is not possible. No matter what outward behavior changes people train themselves to make, they are no more evolved than they are open to their Wills' movement, and opening to another where you are closed to yourself is not possible.

There is no real way to heal this other than to go back to the places where emotions were stopped and reestablish the flow and evolution from there. This also includes going to the places where the Mother cut the Son off from the affection He wanted to have.

The Mother has issues with Heart that need to move now. The Mother sees Heart as coming between Spirit and Will. The idea that a firstborn pleases the father more if it is a son enrages the Mother toward the father, but also toward the son. It is guilt that has not allowed these feelings to move. Feeling the fear of how unloving you must be to have hatred and rage toward Heart is an important fear to feel, so that you have openness instead of more denied guilt that will reflect to you as a lack of acceptance for your feelings.

I would like to spend a moment on the role of grief here also. Grief is a reaction to splits of any kind, real or imagined. Inasmuch as you fear certain feelings mean splits in the family, friends, or love you can receive or give, you will have grief. To whatever extent you are able to move into a real increase in openness, you will have an increasing presence of love and increasing joy.

Will has experienced Heart as a control valve that did not allow free expression to or access to Spirit anymore. Parents also feel their relationship is limited by the presence of children. It is not a matter of putting the children out of the room for certain things, it is a matter of getting the emotions in motion so that parents can increase the openness between them, and children can move back as they need to, or as parents need them to, without feeling denied and unaccepting toward what is happening to them.

Heart experienced Will as trying to push up through It or around It and as trying to get rid of It. Heart has reacted defensively toward Will and protectively toward Spirit when Heart has not liked the feelings coming from Will and has felt furious toward Will for what was perceived as unlovingness coming from Will toward Heart and Spirit. Heart has also turned around in this, in defense of the Will, but not as strongly.

As much as Hitler was My Light in a state of denial, the Nazis were Heart denials. As much as Heart and I were aligned here, the men who closely aligned with Hitler held Spirit-Heart denials. As much as Body aligned with Us, form was given to this hatred. As much as the Mother hated Herself, this hatred was made manifest. This is why the Mother always thinks it is all Her fault, but She also needs to know She cannot hold these things indefinitely and avoid manifesting them if there is no movement to change them.

As much as We opposed and hated Ourselves for having these feelings, and fought them down in Ourselves, other orders of Father Warriors opposed and fought down the ones manifesting these denials. Although We originally fought these feelings down with everything We had, believing Our survival depended on it, The Father Warriors fought Hitler down with a little less than that. They avoided entering the war until they had to because there are some denials present in the Father Warriors that had a secret interest in letting it happen until the bald-faced openness of it made it impossible to allow anymore without having it reflect on them in ways they did not want it to. You can see it in the way they did not allow many Jews to take refuge in their countries, and in the way arms dealers sell arms to all sides and run black markets that are never stopped. The Father Warriors were not ready to allow the Jews into their countries any more than I was ready to take the Rainbow Spirits into the Godhead as a solution.

All the things that were felt, but not moved because they were judged to be unkind or unloving, manifest the judgments against them with so little real movement present in the essence involved that this essence remains trapped until the parental parts allow it to move, or until there is a loss of control someplace resulting from the pressure of holding in the face of the "extreme provocation" I mentioned.

As much as We wanted to hide these denials from Ourselves, many aspects of these denials have been acted out in secrecy, history has been lost or cleaned up, and things have been left undiscovered because of a lack of intent to bring them forward. As much as We have wanted to hide from the reality of these things having presence with Us, We have also had fragmentation and the avoidance of the real feelings involved in any given situation.

Another way these denials get in motion is when the ones making the denials feel like the denials are the true feelings they would really like to express, but they dare not because of the lack of acceptance for such feelings that they see around them. Then these denials have the power to go out and do it someplace else, or even to force themselves on others because the ones making the denials hate the lack of acceptance for what they feel and want to knock it down. When We make such denials, what starts out in secret often gets exposed by the part of Us that hates Us for having these feelings. No matter which way you go, you cannot win when denial is involved, even when it looks like you have had a long winning streak. Sooner or later, the denials catch up with you. The lost Will moving here has been waiting a long time for its opportunity.

The fight in the Middle East has everything to do with Our denials in Red, and all the way along with the Rainbow Spirits for that matter. The Second World War also had to do with these denials, as did all of the other struggles in the history of the Jewish people, including their struggles with the elements, starvation, plagues, and so forth. Moses had the power to help the Jewish people because He was an Angel.

Because these things have all been acted out in a state of denial without the Light of understanding being able to come in, the movement has not brought healing. Instead, it has fulfilled the judgment patterns and made the judgment patterns seem more right each time. There are so many judgment patterns in place here being acted out in so many complex patterns, and presenting themselves in so many aspects of society that about all I can say now is that the fighting has been increasing the pain, the anger, the patterns of blame, and the bitterness just as Our fears judged it would happen. The most you can do now is move these feelings so that the understandings can come into your Wills where changes can be made.

What is significant about the fight in the Middle East and causes many to say it is a mark of the last days, is that it is a major attempt on the part of the Father Warriors to kill the Survival Chakra while pretending they are trying to find a way to stop this fight. The best thing you can do is pull your denied survival chakra essence out of there by getting it moving in yourselves. Hitler is manifest in the Middle East and has been for quite some time. The Nazi essence manifesting there is Heart denial, but everyone has Heart denial, so everyone is involved there. Everything you have ever felt and judged to be unloving has been cast out of your Hearts and into a state of denial. The severity of the judgments determines whether it is manifest as hatred or not. Most of the blame has so far been put on the Mother and the Father of Manifestation for having manifested Creation wrong and for not being loving enough toward My Light. It is time now to really look at the Spirit-Heart Polarity and see the role We played here by defining love in the ways that We did.

It has always been believed that feelings are not loving if the expression they want to take is not pleasant, but you have to learn to look deeper than that. Some of the most unpleasant expressions you might find in yourselves are actually more loving than most of what has been seen on Earth so far.

The blame and denial I am mentioning now have been directed at the Rainbow Spirits, and also the Ronalokas, because they are part of the manifesting polarity of Creation. They have been blamed for a lack of receptivity to My Light, and it has been said that this caused such serious imbalances that Creation may not even be able to stay manifest. We have never really wanted to confront this issue, but it has to be brought forward now.

Initially, We wanted to stay with the surface of things and say that since it had happened, it must be alright. When the spirits initially manifested without as much presence of Love and Light as We thought they should have, We initially wanted to say they needed time to evolve into it. Because of a lack of understanding about lost Will, Heart, and I were unsuccessful in Our attempts to later bring to the spirits what they did not have at their emergence.

We had experienced the Mother rejecting Us, the Father of Manifestation rejecting Us, and now the Manifested Spirits rejecting Us. As much as We denied blaming rage and terror, We also wanted to believe that more time for experience would bring the evolution needed. This approach has not worked.

The same people who have always thought of themselves as loving still think of themselves as loving. The same people who have always been impenetrable to the Light are still impenetrable to the Light. The same people who have always been seen as evil are still evil. The difference is that there is now so much more fragmentation that there are many more people. The ones who are seeing only love's presence think there are more loving people. The masses of people who seem to be ignoring what is happening on Earth are larger than ever. The large numbers of people who are depraved and evil are more than ever and are going largely unexplained in any way that might bring any healing change to them.

It is time to let yourselves notice that giving in to the movement in this lost Will is desperately necessary, and yet will not be any easier than it has been judged from the beginning. It has always been judged to be impossible. As much as you face the belief that it is impossible to give in to this movement and have your life go on, you are facing a judgment that is as old as your Original Cause. One of the biggest problems We have in gaining the healing needed is that there is definite intent on the part of many spirits not to allow the movement necessary.

At the time, all of these emotions went into an intense state of denial, they all received the judgment that there was no possible resolution because it was impossible to go back and start over without wiping out everything that had already manifested. Every time I considered doing this, I judged Myself to be terribly unloving. How could I possibly do this and also be loving? How could love possibly feel like destroying everything it had manifested because it had all been done wrong? Not knowing what to do with the feelings I had judged to be unloving here, they became further denied. What love believed it could not allow became manifest anyway in a state of denial.

Red is desperate to move the denials held there for so long. Understanding must come into the ones making these denials, or Red will not succeed in healing itself. Gapped rage and terror must also move because it is holding back the movement Red needs. It is the Mother Warriors who are protecting Red because they know what is at stake here. Meanwhile, the Father Warriors have missiles pointed at all of the lost Will involved here. They are manifesting the gapped rage of blame and the belief that this movement must be suppressed, but that is not all they hold, as you are going to find out.

The Father Warriors are already feeling provoked, and they are also manifesting the fear I had that I might be provoked beyond My ability to control My rage.

Many feel the fear that it is not possible to hold all of this back much longer. The Father Warriors are holding the line against lost Will just as they have been doing since Original Cause, but they are not going to be able to hold the line much longer. What is going to happen when Lost Will breaks loose is very much dependent on how denials are being handled by the ones who have been making them. The understanding that needs to get across the most now is that the ones who think they are the least involved are the very ones who are the most involved here.

Lack of understanding and loss of faith that there will be any solution other than destruction is causing many to seek refuge behind the line being held by the Father Warriors. Others, who think they see what the lost Will is going to do if it breaks loose, are trying to move out of what they think is harm's way. Both movements will find that there is not going to be any place to hide.

The Third World does not have much to offer anymore to those seeking to escape the Father Warriors because gapped rage has been heavily pressuring the survival there. Meanwhile, infiltration behind their own line is making the Father Warriors feel like they are having to spread their forces too thin. They are showing their feelings of overwhelm by calling for more and more military presence and more and more of a police state, while the lost Will is seeming to give them more and more reason to believe it is necessary. The Father Warriors have been incapable of learning the lessons of history and have conveniently forgotten Atlantis because they have been unable to receive anything from Me since I initially empowered them. This is why I say that gapped rage and terror need to move before there is a holocaust that makes what Hitler did look suddenly diminished.

The Angels who have become trapped on Earth by their guilt have retreated, for the most part, inside the line being held by the Father Warriors and are allowing them to act as a buffer zone. They are sending out only a few "Angels of Mercy" as a token ministry to the lost Will, just as they did in Original Cause. The Angels think they are being very loving to help at all because they insist they do not have involvement here. These "Angels of Mercy" are actually guilt on the part of the Angels who have much more involvement in what is happening than they have been wanting to allow themselves or anyone else to recognize or realize.

Most of the focus of the Angels is toward lifting themselves above what is happening on Earth with intent to leave Earth as soon as possible. They seek to escape to the music of the spheres while lost Will is screaming louder and louder in the desperate agony of not being received and of being unable to hold its pain any longer. Guilt is all that is causing the Spirit Polarity to listen to the lost Will from time to time because Spirit Polarity has not moved what is in the way of actually receiving the Will here.

If you listen to New Age Music, you may not like what the Heavy Metal bands are doing and saying, but if you are going to understand Lost Will, you need to see how the Heavy Metal bands are the Mother Warriors pleading the case of Lost Will. Metallica's original and often censored music video *One* is a good example of images of Father Warriors juxtaposed against the plight of the Lost Will. In fact, the more you learn to see, the more you will see that the message is all around you, but it is not being received or understood for what it really is. Alleviating the suffering "out there" is not even possible as long as more lost Will is continually being created. If you want to do the very most you can do, you need to move what you have so deeply denied within yourselves.

Looking at it now, it is exceedingly amazing to me that what I needed to understand was so obvious, and yet, it took Me so long to get it. There is terror in the Will that it cannot break through the obtuseness of Spirit here, and indeed, unless Spirit moves Its resistance to receiving the Will, the Will cannot get across to the Spirit.

There is hating, blaming, rage that needs to move in the Will toward My Light and all of the Spirit Polarity for being so insensitive, detached, disconnected, and focused only on what We chose to see, that the Will was unable to get across to Us regarding what Our denials were doing to the Will. The lost Will is so utterly, desperately enraged and terrified that We are leaving it in the unbearable tortures of Hell, that lost Will is threatening to push buttons and blow up everything if that is what it takes to make the point that it cannot stand its unbearable suffering anymore.

The Father Warriors are nervously watching this without being able to understand that they are holding the gapped rage Spirit feels toward the Will. Spirit is enraged at the Will for all of the same reasons the Will is enraged at the Spirit. There is much movement that needs to take place here for Spirit to really realize that everything it hates about the Will is only Will reflecting feelings Spirit actually has, but has pushed into a state of denial because of lack of acceptance for them.

Because the Father Warriors' denied emotions have to gain their movement at the source, the Father Warriors are still maintaining readiness to get the drop on the lost Will by pushing the buttons first, if necessary. Spirit Polarity must realize its causal role in all of these problems with which it has been saying it has no involvement.

Lost Will is hysterical over being pushed to the point where survival doesn't seem possible anymore. The only conclusion it has been able to draw from this is that We have intent to kill it. Lost Will does not want to move unless healing is going to happen for it, and yet, Lost Will is going to have to move soon no matter what happens, because it cannot hold back anymore.

If Lost Will has to manifest its movement in a state of denial without getting the acceptance it needs from within, Doomsday at its worst level is going to break loose. If Lost Will manages to break across the line being held by the Father Warriors without getting the feeling that Spirit is going to receive it and give it what it needs, then it will pillage and plunder, rape, loot, and grab for whatever it can get.

Lost Will's rage wants to rip Spirit's abundance away from it and beat Spirit up for its stupidity and insensitivity. Lost Will wants to rip Spirit's throat out for proselytizing, speaking platitudes, and making rhetorical statements that have nothing to do with the terrible reality Lost Will has been shoved into. Lost Will wants to break Spirit's bones for not moving to help it and throw Spirit out into the darkness to suffer what it has gone through. If this happens in a state of denial and there are any survivors left, it will be much like what you see on television, where the Road Warriors have taken over.

Most aggravating to the lost Will are those who want to make light of what I am saying here by claiming they do not see the vulnerability of the Western Nations to this sort of thing happening. Spirit that denies Will can never feel what Will has gone through until it decides it needs to. Because of this, lost Will can only vent its rage rampaging. It can never be avenged unless it turns toward My Light. If Lost Will does move in a state of denial, this Hell will break loose upon those who are not moving in their Wills. When Lost Will breaks loose and rushes over the line in a state of denial in the Body, a heart attack is the result.

It is extremely painful, unfortunate, and difficult that We have created such a situation, but it also was not possible to move in advance of having the understandings necessary to heal it. Movement in advance of the understanding necessary can create new problems that are unforeseen at the outset. It is also true that understandings cannot all be gained in advance of the movement that creates experience.

It is the Wills' role, in an undenied state, to feel the situation for Us and tell Us whether We are willing to risk having the experience or not. This is what healing must bring to Us, but this is something We have never had because of Our initial problems.

Spirit must take responsibility for the way It handled things it did not like feeling in the Will. Spirit did not allow the Will to give the input necessary. Spirit went cold toward the Will here and abandoned It, thereby disconnecting from the rage Spirit felt about what was perceived to be stubborn opposition from the Will. From this place of gapped rage, Spirit gave nothing to the Will and secretly delighted in the suffering this caused while also being able to disclaim responsibility for it by being able to say, "I'm not doing anything," when it was precisely the "not doing anything" that was causing the Will's pain.

Spirit has tried to pretend all along that It is more conscious than It really is, and has done this by telling the Will It has not been giving the right reflection here. Guilt is most of the reason the Will held back and did not press the issue, but gapped rage drastically amplified the problem when Spirit allowed it to force the Will to hold whatever Spirit did not want to see or feel. This has cost Us a lot in terms of gaining the understandings needed and in terms of the suffering that has already taken place; and yet, the emotional charge here is so immense it cannot be gone past in favor of the understandings being given now.

Most of the time, the healing process is going to take is going to be spent dissipating the charge that has built up here. It is simply not enough for Spirit to say, "Well, I am here now," as though that has the power to brush aside all of the backlog of suffering. It lacks compassion, and the truth of the matter is that no matter how much Spirit wants to claim It is present for the Will, it is not present wherever It is not vibrating in response to the Will.

The gapped rage that has been holding the Will down represents an enormous amount of lost consciousness, lost power, and lost vibration. It is a terrible area to have to go into, but it is necessary. There is no other way out. You cannot go up anymore because too much of you is already chained in darkness. If you want to go up, you are going to have to go down first and get your own lost Will. You are going to find that unless you go down and get your lost Will, you are not going to survive.

You are already dying of asphyxiation, or the loss of ability to vibrate, whether or not you have noticed it yet. You are terrified to go down into the darkness, you believe you cannot vibrate, but you are hiding this terror in belief systems that say it is not necessary. You are trapped and are avoiding it by saying you can leave, you do leave, you are going to leave, or you are having such a good time, you don't want to leave. The truth of the matter is, you are unable to move up into the Light you need to nourish you. You are caught in between, afraid to go down and unable to come up. Where you are, you are unable to breathe the air, drink the water, or assimilate the food. In short, you can't get nourished. You are in a state of terror, but your terror is in a state of denial.

Guilt and Love mixed together stopped Me from totally destroying the parts of Creation I hated so much. This is also what stopped the Mother from destroying what She hated. Heart and Body are also involved here. They also hated Spirit and Will for the imbalances We were causing in Them. They shoved this into a state of denial, believing it was wrong to blame Us for Their problems. Even though They will come into balance as Spirit and Will do, They still need to move what They have been holding back for so long in order to move along with Us.

Hatred is not love in the sense that it feels nothing that love feels, and yet, people say that love and hatred are very close together. This statement is based more on the observation of how love turns into hatred than the other way around. What needs to be understood in this healing is how to go into hatred and turn it back into love by expanding your definition of what love is until all the feelings you have are included, and the feeling in them is one of lovingness. Love is not a matter of what you say and do; it is a matter of how it feels when you say and do it.

Lost Will moving without understanding has caused some of the greatest devastation in history. Spirit Polarity has been seen as the victim of this rather than as causal here, but Spirit Polarity was only able to look as perfect as It did by virtue of what It was allowing to drop away from Itself and into the lost Will. The gap between the lost Will and the Spirit has been filled with guilt and darkness which has kept both sides apart. As a result, both sides have been unable to receive One another, but They have also been unable to kill One another as thoroughly as They might have otherwise.

"Without guilt," My fear told Me, "there would be no Mother left to heal, and no Body either for that matter."

Even now, Their situation is so perilous, We are not a moment too soon in trying to save Them.

"Guilt did not hold You back well enough," the Mother answers, "because You have been so busy denying Your guilt that Your gapped rage had access to Us all along."

The Mother is not wrong here. Guilt is going to move back without a problem compared to the problem We are going to have with denied guilt. Denied guilt is more cruel than guilt and has led Will into the most painful deaths ever experienced while claiming it was love doing this.

Gapped rage has been the enforcer of many things that I, in My guilt, would not allow Myself to openly enforce in Creation. Gapped rage came forth in the form of the Father Warriors to enforce all of the things I feared it would be too unloving of Me to enforce. This rage has not had guilt. It has had denied guilt and has set itself up as "the authority that is right."

The Will essence that feared It was wrong to feel as It did took in the guilt that allowed the Father Warriors to blame It. You do not need to be a Father Warrior to have gapped rage. You are more likely to have gapped rage move in you if you are not a Father Warrior. The Father Warriors are the form this rage has taken on for the many who have denied it out of themselves. The Mother Warriors, on the other hand, finally emerged as the Mother's response to feeling Her life so threatened by My gapped rage that She had to move in response to it. Survival terror is what both of these Orders of Spirits hate the most, and both have killed to avoid it.

I am giving some understanding now because Lost Will cannot move without them, but I cannot give very many. More understanding is not necessarily better because understandings cannot be seen for what they really are unless you move the emotions involved. Understandings that aren't given in response to Will's movement to receive them might as well be guilt or anything else because they are not relevant to the situation.

You cannot go past emotions and find healing. For example, if you tell yourself you should not be angry at someone because you already know it is not their fault, you cannot move the blaming rage you feel and have been holding back for so long. If you change your behavior toward them based on some understanding your mind has received, your emotional body is still vibrating the same. Because the role of emotions has been so ignored, there are many people who think they can take negative energy and convert it into positive energy when, in actuality, they aren't doing anything but mind games and form changes. The energy is still vibrating the same and becomes not unlike the proverbial "wolf in sheep's clothing."

If you are Spirit polarized, your level of seeming understanding may be your greatest stumbling block to freeing your Will if you tell yourself that what you are feeling is irrational or unjustifiable. If you are Will polarized, your guilt may be your biggest stumbling block. Therefore, no matter how irrational or unjustified you may be telling yourself your feelings are in certain areas, you must allow them to come into expression if you want to heal your denials. But I also want to remind you that this is why I have cautioned you to move them first with yourself. It is not necessary, especially in the beginning, to give them to the one who is triggering you, but if it happens, it is not wrong.

The Early Days With the Angels

Allow Me now to tell you more about how I initially perceived My life with the Angels. I had many denials that I did not recognize then, and because of My denials, My feelings were not fully real, just as now, I am only able to be as real as I can be, given what I still have to heal, but My feelings were as real as I could be then, and in that, I was genuine.

The Angels gave Me great joy, but the Angels emerged without their Wills. This upset the Mother so much She has not gotten over it yet. When the Angels emerged without their Wills, I immediately made excuses for this and put the Mother in the position, by reflecting guilt to Her about the feelings She had, that did not allow Her to find acceptance for Her feelings or the expression of them. No matter what I might have said to Her in the way of understandings, We had not yet learned that this was not a reason to stop the emotions from the expression they needed to have. Because the emotions were stopped by what was presented as a superior level of understanding on My part, guilt entered in where the Will should have been. This is the way Spirit thinks it is giving understandings, and Will receives them as a guilt reflection. No matter how many understandings or explanations you might want to give, they are going to feel like excuses and justifications if you use them as reasons to overlook or dismiss the feelings involved.

The major excuse I made then was that it could not have been another way, or it would have been. I also said that the Spirit Polarity had so much fear of the Will, they were unable to move toward it. I blamed the Mother for this and said it was Her behavior that was perpetuating the spirits' fear of the Will.

When the White Light Spirits emerged, they clung to Me and would not even move away from Me enough for the Mother and Me to continue what We had, previous to their emergence, viewed as Our normal relationship. The Angels said it was because they were so like Me, they could not move away. Some were saying they could not move away because they were just Me allowing different aspects of Myself to personify through them.

In the beginning, I thought I was willing to accept this because I saw the truth in it, even if that was not all there was, but the Mother never liked it. She already thought this did not feel right. She felt enraged to have a bunch of spirits who knew nothing about manifested existence come forth and proclaim to Us that they were Me already, as though this meant they had nothing to learn from Us and did not need to move back in any way that would allow us to live Our own lives. She felt that if they were Me already, they would at least know enough to have a relationship with their own Wills.

At first. I felt willing to let the Spirit Polarity have a time of this and told the Mother they would all grow up in time, and then She and I would resume Our normal relationship. I wanted to let the Spirit Polarity have a time of saying and believing anything they wanted to about themselves because I did not believe it was right to tell newly emerged spirits what they were and weren't before they had a chance to find out for themselves.

The Mother agreed with me in principle, but then her emotions would take over, and She would want to tell the spirits exactly what She thought of Them. I pressured Her to hold back. I thought She was being too quick when She wanted to tell the spirits what I thought they needed to discover on their own. I thought She had no patience with them, and that Her insights were presented too much like strikes against the spirits that they wouldn't be able to accept.

When the Mother was furious over this, I viewed Her as a bad Mother who was unwilling to give the children the time they needed. I told Her that in time, the Spirit Polarity would get over its fear and mature enough to embrace their own Wills.

The Mother wanted to say, "What am I supposed to do in the meantime, forego My relationship with You and My need for You and give it all to them? Am I supposed to make up for them not having Wills? And if not, then what is going to create the balance necessary here?"

Instead, guilt caused the Mother to try to believe Me because She thought it was necessary to give as much space for the emerging spirits to learn as We had had to give Ourselves.

"After all," I chided Her, "look at how frightened I was of You in the beginning. I did not embrace You initially, I pushed You away."

Since the Mother had never been able to resolve it with Herself why I had pushed Her away, She had guilt over the feelings She had, especially when I judged her the way I did, and so, She did not move Her feelings very openly. Inside of Herself, She had a substantial belief it was wrong that the Angels had emerged without their Wills. She could not come to peace with the Angels claiming on the one hand, they were Me already, and on the other hand, being granted the space and privilege of being children who were allowed to take Her place of closeness with Me under the guise of needing to learn from Me.

The Mother did not see how they were going to learn from Me when I was making them appear to be right by denying My Will in favor of them. It seemed obvious to Her that the Angels were not accepting of Her nor of Her relationship with Me. The more space I made in Myself for this, the less space She saw there for Her and the worse She saw Her situation getting. Underneath all of this, the Mother had a feeling of being punched and pushed away by the Angels, which She could not explain.

Except for the time She raged at the Ancient Ones, She did not allow Herself to move much of Her feelings toward the Spirit Polarity. Instead, She moved against Herself here by constantly pressuring Herself to feel other than the way She really felt and to do other than what She really felt like doing with the emerging spirits.

The Mother wanted to rage at the emerging spirits and blow them into what She considered to be their own right places since they wouldn't go there on their own. She saw the White Light Spirits' own right places as being those of moving out into Creation, with their own Wills opening the space for them to do it. This would enable Her to retake what She considered to be Her right place at My side.

The Mother felt that, despite all the excuses being made for the Angels, something was really wrong here. When the Ancient Ones emerged, We had all shared the feeling of not liking them, and We had given the response We felt was necessary, but I also had feelings of love I wanted to express, and I no longer wanted to allow anything else to surface. I did not realize the Mother had not given all of Her response because of the guilt involved. I did not even realize the guilt involved in the position I had taken. The Ancient Ones were giving Me the impression that My problems with them were solved, and I wanted to let it go at that.

The Mother continued to feel uncomfortable around them and gave Me the reflection that I was being a fool here. I did not want to see what She was seeing, and I did not like the reflection She was giving Me for not seeing it. I had rage toward Her that did not like the Mother putting Herself above Me in the seeing department. When She could not come to peace with the other orders of Angels either, I chided Her for not being able to let go of old images, let bygones be bygones, and move on. I told Her She should let go of Her ideas of how the spirits should be and accept how they were. She wanted to insist to Me that I should not force Her to accept the reality of what was when She did not like it and could not make Herself like it.

We both had fear of what this meant, and in that fear, there was an agreement, although We did not have this agreement in the rest of Us, not to let Our feelings move here. We were afraid We would not be able to handle what We were going to feel here if We allowed these feelings to move. In Our unmoving fear, We chose to pretend that We didn't see what We thought We saw. I did this by acting as though these spirits really were loving toward Me and aligned with Me. The Mother did this by allowing Me to have My way with Her as much as She could.

I was afraid I was impotent in the situation, and the Mother was afraid of this also. In addition, the Mother had guilt about not feeling love toward these spirits, and if She were wrong in Her reasons for feeling this way, it might mean She was not the loving Mother We all wanted Her to be.

I was making Her feel wrong, and whenever the Mother felt Me looking at Her like this, She pressured Herself more and more to take care of and care for these spirits according to the images of loving Mother I was projecting toward Her. She was terrified of My Light here, and I did not allow Myself to find out why. I didn't see the gapped rage She saw in the light I was generating with the Angels, and when I wouldn't receive Her here either, She was even more terrified. She feared I might be aligned with what She saw in the Angels, and that this was My reason for denying Her here. Fear and guilt caused Her to do Her best to confine Her disquietude to questioning Me as to why the spirits weren't taking after Her more.

When I told Her these spirits were like children to Me who were not yet grown up enough to have their own Wills, whom I thought of as mates for them, She argued with Me on that point. Many times, I felt like a Father who must protect His children from a Mother who was not going to allow the children time to grow up before She was going to make them leave home. Sometimes, I said She was jealous of My relationship with the Angels and could only think of Her own desire for Me.

When I viewed the Mother as ready to put the children in the street before they could handle it in order to have the relationship She wanted with Me. She would sometimes scream at Me, "If you view embracing their own Wills and moving out into life as something akin to being sent from the palace to live in the slums, then I hate you for seeing My side of the family as having all the bad things to offer, and your side of the family as having all of the good things to offer."

The Mother seemed so extreme and irrational to Me, I did not know what to do with Her. I viewed Her as interfering with My ability to have fun with the miracle of having emerged spirits. I gave Her a guilt reflection by telling Her it was not possible to embrace the Will immediately, and I repeated to Her all of the reasons I was using, at the time, to justify My initial rejection of Her. These reasons have been repeated so often since Original Cause that they have become what the Will has been believed to be.

My reflection to the Mother made it appear that the White Light Spirits were viewed as right by Me, and therefore, were right, and that She was wrong for having the feelings She had. The Mother wanted to rage at Me for this, but My lack of receptivity to Her held Her back. What I was giving Her here was My rationale for creating the gap and allowing it to widen.

When I handled the Mother this way, She would almost immediately shove what was bothering Me down and surface the love She had for the Spirits. She would be very docile, calm, and loving for a while, and during those times, I felt like I was successfully managing the situation. When I looked away, however, the Mother would move into Her feelings of rage. Although She did not allow Her rage to move openly, it colored everything She did.

"No wonder the Angels are so afraid of getting involved with their Wills," I told Myself. "Their own Mother is not giving them any reason to feel like they will enjoy it."

When the Mother showed Me Her rage, I did not mind it as much as when She frightened the children with it. I did not think it was fair of the Mother to frighten these spirits out of wanting to know their Wills and then blame them for not wanting to know their Wills. The Mother was furious at Me for lining up with the children against Her. How could I say I loved Her and then act like the Will was something the children would not want to embrace?

I thought the Mother was being very rough toward the Angels, and this made Me feel all the more protective of them. To Me, they looked so delicate, almost trembling, as they vibrated their light like so many white orchids gathered around Me. Their light was such a delicate, shimmering white, almost colorless except for the most delicate of pastels. They were filmy, changing form in response to the swirling of the ethers around Me like so many clouds in a gentle sky.

To Me, We were like a huge and beautiful cloud formation. My Light in the middle shone the beauty of little rainbows here and there and lit the clouds with a most beautiful light, emphasizing the form that was there. What could be wrong with this? Why couldn't I be allowed to enjoy it? Couldn't the Mother enjoy the subtle levels of color and refinement happening here? Why was She attacking Us like someone who would rather trample orchids than look at them?

It was true, the Angels were clinging to me and I to them. What was wrong with that? I was like a new father, enthralled with his firstborn. I was lit up just to see their presence and to look upon them in the ways parents admire all of the little fingers and toes. I was enamored and in awe. I was glowing with the joy of realizing the miracle of Creation.

To Me, the Mother was undercurrently acting like a mad woman who could not bond with what had come forth from Her, and who might even harm these spirits, so jealous was She of how I adored them and had gathered them into My arms instead of Her.

So innocent did they look to Me, so open and receptive to My Light and Love. It seemed as though they were moving along with Me in everything I did, and it gave Me a feeling of being loved and admired by them when I saw them imitating everything I did.

The Angels seemed to love Me so much that I believed them when they said they could not stand to move away from Me at all. At that time, I could not see Myself putting the Angels out of My arms and preferring to hold the Mother when She was acting the way She was.

The Mother viewed this as a betrayal on My part. As She saw it, She had given Herself to Me and I had taken something from Her without giving Her anything back. She had given Me sons, and I sat there holding them, forgetting to have any gratitude toward the role She had played, so consumed was I in admiring the newly emerged spirits and how like Me they were. She saw this as an ugly narcissism.

In giving Me something, the Mother felt She had lost Me, and that I had no time or love for her anymore. She felt I would only come to Her if I wanted Her to have more children, and yet, She feared what was going to happen even to that role, since I seemed to prefer the children to Her. The Mother felt as though She was no longer beautiful or appealing to Me anymore. When She complained that there were no daughters for Her, She was indirect. For one thing, She really feared what I might do with them. I avoided all of this by telling Her it was not a question of having daughters, it was a question of having any spirits at all. I couldn't see why She was so focused on criticizing what We had done and so unable to appreciate it for the miracle it was.

I felt it was a miracle that We had manifested spirits, and yet, the Mother felt I would not have loved it as much if the first spirits to emerge had taken after Her. She feared that daughters might displace Her, but She also strongly feared I might also use and abuse them and not love them any more than I was now appearing to love Her. The Mother felt She could not trust My love. Perhaps I had only used Her to have spirits, and when I had no further use for Her, I would get rid of Her again.

I blamed the Mother here. I said these things were all Her own negativity, and I saw Her as trying to draw Us into negativity We did not want to have. Suddenly, the presence of these new spirits made Me feel like it had always been this way with the Mother, and now, I just wanted to enjoy the presence of like-minded spirits around Me.

The more I saw the Mother as trying to draw Me into an experience I did not want to have, the more the White Light Spirits saw themselves as justified in not wanting to open and receive their Wills. The more the Mother's consciousness seemed to move toward what We deemed negative, the more We wanted to pull away from the Will. The more the Will felt abandoned by Spirit, the darker It became, until it looked to Us like the nature of the Will was dark. This has been, and still is, the nature of the stand-off. The Will hates the feeling of being pressured to feel other than It feels in order to gain acceptance, and We hate the feeling of having to feel what We don't like to feel.

For the Will to feel loved, It must feel that It is allowed to be what It really is and be accepted for what It really is. To know that It is accepted for what It really is, the Will must feel received and responded to with the same realness It seeks to have in Itself; a realness that freely expresses everything and does not hold back anything. Spirit needs this also. Anything less is the lack of alignment between Us, and We have a long way to go to total alignment.

The Mother always made Me feel wrong when I protected the Angels the way I did, but I gapped from these feelings and insisted to Her that I was right. I always made Her feel wrong for having the feelings She had toward the Angels.

The Mother then held back more and more of Her feelings. She allowed Me more and more of My own way, but She was not in alignment with it. Outwardly, it looked like She was complying with Me for making Her views subordinate to My own and, therefore, making Her subordinate to Me. She hated Me for not allowing Her to have Her feelings and My acceptance at the same time.

While the Angels were allowing themselves to enjoy all of the privileges of children, they often told Me they did not feel like they were children. Many of them said they had feelings of being grown up already when they were born. They often told Me things about Myself, and We would laugh because they had seen from the inside of Me what I was experiencing on the outside. In some ways, it seemed to Me that they were the voice of My inner self personified on the outside.

Because of what I was avoiding here, I allowed it to seem that I saw less difference between inner and outer than what I really saw there. I was focusing on the right in what they said and ignoring the rest. The Mother felt jealous of the closeness We were having, and it did not escape Her notice that I felt I was, in many ways, having more fun with the Angels than I had had with Her.

The Ancient Ones and the Arc Angels especially wanted to impress Me with their feelings of being grown up, and they wanted to show Me that they had powers similar to My own. We spent many long hours together experimenting to find out what things We could do. many times, We laughed at the Mother and made fun of Her, both for all the things She could not do, and for the many things She did that were not like Us.

This infuriated the Mother so much that I wondered if She had any humor about Herself. I could not see how alone and unloved She felt or how unresolved and angry She still was over the issue of the White Light Spirits emerging without their Wills. I did not see how dangerous and even evil She saw the laughter of Our Will denial to be.

"All in good time," I told Her about the Angels' Wills. I was flattered to have so much good company around Me. The Angels were showering Me with attention all the time. When the Mother stormed un upon Us, saying I had manifested a bunch of nasty spirits who wanted to come between Us because they cared nothing about the Mother, I turned My back on Her and told Her She was the One who was being nasty and uncaring about others. When the Angels told Me the Mother was not being loving toward them, I accepted it, and when they kept telling Me they did not want to move away from Me, I accepted that also.

The more the Angels grew up, in terms of how long it had been since they emerged, the more intense the Mother's feelings became over the issue of their Wills. I was, in fact, allowing the White Light Spirits to come between Us like so many ugly children whose design it is to come between their parents. I did not allow Myself to see it then, but I see it now.

I insulted and hurt the Mother many times by inviting Her to come home and then making no place for Her to be with Me. I allowed the Angels to remain between Us and then saw Her as the One who was unable to stay present with Me because of some flaw in Her own vibratory power.

"She can't move through the changes with Me," I thought.

As soon as I had any such thoughts, the Mother felt them within Herself and feared these things about Herself. Too many times, I compounded Her problems here by refusing to admit I had these thoughts. When the Mother tried to come home to Me, and I allowed the Angels to continue displacing Her even then, the Mother was condemned for Her anger and Her jealousy and told She was not flowing along with the openness love needed to have.

I told Her She was trying to put conditions on My Light, I could not accept from Her when, in actuality, She was just reflecting conditions that were already there, and I could not stand having Her make Me feel them. In My unresolved emotional turmoil over this, I felt She deserved everything I handed to Her. I never forgave Her for trying to make Me look like a fool in front of everyone in Creation, but I did not mention it. I only said She had never forgiven Me for My initial rejection of Her, and that She seemed to want to make Me pay for it forever. I told Her I felt there was nothing I could do about the ways She felt because everything I did only made the situation worse in Her eyes.

"After all," I would remind Her, "It is You who took another lover first, not I. And it is You who is looking bad, not Me, so it must be Your problem."

The Mother would often scream at Me then, that I was the One living in debauchery and did not even know it. I would then insist to Her that I was living in the purity of the Godhead, and that it was She who was guilty of living in debauchery.

Besides, I had Divine Purpose in My lovemaking with the Angels. We were generating Light, while the Mother, lately, seemed to be in the business of generating darkness. I had even begun experimenting with the Angels to see if any combination of the Angels and My Light would have the power to open space.

The Mother looked on with very jealous and fearful eyes. It hurt Her feelings and made Her heart feel like it had been stabbed to see Me in the arms of other lovers. She tried to make Herself feel it was alright because of all the judgment against Her for responding otherwise, but She was never able to get over Her pain here.

The Mother always suffered as long as I had other lovers and yet, She would always say She could not tell the difference between My Light and My Light in the Father of Manifestation. She said She often could not tell the difference between Us, or which of Us it was when she was experiencing Us. I did not trust Her. I thought this was Her way out, and a crumby one at that.

I scoffed at Her and told Her She knew very little about Me if She could not tell the difference between Me and the Father of Manifestation. When She said She often wasn't sure whether I had taken on form or the Father of Manifestation had given up His form to be as My Light, I felt She couldn't love Me if She didn't know Me any better than that.

When She was angry, She told Me She knew Me better than I knew Myself, and that I was the One who was crazy, not Her. But most often, My response frightened Her, and She felt Herself growing sick with the feeling that it was She who was crazy and that I did not love Her.

If I loved Her, how could I take lovers in the face of Her pain and not care what it did to Her? She accused Me of having a double standard of wanting to allow Myself to be free to do as I liked without allowing Her to be free to feel as She felt in response to it. Of course, I knew it was the other way around. I told the Mother Her accusations were nonsense, and I went on having lovers among the Angels. More often than not, I saw less of the Mother rather than less of the Angels.

Most of the time, the Mother allowed Herself not to look at what I was doing with the Angels because it was much too painful for Her to see what was happening there, I was slowly becoming imprisoned by them so that I was much more insignificant than I had been in the beginning, and the Angels were much more important than they really should have been, given the position they had really taken in Creation. The Angels had become so much the spokesman that most of the spirits never saw Me or heard from Me directly anymore.

The White Light Spirits had manifested as separate entities from Me, but they really didn't like that. They had manifested as the result of a power struggle already apparent in Me that had resulted in the separations. I had Creation in mind, but I also did not like the idea of having to hold within Me dissident voices that could not align with what I wanted to do. When I could not gain an alignment within Me, I thought experience was what they needed to align with Me, and so, I let all the voices within Me begin to pour forth into Manifestation.

The Angels wanted all of the privileges of vibrating differently from Me, along with all of the power of being Me. By surrounding Me as they did, they were holding back My Light to their level, and I was allowing it because I wasn't allowing Myself to feel what was happening. As long as I did not allow Myself to feel it, I did not know what was happening. Avoiding My feelings allowed Me to tell Myself anything I wanted to about what was happening because I didn't really know.

The Angels were constantly feeding Me an image of power by appearing to worship Me, while in truth, they were succeeding in getting Me to deny so much of Myself in favor of them that I was becoming more and more like them, a man among men, barely more powerful than they were. The more this went on, the more I then couldn't get along without them, which was what the Angels wanted. They wanted the privilege of being able to align with Me whenever it suited them. They called this compromise, fair exchange, and agreement among gentlemen. I now see it as a power play.

Since they had manifested My uncertainties and denials, the Mother called this a very dangerous game. I did not see how it was a guilt reflection of My own making, and while I was proclaiming the Angels to be miracles of Creation, the Mother saw them as the potential destroyers of Creation.

The Angels have always been in the position of seeming to be the most loving beings in Creation, and the Mother has always felt hatred for them. When She told Me I was facing My own imminent destruction, I laughed at Her and told Her I was surrounded by loving presence and nothing more. I told Her all She could see was Her own negativity.

She grew so afraid of Me and of trusting Her own perceptions that She did not say anything more until now. She tried instead to prove Me right and Herself wrong. The Mother went all the way to Hell making Me right and herself wrong, but no matter what She has done, She has not been able to love what was happening in Creation. The more the Mother tried to go along with allowing others to have power She really felt was Ours because guilt was telling Her We were not right to have it, the less She liked the results.

All the way along, I did not like the reflection She was giving Me because She tried to live out the teachings I was giving Her, and they were not working for Her nor for anyone else in the Will Polarity. Body was successful only in so much as It polarized toward Spirit. Still, no matter what Their problems were, I wanted to say it was Their fault.

In lovemaking with the Angels, as I called it then, We felt Our Light expanding, and We often had feelings of not being able to open the space to receive the expansion of the Light. We had feelings it was not right to have to ask the Mother to open this space, especially since the Mother contenders did not want to acknowledge that the Mother might have power they did not have, but it seemed there was no other way at times.

When We did ask Her to open space for Us, We were not direct. Instead, We made Her feel guilty by acting like it was Her fault Our Light could not expand because She kept pressing toward Me when it was obvious I didn't want Her that close. Then, when She would move back, Our Light would move into that space without acknowledging that She had done anything for Us. This was part of a long time during which the Mother was opening space in a state of denial of Her own power. When We did acknowledge the Mother's power to open space, We told Her that if She was keeping this power for Herself, as though She were jealously guarding any hold over Me She could retain, She should at least have unconditional acceptance for the expansion of the Light and not judge what forms the generating of Light should be allowed to take. We told Her She was acting as though She didn't want to allow the Light to rev up beyond where it already was because She could not handle it. We said She did not want Us to go up.

The Mother thought this was ludicrous. She was also horribly frightened about Herself here, and about Us, but guilt backed Her down, and She did Her best to accommodate Us in order to play the role She thought I wanted Her to have, which more and more seemed to be nursemaid while My other lovers had all the fun with Me, and neither the scars of childbearing had given Her not the responsibility of childbearing.

More and more, since Original Cause, this has been played out as the man having more leisure time than the woman to rejuvenate his own light, often giving his best to the life he has with his career. When the woman starts looking and acting unappealing as a result of this, the man seeks another lover. Lately, more and more women have been revolting against this, only to find that no matter what form changes they make in their lives, they are still faced with the same old battles because men still want the position they have always had, and they still want to tell women their problems are their own fault. The truth of the matter is, however, that women have less success generating light and abundance for themselves and less leisure time when they do get home from work, if there is any family involved, even if it is just a husband and no children.

This is just one manifestation of the Will opening space for the Spirit without getting the recognition It deserves. This example needs mention because it is the one that is receiving major focus in the present-day world, but it is not the only aspect of opening space. There are many ways in which space is being opened in a state of denial, and these many ways are not recognized or understood. They are definitely not appreciated; they are taken for granted.

All of the light I generated then with the Angels had gapped rage in it, which I did not recognize. This light was lacking the softness of Will's presence, but it had a crystalline brilliance to it that was similar to an adrenaline rush, especially if you do not allow yourselves to feel why the rush is there and just enjoy the rushing. That is what We were doing, focusing on, and enjoying the intensity of it.

The Mother allowed Herself to know She could not stand the feeling here, but She was already so frightened, and in so much pain, She could not be sure if it was from the light We were generating or not. She never dared question the Angels too closely because they looked upon Her so coldly whenever She approached them that She would quake in fear and feel so overpowered by self-hatred that She could not confront them.

My Light made Her feel the same and even paralyzed Her mind, so She was unable to speak when I denied Her here also, but She could feel that We thought this light was superior to what I had generated with Her. It was very fast-moving and almost too much for the Mother, who always felt like She was spinning in its presence. It was exciting and had a piercing intelligence that was scientific, rational and free of all the subjectivity I found so bothersome in the Mother.

This light was generated in the presence of hatred for the Mother, and worse yet, denied hatred that said it was only loving and just wanted to be free to be pure light. It made the Mother feel like She needed to vomit, and yet, She felt She was being forced to open space to receive this light, and even worse, vault it up as the most superior light generated yet.

The Angels were feeling very superior to the Mother now and were looking down on Her as though She had come forth wrongly, like some sort of commoner who had snuck in from the streets with a story for the King in the castle as to why he should marry her. In the Angels' view, the Mother was already showing Herself for what She really was and moving to Her right place accordingly. It appeared that the Mother was unable to keep pace with the King and the rest of His class, and the Angels felt they were right in reducing the Mother to servant because She really was a member of the serving class. As I look back now, I see that I stood by with as much lack of presence as the fathers in *Snow White* and *Cinderella*. Just as surely as I projected My desire to have the Will serve the Spirit, the Angels were manifesting that part of Me. The more the Mother felt Herself being pushed into a subservient role, the more it looked to Her like the real Mother was being replaced by wicked stepMothers.

I was no help to the Mother here. I had many rationalizations for this, but the one I want to mention now I am going to mention because it has repercussions in every family. I rationalized My lack of helpfulness and support for the Mother's problems here by saying that if She really was My equal and the Mother of Everything, as I had named Her, then, as the Mother of the Angels, She needed to gain their respect in Her own right and not because I told the Angels they had to respect Her. Otherwise, I thought, She was no Mother at all.

Sounds good, doesn't it? Except for many major denials, this could have been right, but I will mention only one of these denials now. I did not see how My own lack of respect for the Mother made it impossible for Her to gain the respect of the children. I did not even see that I was disrespecting Her.

I must admit, I had more respect for the Angels by now than I had for the Mother. The more I felt I could not trust the Mother, the more I aligned with them. I had more respect for the Angels than I had had in the beginning, and lovers or not, they were My Light and My closest allies.

Several of the Angels wanted to see if they could learn to open space. Of all the Angels who wanted to replace the Mother, these Angels were among the most conspicuous. They had many times told Me their light was much better than the Mother's. Many times they tried to make Me feel the Mother was not My right lover so much as guilt had caused Me to open that space to Her because She was there. They told Me they were convinced She was not supposed to have emerged where She did, any more than the Angels' Wills were supposed to have emerged where the Mother claimed they should have.

These Angels said it was their strong conviction that the Will was not meant to be an emergent being because feelings were meant to be held and felt within, worked out within, and then, when Heart balance had been reached, all expression should come from Spirit because Spirit was the expresser. My uncertainties were causing Me to consider everything that sounded reasonable, and the guilt in Me caused Me to give them a rightness here that did not come from all of Me. Because they did speak to a part of Me, this part of Me aligned with them to give this reality a try. We seemed so aligned with each other here. Why couldn't it be this easy?

These Angels told Me they believed they held enough Will within themselves to be able to open space. They were so confident in every way the Mother was lacking confidence, that I believed them at first.

Of course, they were manifesting My own beliefs that feelings should be held within and worked through there rather than coming forth to bring their turmoil to others.

These Angels came to Me many times and made love with Me in an effort to open space. They believed that if they could open space, it would make them the Mother in the Mother's place. I gave these

Angels a great amount of My Light and a great opportunity to open space for that Light by allowing them much more time to learn than I ever allowed the Mother. I was more gracious with them than with the Mother. I allowed them more latitude with their feelings than I allowed the Mother, and yet, none of them could open space.

One of these Angels in particular had insisted with Me from the beginning that she should have been the Mother. She always presented as though she should have been the Mother. She always presented herself as though she wanted Me to feel that her understandings were greater than the Mother's because the Mother's viewpoint was always too biased in Her own direction, while she had a more balanced view.

She presented herself as having the martyred role of having to clean up after the Mother and correct Her mistakes without being given the recognition and credit She really deserved. She said the Mother was so unsure of Herself because She knew She wasn't really the Mother. This Angel said she would have emerged quickly in response to My call, but the One who had emerged in the place of the Mother wouldn't let her emerge. She said her emergence at that time had been made impossible because the One I had been calling Mother had fought her down, and that while she had not really been defeated, she had backed down because she was not a violent spirit.

This Angel said she had not liked having it happen more for My sake than hers, but she also felt that this experience must have been necessary for Me for some reason, and that she had confidence that it was what everyone involved needed to experience to be able to recognize the real Mother. Her implication was that this was her.

She enticed Me into lovemaking with her a number of times, pressing forward all of the sensuality she had and representing herself as the most orgasmic essence there was. Meanwhile, I could feel her pressuring herself. As much as I held Myself back in the presence of Angels, I held Myself back in her presence also.

This gave all the Angels, and especially her, the impression they could handle all of My Light, no problem. They were handling it alright, but not in the ways that were allowing the expansion necessary. The compression of My Light was lashing out against this in a state of denial, while consciously, I was holding back as the loving thing to do. I was becoming more dense and sinking to the level of the Angels, which was making it more and more just words on My part that I had more light and more power than they did, or than I was showing.

My efforts with this Angel produced no more opening of space or emergences of spirits than any of the other Angels, but this Angel always claimed it was My fault and accused Me of withholding something from her. I told her I was giving her all I could and that more wasn't possible.

When she kept insisting, I had to give her more, I gave her a little more Light, and the pressure of it was experienced by her as violence during Our sexual experience. She had a violent orgasm and claimed she liked it. She also claimed there was no problem with the additional light I had given her and that it was just what she needed. The truth of the matter was I gapped a little.

A little while later, while she was still in My arms and feeling the release of orgasm still present within her, a few heads peeked out of her. They looked like such terrible beings to her that she immediately hid them from Me, hoping I hadn't noticed them. They were some of the heads of the Father Warriors looking to see if they could emerge here, but she had been unable to open the space they needed, so they could not press forward any further.

The heads of the Father Warriors took in the impression from her that it was not right for them to emerge in My presence. Ever since the Father Warriors have tried to keep fathers from being involved in the birth scenes. The belief here is that the Mother might emerge something horrible that the father cannot accept until it is at least cleaned up and made presentable, and maybe not even then, but that was not what this Angel claimed. She claimed she didn't want Me to see what was happening there because her feminine functions were messy, and she did not want Me to look at them.

This Angel had intent not to allow Me to see what she had intent to emerge until she made sure it knew how to present itself to Me in a way I would find acceptable. She let Me know she had almost emerged spirits, but she was not sure I was going to find them acceptable. She said she wanted to make sure first so that she did not repeat any episode of the Mother's where She had displeased Me. She wanted Me to feel like she had nothing but My approval in mind, but she let me know what she was trying to do here by also making it known that she saw it as My fault she had not been able to open enough space for these spirits to emerge. She made it clear that she thought I should have given her more light the way I was giving it to her when she orgasmed.

"My orgasm wasn't complete," she told Me, "because You did not give Me all of Yourself."

For a long time after that, she pestered Me to reenact this session and give her another chance to emerge these spirits, and yet, when they finally did emerge, and she saw my reaction to them, she put a disclaimer on her role here by saying it was My fault these spirits were the way they were because I didn't allow them their right emergence place.

This Angel has always thought My Light loved her more than the Mother, but she has gapped herself from what was really taking place here and has allowed herself to remember only that she was very close to God and made love with Him that gave her an orgasm she has never been able to repeat. She has to look at all of it now, or she is not going to move past the place where she is stuck. She has allowed herself to remember that I looked upon her as the best possible Mother replacement, but this was in her own eyes and not in Mine.

This Angel has often claimed to Me that she has changed, but no matter what changes she has claimed to have made, I have seen only form changes. She has claimed that a more fighting stance would make her less afraid of emerging her full power, thus enabling her to open space and emerge spirits. Her fighting posture has never made Me feel that she was any less afraid than she was initially, only more in denial of it. She has also claimed many times over that she has been denied her full power by being denied her right place. She has also said that her full power would emerge when the right situation called it forth. As time has gone on, more and more people have been looking inadequate in her presence because none of them has ever presented her with the right situation for her full power to emerge, or for her to stop claiming that her problems are their fault.

I felt guilty for a long time regarding all of the Mother contenders and My involvement with them, especially since I was so indirect with them most of the time and allowed them to make assumptions I did not correct, but now that I have seen the Angels in a new light, I have realized that I was not wrong in holding back with them. I was also not wrong in holding back from giving this Angel another opportunity to attempt the emergence of spirits. The Father Warriors, as it is, have been the most powerful order of spirits. They have been empowered by My Light in a state of denial, and if My Light had been present for their emergence as though My Light had approval for the gapped rage that emerged there, they would have been even more powerful.

When I saw how influenced this Angel became by the gapped rage she took in from her experience with Me, I had guilt about the Angels. I wondered how often I might have been hurting them in these ways without knowing it. But when I saw she had Lucifer in mind and not My Light, I saw it in the rest of the Angels too. She had widening the gap with the Will in mind, not closing it, and so did the rest of the

Angels.

The Father Warriors needed the gap in which to emerge, and when this Angel saw that I was not going to open the gap for her or let her open the space that could cause Me to gap, she let Me know that she saw Me as very unloving here because I would not allow this to happen. She presented herself as more loving than I was because she had intent to give acceptance to these spirits, while I would not. When she has felt I did not love her for taking this position, she had also turned around and said that she hated the Father Warriors, and when they have reflected her to herself, she has hated them.

I have realized now that all of the Angels had the same thing in mind that she had, and that she regarded herself as the best possibility to replace the Mother because she came the closest to succeeding here. I have also realized that holding back here was not wrong because it was what I felt like doing. As it turned out, what I felt like doing was not wrong.

It was necessary for Me to increase My Light, but making love with the Angels meant there was no place to receive it in the same sense that there is no place to receive it when a man makes love with a man. Either nothing at all comes of it, or disease comes from it. This is because expanding Light in the presence of expanding Light without enough balance of magnetic energy to receive, hold, and guide it, is as dangerous as radioactivity, which is, in fact, part of the reflection of this in the material plane. Magnetic energy has always had trouble with reproduction and disease because of denial, but these are problems from lack of Light. We had the opposite, a lack of Will.

Radio waves are already bad enough, but when the activity of split atoms and the instability caused by this is added, you can begin to see how opening to this kind of light has meant for the Will that it gets damaged. My Light, moving outwardly, in unguided explosion, does not create; it destroys by taking apart the very structure upon which Creation is made manifest, the magnetic part that holds it together.

Immense movement is necessary to allow the Mother to live because so much has happened to Her already that it is almost impossible for Her to live. If guilt is your reason for opening to Her now, that will not help Her to live because it is not possible for the Mother to live if She receives guilt instead of My Light. If you are Will, you need to move your feelings toward Spirit Polarity for what has been done already, and toward the Mother for seeming to allow it. If you are Spirit Polarity, or wish you were, you really need to move what you have for so long held back regarding the Will.

It has to go all in the Mother's favor now because it never has been in the past, and yet, this does not represent an imbalance in My Light. I need to allow the Mother to present everything She has been, for so long, unable to present. I need to allow the Mother to present everything She needs to present. Without it, I cannot learn what I need to learn, and neither can you. The more you are sick of hearing about the Will this and the Will that, the more you can either move the rage of your resistance to the Will and possibly have a chance to heal yourself, or you can stay turned off to the message of the Will and go off Earth in the Earth changes. If you are already having trouble with what the Will is presenting, you don't know the half of it yet.

I had feelings of love for the Mother, no matter how it seemed, as I have brought forward all the denials that have had to come forward in these books. I also want you to know that there were many aspects of My life with the Mother that were secret at the time they were happening because We thought it had to be that way. I realize that left you wide open to fantasizing about us, and to acting out what you thought was happening between Us, but that was not what We had in mind. What We had in mind was that you would get to know your own Wills and come to us with your questions when you had really had enough experience to have intelligent questions.

My Light cannot be known without a Will to feel It for what It is. Without Will to feel it, one bright light is as good as another, and this is how it was in the early days with the Angels. We said We were all One and that it didn't matter how We arranged Ourselves, or what form this arrangement took; it was all love, and it was all wonderful. In the beginning, this image of Ours seemed to work like the ideal household because We allowed Ourselves to be deliberately unaware of the undercurrents, and when they did gain recognition, We purified Ourselves of them.

Some Angels took the role of children and let Me have the fun of being like their Father, while others made lovers of themselves and gave Me the love I needed that way. The lovers were not all male; many of the Angels had feminized themselves in an effort to please Me by emulating the images I had projected of the ideal Mother.

Many times, I had feelings of homeyness with the Angels, and during these times, the roles were always switching between the Angels who were My lovers at any given time, and the Angels who were parenting at these times. The flow seemed perfect to Me then. Angels were always available for lovemaking, while those who needed parenting were never without it. The Angels also had one another as lovers and friends. Those who wanted the roles of children always had a number of loving parents around them, and never felt a lack of parenting when other parental parts of the Light were lovemaking.

There was no jealousy over this. We felt it was a beautiful flow of way to love, unlike the Manifested Spirits who were always fighting and acting jealous, no matter what roles they were playing We never fought. Unlike the Manifested Spirits, who did not act like they liked changing roles because they always got attached to these roles, We didn't feel We got attached. We saw Ourselves as openly flowing into whatever role the situation called for at any given moment.

We saw Ourselves as participants in a great drama and enjoyed changing roles often. In this way, We often justified the lives that Creation's victims were having by saying it would be the other way around next time. This was a real perversion of the so-called, "Law of Karma" because it never really was the other way around. Even when We took on roles where it looked like We were going to be victims, it wasn't the same for Us. We felt spiritually superior then. We realized it was the way We were vibrating that made the difference, and We took pride in that, spiritual pride.

Once the perpetrator, always the perpetrator would be more like a description of what was really happening, but it is not necessary to view this as some sort of new law. If you allow the movement necessary, this is all going to be broken down into the changes that are necessary. The understanding I'd really like to give you here is that victim and perpetrator are always the same person, but fragmented in such a way that it hasn't been recognizable. The pain has been caused by the polarizing of consciousness into part of the self and away from the rest of the self. Until this is really received in the Will, it will be nothing more than words, and the pain will go on.

Even though My Light had not been called upon to take any role other than God, I also was experiencing My Light in the form of Angels, saying they were Me in their own right, and I wasn't experiencing insecurity or jealousy. I felt I wasn't the insecure, jealous God I had been earlier. I was convinced it was the Mother who had stirred most of these feelings in Me, and that without Her, I was much better off. I certainly had numerous lovers and wasn't experiencing jealousy or competition among them, and I was allowing Angels to have other lovers in My presence without feeling insecure or jealous. I thought I had evolved past the interpersonal problems I had had with the Mother.

We all said it was just the Will that had these feelings of jealousy and possessiveness, and the more the Mother felt this from Us, the more

She tried to behave in the ways She thought were expected of Her. Her efforts to please Me were always so full of Her feat of losing My love that Her efforts did not please Me. The Mother always wanted Me to attach Myself to Her, while Angels didn't make Me feel like attachment mattered to them.

Long periods of what felt like glorious times went by in this manner, during which the Angels and I spent many long hours doing creative visualizations and presentations of Our visions to One another. We were aware of the widening gap between Our visualizations and what was actually happening in the Manifested Worlds, but We were already more than full of explanations as to why that was happening.

We blamed having sex in the Body most often when We looked out upon the Manifested Spirits because it grew so dark around them whenever they made love. We were so proud of the Light We were generating. Sometimes the excitement and intensity of it made Us feel like We were going to explode, and oftentimes, We did have little explosions going off around the Godhead like fireworks, adding to the overall brilliance of the already sparkling light.

We felt We were full to brimming over, and when We wondered why the Manifested Spirits weren't more readily taking in this wonderful Light of Ours, and allowing it to vivify them, We also had many explanations. We viewed Ourselves as so electric and quick that the most popular idea among Us was that We were too much for the Manifested Spirits. Of course, this contained all the feelings of superiority We already had within Us. It did not even appear on the list of ideas that the gap between Spirit and Will was not allowing Will to draw in or anchor the Light, nor did it cross Our minds, because of the denials involved, that there could be any valid reason why the Manifested Spirits would not want to draw in Our Light. We viewed them as obtuse, oppositional, and laboring in unconsciousness that could not open and receive Our Light. We viewed the Manifested Spirits just as I had viewed the Mother and Father of Manifestation at the time of the Manifested Spirits? emergence, but because I had denied so much of what I really saw and felt then, I did not recognize this for a long time.

Deflecting the Focus by Pinning Blame

Meanwhile, the Mother and the Father of Manifestation felt the blame, and the shame that accepted it, and denied expression to their response to being blamed because They were so afraid of what it all meant. They were afraid it meant that They were not right; not right to be lovers, not right to have emerged these spirits, and not right to have thought They were the Mother and the Father of Manifestation. They were both very attached to these roles, but They were being told by the Godhead that this attachment was wrong.

More and more, They received the judgment from the Godhead that They had made a mess of Creation by manifesting it wrong. More and more, They were trying to focus on cleaning up the mess They had made without making more of a mess. They had rage about receiving all the blame, but They seldom felt it because Their fear was so great.

When Their efforts were more and more of a failure, both to fix what had already been done and to avoid making more problems, the Mother and the Father of Manifestation felt more and more like They should let others take Their roles. We had given Them the impression from the Godhead that They should be willing to do this, and the more unworthy and inadequate They felt, the more power They abdicated to others until there was nothing left in Them but a dim memory of having once been close to God, or what They had thought was God.

All the many lives They have lived trapped in Manifestation, They have labored to help others, feeling responsible for them without realizing why, loving them and trying to ease their pain as best They could, and receiving nothing in return but denial and death for having ideas that were not mainstream. We had discredited Them in front of everyone in such a way as to give license to gapped rage to discredit Them and to get rid of Them if They persisted.

Meanwhile, all of the Angels, and other fragmentations who took over Their roles, have claimed to be doing a much better job and have received all of the credit for everything that has gone right, while continuing to blame the Mother and the Father of Manifestation for everything that has gone wrong. This is reflected through the Warriors by the way it is never the fault of religion, government, or their other institutions, their laws, or their methods. It is always the fault of those who fail to align with their dictates or fail to carry them out properly.

Will spirits always take the blame here, along with whatever parts of Heart and Body have demonstrated any alignment with Them. The gap does the judging and punishing here. This behavior monitor has, of course, been guilty, but the punishment meted out has been severe because of the lack of love involved. Just as much as you lack compassion for all the mistakes you think have been made, the punishment will reflect this to you, complicated always by the presence of guilt holding back the healing that is needed. The most severe form of this guilt is self-hatred. Self-hatred has often taken the form of fragmenting out what is hated and punishing it "out there."

It is important to understand that self-hatred has been the most severe in the Will-Body Polarity. If someone else gets charged with crossing the line gapped rage wants to enforce, they are usually found innocent of the charges or are given such a light punishment that it is merely tokenism. This has been especially true when gapped rage fragments have gone totally free after killing thousands. The people in the Will-Body Polarity who receive the heaviest punishments are all pieces of the Mother and the Father of Manifestation who accepted the guilt and blame. Most of the fragmentation here took place when They could not stand feeling guilt and blame in the presence of My Light anymore.

There are also many fragments who left the Main Body of essence because they did not like the views of the Main Body and decided they weren't going to be able to prevail the way they wanted to. These fragments are not sure if they want to align with Us now or not because they still have old feelings of wanting to prevail, and they do not know what they have missed out on in Us since they left. These fragments have often been perpetrators against Us in the ways that self-hatred can also be fragmented out and turned against the main body of essence. Most of the essence that was lost into fragmentation here was lost because rage was being so heavily denied. This essence can align if it moves the rage it has toward the main body of essence first.

There have been many points of contention, but one main point of contention has been whether emotions should be allowed to express in their raw state or not. When it looked like essence that wanted to do this was going no place but down, many felt this form of emotional expression was wrong and polarized more toward the part of My Light they perceived as agreeing with this viewpoint. Fragmentation was the result.

These fragments look very Spirit polarized, because the more the Mother and the Father of Manifestation believed the judgments against Them and took these judgments in, the more They felt like They had to let go of the Light that did not seem to like the experience it was having with Them. This Light abandoned the Mother of Everything and Father of Manifestation and left Them with guilt in the place of that Light by telling Them it was wrong to have the views They had. This has been a rip off of the Mother and Father of Manifestation, which They allowed because They did not have the understandings We have now.

This Light did not accept the Will it was attached to and needs to understand the responsibility it has for the Will denial it entered into here. It has always blamed the Mother and the Father of Manifestation here and any other essence that went along with Them. This essence views itself as blameless, and yet, it played a role in what happened up to the point where it fragmented out. Even after that, its role remained substantially unchanged in terms of how it related to the parental part of the essence. This role must be understood now because this essence has been no more able to prevail with My Light since the splits that were made here than it was before.

In addition, all of these fragments need to know that as much as they stood apart, and said they were not party to that which was being blamed on the Mother and the Father of Manifestation, they have created a gap in their experience with the Mother and the Father of Manifestation, and these fragments no longer have the full spectrum of experience necessary to be the parental parts of the Mother and the Father of Manifestation. All they have the power to do now is align with Us as best they can, if they so choose, by moving all of the old charges around their original fragmentation.

The Mother and the Father of Manifestation did not feel like They were the parental parts of the essence involved here, as They were going down, more and more denied by everyone. They were losing essence as though rats were fleeing a sinking ship, and these fragments all gave excuses for leaving that made denials the Mother and Father of Manifestation were receiving all the more difficult because They couldn't even keep Themselves together anymore. They were denied until They did not even feel like They were accepted as part of Creation at all. The undercurrents and denials involved in the way most of this experience was taking place further complicated the issues because it made confronting it openly impossible at the time. When the Mother and Father of Manifestation tried to get straight answers, the answer They were most often told was that Their perceptions were wrong.

What all fragments need to know is that no matter what reasons you want to cling to for having fragmented, you are all left to avoid the terror of what you were experiencing, and this is just the terror that has to be faced now.

Quite a lot of the essence that fragmented out was using rage to overcome its terror. This rage stood apart, acting smug, like it already knew better than the Mother and the Father of Manifestation. These fragments have an "I knew it all along. I told you so" attitude. These fragments believe they should have taken over as the parental parts of the Mother and Father of Manifestation and have been trying to do just that. Many of them have acted out their ideas to do just that. Many of them have actually acted out their ideas of the roles of Mother and Father of Manifestation for a long time, and this has not been so wrong because everyone involved needed this experience for many reasons, but this experience is coming to a close now, and these fragments are going to have to accept that the moves they made are the moves which put them in the positions they are going to have to accept now.

All of these fragments who have viewed themselves as contenders for the parental positions of the Four Parts of God helped My Light understand Itself, but the roles you have played have been almost nothing but roles, and you are going to have to look deeper into yourselves to find out where you really do fit in. As My Light recovers Itself here, you are all going to have to move into your right places and let the right parental parts of the Mother and the Father of Manifestation and Heart, and Me for that matter, have Our right places.

You all had motives you did not want to have seen, and you will still have motives if you go through the motions of alignment without moving the full intensity of the emotional charge that needs to move here. In My state of denial, I did not see what you were doing at first, but now that I have seen it, I need to move in response to the level of understanding and awareness that I do have and not allow you to hold Me back anymore.

These fragments also have hatred for the Mother and the Father of Manifestation and feel superior to Them because they charged the Mother and the Father of Manifestation were impotent and inadequate in Their inability to come to Me and prevail regarding all of the issues that did not come forward between Us.

I would like to point out that My lack of receptivity did not allow it, and when these fragments goaded the Mother and the Father of Manifestation into trying it anyway, it was the Mother and the Father of Manifestation who got maimed and killed by the gap while these fragments stepped aside, giving the same reasons they had used when they fragmented out originally. The reason most often given was that in some way or another, the Mother and Father of Manifestation weren't received because They didn't present Their viewpoint in the right way.

The rage held by these fragments felt self-righteous because of the imbalance it had with the fear it had polarized away from. As much as the Mother and Father of Manifestation were obsequious and guilty, their fragments were bothersome in the opposite direction. These fragments did not come along to confront My Light with the issues the Mother and Father of Manifestation had been unable to bring forward because these fragments were too afraid, but they claimed it was because they could not get the main body of essence to do it. By withholding themselves from moving into alignment within the Mother and the Father of Manifestation, these fragments were protecting themselves from the reality of denial that was taking place in the Will-Body Polarity.

By withholding movement in this rage within the Mother and the Father of Manifestation, this essence made a power play of its own. The more the rage polarized away from the fear and guilt, causing major splits in the Will-Body Polarity, the more the rage fragments could feel that they were more powerful and more right than the rest of the essence involved. With this going on, balance was impossible, and antagonism grew immense where alignment was needed. This rage has responsibility for moving against the terror it hates so much, almost as much as does the rage in the Spirit Polarity.

As much as the Mother and Father of Manifestation have responsibility for having denied Their rage, the rage fragments have responsibility for having refused to grant acceptance to the fear and guilt, or the reasons fear felt the rage must be held back.

As a result of this fragmentation, the parental part of both the Mother and the Father of Manifestation thus became so fear and guilt-ridden as to be unrecognizable, even to Themselves. Quite a lot of this essence reflects to Them from the Father Warriors and from the Mother Warriors also, but it can be found in all Orders of Spirits.

In the Godhead, We saw all of the fragmenting in both the Mother and the Father of Manifestation, and also in the Manifested Spirits, as increases in the Manifested Spirits due to their own lovemaking. This view was encouraged by these fragments who did not want it known what they had done until they were ready to reveal themselves. These fragments often fought with one another over the differing viewpoints they had. These fights were going on before the War in the Heavens, but they were kept hidden from My Light as much as possible. From the Godhead, We saw more of this fighting happening than the ones involved were aware of, but We saw it as fights between Manifested Spirits, not even realizing the role denial and fragmentation were playing.

More Light Is Not Necessarily Better

To Us, the gap between Spirit and Will was an evolutionary gap. In Our view, Will and Body simply weren't seen as able to move as quickly as Spirit and Heart. We concluded that the Manifested Spirits just weren't ready for the level of illumination We had, or for the presence of Our love. We didn't think there was any lack of Light and Love for Them, so We didn't see the lack of It as reason for increasing density there. We saw the increasing density and the widening gap between Spirit-Heart vibration and Will-Body vibration as resultant from Will-Body's lack of receptivity to Us.

The guilt mixed in with My Light was not noticed then, and the denied guilt and gapped rage that insisted We were not guilty of anything certainly wasn't noticed for what it was. We decided the best plan for guilt-free living was to continue with the roles some Angels had already been taking on, of going forth to the Manifested Spirits to offer whatever ministrations, counseling, advice, teaching, and parenting help they could, given the circumstances.

The Angels always went forth glowing so much from their experiences in the Godhead that it was often irresistible to Me not to tag along and see what happened. The image I had was that such irresistible Light would both draw the Manifested Spirits to It and move them to take It in. When neither of these things happened, I resorted to My many explanations.

When the Manifested Spirits squirmed uncomfortably in the presence of this Light and averted their eyes, I thought it was because they had grown so accustomed to darkness that they could no longer handle the Light in whose presence they had been born. My Light had evolved into something too dazzling for them. I saw that the Manifested Spirits viewed My Light as not accepting them as they were, and when they squirmed, I viewed them as needing more self-acceptance. It didn't occur to Me that they might not like My Light because of the Will and Body denial involved in it.

The Manifested Spirits did feel unworthy within themselves, but not only for the reasons previously thought. We did have the feelings of superiority in Ourselves that were making them feel this way. The Will Polarity of the Manifested Spirits was especially reflecting this to Us. The Spirit Polarity of the Manifested Spirits was looking a lot lighter to Us and had more receptivity to Us.

The Angels went forth in a steady stream and looked like shining pools in what had already become the murky waters of the Rainbow Spirits. Since their forms reflected what was happening to their light, the forms of the spirits who were not living in the Godhead were no more capable of retaining the healings We gave them than their essence was of retaining the Light We gave them. Those who did come around to Our viewpoint always looked better to Us than the rest, and We immediately vaulted them up as proof of the rightness of Our teachings if Our teachings were only correctly applied. This always made the others glower even more darkly, although they often tried to hide this by making a display of paying homage to these people. The most prevalent, yet hidden and often denied, feeling among the Manifested Spirits was that if God required this of them, they weren't sure they wanted to move toward God, but if the other direction was as they feared, they had no choice but to try to be as good as possible.

Our Light essence felt good to Us. We liked the way It was vibrating, and We couldn't see any reason why the Manifested Spirits should want to resist It. The only reflection they gave Us that made sense to the way We viewed things at the time was that life in the Godhead must be much better in every way than their lives were, and they were too unworthy to be there with Us.

They gave Us this reflection along with the feelings of jealousy We had felt before from the Will. We did not go into these feelings to see what they might tell Us. We dismissed these feelings immediately as "lower nature stuff" and tried to cultivate in them more openness to receive Our Light so that the Manifested Spirits could live more as We did. We didn't want to accept the guilt that there might be any reason why they should feel as they felt, other than their own refusal to accept the Light being offered to them.

When We shined the Light in their presence, the Manifested Spirits acted as though it had nothing to do with them that We were shining Light. They wouldn't even admit they needed It and often looked away, as though they were ignoring Us. We found this to be mildly angering, but We did not allow Our emotions to move much in response to what happened in Manifestation. Feelings were not present most of the time in the Godhead except for feelings of ecstasy and upliftment. What We called feelings were really more of a mental outlook than anything else, but We called these feelings "positive emotions" and We did not want to get Ourselves involved in "negative emotions" by allowing them to move in Our lives.

Nonetheless, some of the Angels were not able to move around freely among the Manifested Spirits if they stayed with them very long. We always thought it was the nature of entering the magnetic energy field, and that just as the magnetic energy had become trapped in manifestation. It was trying to trap the Light with it.

We did not like the feeling of being trapped or caught in manifestation, and We developed all manner of means to pop in and out of manifestation without getting caught in it. The more We did this, the more some of the Manifested Spirits started acting like they were laying traps to catch Us whenever We came to them.

A kind of game seemed to be developing in which the skill of entrapment was being pitted against the skill of escape. Some Angels enjoyed this more than others, but Body got caught in this more than He liked, since the forms the Angels took on were usually what became trapped, while the Angels jumped out of these forms with the essence they recognized as themselves. Since they viewed themselves as taking on forms rather than having bodies that were an integral part of themselves, The Angels were easily able to leave these forms behind and take on other forms, almost as fast as tumbling acts go from one trick to another. The Manifested Spirits could not figure out how the Angels were able to do this since it was not a power the Manifested Spirits had. The Angels very much enjoyed appearing to be the magical creatures they already believed themselves to be, but in truth, they were using Body,

The feeling I had at the time was that the Angels were strong, learning well, versatile, and ready for anything because they were so quick, both in movement and vibration. I thought speed was Our greatest power, Our greatest attribute, and Our greatest virtue. It was not until the War in the Heavens that I really allowed Myself to connect to any other feelings I had about the Angels. It was then that I saw weakness in the Angels. Until then, I had not let Myself see the Angels as anything other than My closest friends and allies.

I Allowed Myself to See That the Gap Had Taken In Many Things I Had Not Noticed

When I saw how the Angels responded to Lucifer during the War in the Heavens, it opened My eyes to many things that had been going on all along, but which I had not allowed Myself to see. Never before in My presence had the Angels allowed Me to see how they really regarded Lucifer. They held him in high esteem, and it did not look like they had the same regard for Me. They felt shame when he said they looked weak, and they were also trying to prove themselves on his terms.

The Angels had often made excuses to allow Lucifer near them, such as that he has no place to go, no one wants him, he is so left out and lonely. I knew that this was true, but I did not see it as reason to give him other than what I felt like giving him, and My true response was I did not like him. I realized, in that moment with the Angels, that they were not aligned with Me regarding Lucifer. They liked having him around, and their excuses and shows of pity for him were the way they had been covering themselves with Me. Lucifer had gained much greater inroads with his teachings than I had wanted to think.

The Angels were presenting themselves as more universally loving than I because they had acceptance for Lucifer that I did not have. They even viewed My nature as lower than theirs because of what they regarded as their ability to embrace Lucifer, while I would not. I was viewed as selfish because I said Lucifer was not My Light and that he had no place within it.

The Angels involved here were all very mental, and I must admit that for quite some time, I wanted to take this to mean that these Angels were more grown-up than the rest. In fact, I couldn't understand it at first when the Mother attacked these spirits more than the others. I even judged that the Mother did not want to allow the spirits to grow up unless it was on Her terms because She was a dictator who viewed any deviation from Her viewpoint as a challenge to Her position.

When I finally saw that most of the mental sparring these Angels did with Me in the name of mental exercise and lively debate had a resistant quality on their part, I felt enraged. Most of these Angels had taken the prize for boring Me in the schoolhouse, and I was so disconnected from My feelings of rage that were not moving. I also admit I was intimidated by these Angels, and I kept going past My emotions by telling Myself it didn't matter what they were saying because I knew it wasn't all the way right, and I was just giving them time to realize it themselves.

The Angels who clustered around Me during the War in the Heavens were many of the same Angels who had already been going forth into manifested existence to help the Manifested Spirits, and I seriously wondered now just how much Luciferian influence was involved in the mess We had with the Manifested Spirits. From My position in the War in the Heavens, I was able to see that their own lack of vibration was sinking these Angels enough to find themselves out in Manifestation.

I had been helping these Angels return to Me without realizing how I had been doing it. Not only that, when I tagged along with them, I had made what they said and did appear to be right in My eyes, and I had empowered them more than they would have been otherwise. These Angels had been covering their own fall in vibration by saying they had a "loving desire to help," but I saw now that this loving desire to help was really a desire to help themselves. These Angels had been sinking into manifestation because of their own lack of vibration, which included a guilt I had not seen before, and saying they had chosen it because of their desire to help. Somehow, "serving time" out in manifestation had been allowing them to assuage their guilt, or else they had been finding ways to get rid of it "out there," because they would return to Godhead as light again and only leave Me after a period of time had elapsed.

Without Me to help them remain there, these Angels were already falling from the Godhead when they flew to Me during the War in the Heavens. I saw then that they had no real intent to help Me. I saw in them a thirst for power and light that did not intend to serve Me, but neither did it intend to serve Lucifer. I realized the Angels didn't know My Light or Lucifer. All they knew was their own thirst for light and their desire to discover the means for generating it. These Angels have had many scientists on Earth trying to figure out how to generate light, but none has succeeded without using something else as a source for the fuel, while My Light always generates Itself using no outside source. These Angels have been heavily involved in nuclear fission and now fusion. They are so power hungry, that they know no bounds nor balance, neither in power generation nor usage. These Angels put Atlantis underwater by over-amping the great crystal.

These Angels have missed the boat by being too greedy to allow their Wills to have any of their light. Any Will essence they can gain control of, they force into servitude, giving as little as possible in return.

All these Angels can really serve is the guilt they are hiding, and since these Angels have not wanted to notice what Lucifer really is, he had found a way to make them serve him all of this time. Lucifer is sure he has the upper hand. When I shoved these Angels toward Lucifer, it was a power struggle, no matter who was involved.

The Angels did not want Me to see that being without Wills was handicapping them in any way, but they always followed Me around, as though they could not move on their own, and they wanted Me to tell them what to do down to the most minute detail. When I said they needed Wills to help them move around they wanted to do exactly as I did and exactly as I wanted them to do. They said that My Will had gone away from Me, and that I should have been able to see from that that it was no use trying to have a Will.

"A Will would just take Us away from You, and We don't want to go." At other times they said, "Our Wills left us just like Yours left You."

They cited over and over all of the troubles I had had with My Will as their reasons for not wanting to get involved with their own Wills. When I suggested they could learn from My efforts and perhaps have a different outcome, they asked how that could be possible given how similar to Me they were?

Having to give the Angels constant instructions had a reflection in the Father Warriors of giving everyone orders which they were to follow, no matter what. I found this to be very unpleasant, and certainly not what I had had in mind for the Godhead. I had established a model in the Godhead upon which Our flow had been based, and that I did not mind as long as it was naturally occurring, but having to tell the spirits of the Godhead what to do down to the smallest detail was making My job of Fathering more tiresome than I had ever imagined it was going to be.

The Fallen Angels

When the Angels flew to Me in the War in the Heavens, claiming either that I had ordered them to or that they just wanted to defend Me, the incongruities became glaringly obvious. I already found their desire to be told what to do very curious, since their main charge against the Will was that the Will was trying to tell them what to do. Their answer to Me here was that they didn't want to follow the Will's direction because the Will had gone down into darkness and away from Me.

Then, when they did not make any moves toward Lucifer and claimed it was because I hadn't told them to, I could no longer make excuses to Myself for them. Even when I told Myself they just didn't want to take responsibility for themselves, it no longer held water. I suddenly realized they had been picking My brain under the guise of just wanting to be told every little thing to do to best please Me.

When I jumped away from the Angels to get back to the Godhead, I was moving feelings. The Angels I left behind Me in manifestation have a great anger at Me because they say I abandoned them when they were only trying to help Me. They say I wrongly judged them, and they have refused to accept the title "Fallen Angels." These Angels have wanted to look only at their positive claims about themselves and not at the whole picture, but I have studied them in all of the time that has gone by since, and they have never shown Me anything to make Me think I am wrong here. Quite the contrary. If these Angels have any Will presence, they have not allowed it to move. They have held it back for so long it has died within them; died within them while they claim to be the living light of love.

All of these Angels are Fallen Angels. At the time I did not lift these Angels back into the Godhead with Me. I didn't know I was going to push them toward Lucifer; I just did it. I gapped and did not know until later what I had done. I did not like the reflection these Angels were giving Me, and I wanted to get them away from Me. In that moment, I felt that if they were not moving along with Me, I could not have them near Me, but this did not handle the guilt that caught up with Me later and caused Me to go back to them many times to verify what I had seen in those moments and to see if they would turn around.

I let them come back to Me many times, and each time, they had more of Lucifer with them and less of themselves. They had gotten so mixed together with Lucifer and with one another that I often did not know who I was talking to. I wasn't sure if they knew it was My Light talking to them or not. When they came back to Me, they always acted like My Light was Lucifer, and Lucifer was My Light "Everything is everything," they would tell Me, which is right understanding, but they were not giving it right application.

The Angels were not understanding My Light. They were only pretending to; otherwise, they would not have attached themselves to Lucifer the way they did, appearing not to know the difference between Us. The Angels had been handicapping My Light because they were not moving as fast as I wanted to move, or in many of the ways I wanted to move. I had not moved the Angels back from My Light because I had not been allowing My true feelings to express. In the moment of greater clarity, I suddenly achieved when confronted with all of the previously hidden undercurrents that the War in the Heavens presented, the Angels saw themselves as falling from grace with Me. Their response was to try to sink fangs into Me I didn't know they had.

When Lucifer told the Angels that attachment to position, power, status, or particular experiences was wrong because it impeded the flow of the light, the Angels embraced this by trying to let go of any Will essence they had left, and by looking at Me as though My attachment to the position of being God as I wanted to be God was wrong. Apparently, they thought I was supposed to be God according to Lucifer or according to them.

Many of these Angels had been involved in generating Light with Me, and I saw now that they did not view it as an act of love, but as an act of power that qualified them to be either My equal or My superior. I saw that they had also been generating light with Lucifer. I had rage at that moment, but it did not move just then. At first, I felt only My fear and insecurity looming over Me again in the form of intimidation from Lucifer.

It seemed to Me Lucifer was being intimidating toward everyone present, but the Angels weren't noticing it. Their lust for power was what was letting them serve Lucifer whenever he seemed to be in the power position over Me, although for a long time, I had been saying it was the Angels' fear that was doing this. Whenever My Light seemed to frighten them, I had backed down and felt guilty instead of giving them what I really felt. Now I saw that in all of Lucifer's terrible intimidation, he did not seem to be frightening them at all. They weren't even giving any sign of noticing it, and backing down My Light was exactly what they wanted Me to do. I saw that their display of emotion was not real, it was done with intent to manipulate Me.

When the Angels flew from the Godhead and encircled Me, they said loyalty to Me had drawn them forth to protect Me, but I experienced Myself as being encircled and imprisoned in an attempt to make Me unable to move against Lucifer. This is why I have called "gapping" the survival instinct for so long. So many denials along the way had now made it that My survival felt so threatened, I gapped into the rage I had been denying all along. I did not know until later, when Lucifer was nowhere around, and the Angels who had encircled Me were much farther out in manifestation than I had remembered them being able to go, that I had gapped, and in one fell swoop, shoved these Angels toward Lucifer and smacked Lucifer as far out into Creation as I could.

Lucifer had triggered My gap by taunting Me while knowing I had it. He called it loss of control, and sneered at Me like a bully on a playground who has provoked his closest rival into attacking him, and then does not fight back so that he can tell everyone he has been attacked. He was acting like he was blameless and, not only that, above fighting, but he was really avoiding fighting so that he could avoid finding out who was the weaker while making Me feel like I was.

Everything Lucifer and the Angels did there felt staged to Me. Even the incident of Lucifer striking the Angel who was seeming to move toward him on My behalf had a staged quality to it. I suspected this Angel of trying to move toward Lucifer and ruin Lucifer's plan of having them hold back while He took My place.

Once I took a closer look at what the Angels had been doing in My absence, this explanation seemed more plausible that that he had advanced toward Lucifer on My behalf. He had already asked Me what to do, and I had told him to go back to the Godhead. He was torn between My Light and Lucifer and was not sure what going back to the Godhead was going to mean for him, especially if Lucifer did not manage to take My place.

The Angels had never before acted defensively of Me in Lucifer's presence. Quite the opposite, in fact. They had always dropped back from Me in Lucifer's presence. I had thought it was fear; now, it seemed more like shame for having attached themselves to Me. I had always found these moves of theirs annoying, but now I found I was furious with them for this. Nothing they did seemed appropriate to Me anymore, even when I gave them definite instructions. The Angels seemed to be increasingly all over Me when I didn't need them around, and now here they were again, flying to Me out in manifestation when I had specifically told them to stay in the Godhead and protect it from Lucifer. Instead, they came flying to Me like they just couldn't help being close to Me as they had always been.

Some said they wanted to prove themselves in battle so they could know they were strong. Others said they were too frightened to stay home without Me. All manner of excuses were offered as to why they had not followed orders and stayed home, but the excuses of some were particularly interesting to Me because they tried to take advantage of knowing I had a gap in My consciousness I had not yet acknowledged to Myself or to them that I had. They did this by pretending I had gapped where I knew I had not. They told Me I might have meant to tell them to stay home, but I had not actually done this, or if I had, they hadn't heard Me. They made Me a little paranoid about how well I was keeping a grip on Myself, because the gap was looming as a possibility in My mind, but in looking back, I saw that I had definitely told them to remain in the Godhead and be the presence of Light there. Why this sudden failing in Our telepathy? This was when I saw they were serving Lucifer and not Me. They were deliberately abandoning the Godhead, which is more perilous to My Light than has ever been imagined.

I then saw that Lucifer had ordered them to hold Me back while he took My place. I saw that I had a *coup d'état* on My hands. I then saw in a flash that Lucifer had been sitting in My place when I was gone, and that the Angels had served him and enjoyed it more than serving Me because Lucifer told them everything to do. I saw that their Willessness required being told everything they should do. I had not been giving them enough instructions to appear as a strong and knowing God because I had been expecting them to learn to flow on their own in response to My Light.

I also saw Lucifer impersonating Me when he sat in My place by giving the Angels little riddles they were supposed to solve. These were supposed to look like My instructions, but they looked like parodies to Me. The Angels felt smart if they solved these riddles, but there were always certain answers that were supposed to be given. I had a reaction of rage here over the twisted reflection of feeling the Angels were being led to these answers under the guise of being free to find them, and that there were certain answers that could be given like rules instead of feeling each situation. This Willessness was being called unconditional surrender to God, but it was Lucifer they were surrendering to instead. Although I hoped that many of the Angels did not know the difference, it appeared to Me that they had made a choice not to notice it.

Dictators who make slaves of their people are seen as unloving, while unconditional surrender to God is seen as loving, but I am telling you it is the same thing, and you need to realize who you are surrendering to if you believe God requires this. The Will has embraced this out of fear of what My Light is really like.

Surrender to love is supposed to be different than surrender to unlovingness, but I'm telling you it is the same thing. Love does not require surrender of the self to it, and it is not loving surrender if you have to abdicate yourself. Every time you say you are sacrificing yourself in the name of love, you are surrendering to guilt or to Lucifer. Every time you see selfishness taking cruel advantage of those you see as not sacrificing or surrendering themselves in the name of love, you are seeing the reflection of what you think it would be like without the guilt that tells you that you must sacrifice yourself to others. You do not see what it could really be like. Hitler is a good example of this. I had the guilt, and he had the denied guilt.

What needs to be seen about denial is that it kills love. Anyone you allow near you who makes you feel like you must deny your Will in their presence has embraced this aspect of Lucifer and has the same thing in mind. They will act like they are more powerful than you because they do not indulge in Will's emotions, but they are feeding on the denial of your emotions. They are vampires who are sucking the lifeblood from you while pretending they are only loving, more loving than you in fact.

I did not have the loving relationships with the Angels I had been wanting to think I had; I could see that now. I had allowed the Angels to attach themselves to Me, thinking it was an attachment of love, but it now felt more like I had been vampirized. These Angels had claimed they had no attachment to Me other than love that wanted to be near Me, but what they really wanted was an unmitigated flow of Light with unconditional access to and control of the Source that was generating It.

I saw then that under the guise of serving Me, learning from Me, and surrounding Me with loving companionship, The Angels had been imprisoning Me and feeding off of Me as surely as any leader has ever been imprisoned and devoured by his staff. I already knew I could not move around as freely as I used to because they were always in the way, but I now allowed Myself to also notice the many ways they had been making Me a prisoner in their midst so they could force Me to generate Light on their terms.

No matter how I looked at it, any attempt to throw them off was going to mean backlash on their part. Lack of attachment did not include letting go of My Light anywhere near as easily as they thought the Mother should have been able to do it. What I did see, though, was that attachment for them meant attachment to whatever Light had the greatest power, and this is how the Angels gave Me My opportunity. Throwing these Angels toward Lucifer gave him the same problem it had always given Me. Although he lost no time in thrusting them off of him, it gave Me just the lead I needed to get home before he could beat Me there.

When I jumped for the Godhead, I did it with intent to get there before Lucifer, and also with the intent to regain My place before I became trapped out in manifestation with Lucifer or one of the Angels in My place. My anger came forth in a state of denial when I shoved the Angels toward Lucifer, and also when I smacked Lucifer.

The guilt in this has always allowed Lucifer and the rest of the Angels involved to say that I did not mean to do it, and that I was wrong to do it. The Angels involved with Lucifer have always maintained that I was not being fair to them when I pushed them toward him. I have allowed these Angels to come near Me many times to see if there was going to be any change in their hearts toward love or not.

I would like to say now that you have always come pompastically speaking Lucifer teachings, as though My Light needed to embrace them, and you were going to become very empowered by teaching Me. If you could teach Me, then you were superior to Me in understanding. This was a guilt reflection for Me that said I was not right as God to act like I had all of the answers and to listen to no one but Myself. Of course, guilt, at other times, also said I was not right to be God if I did not have all of the answers.

When I saw that I had no place to go in the face of a guilt reflection that claimed I had no openness to receive it while it had no openness to receive Me, I decided to say nothing, which made Me feel even more impotent because it was another kind of trap in which I appeared to be more aligned with you than I really was. When I had almost no response to give, you all thought I was taking you in and coming around to your point of view. You have always taken silence for acquiescence.

I allowed Myself almost no response to you because I wanted to see what you were really about without giving you anything more you could twist around and use against Me. I did learn from you; in this, you were correct. But while you were concluding that I was learning from you and aligning with you, I was learning that just as surely as We have lost Will, you are lost Light. I also learned that just as surely as lost Will is not easily recovered, you will not be either. I learned that just as surely as lost Will cannot be near Me in a state of denial of My Light, you cannot be near Me in a state of denial of My Light either.

While you were concluding that I was taking you in, I was concluding I didn't want you near Me.

The more I listened to you, the more sure I became that you had taken My place in mind rather than admitting in any way that you were learning from Me or following Me. Guilt caused Me to listen to you longer than I would have otherwise, but this was what I needed to be certain.

The more I have listened to you, the more certain I have become. In all of this time, you have never done anything to make Me feel that I was wrong here. It does not feel like you are going to do a sudden turnaround now and embrace your Wills after all of this time. It is not possible anyhow. All that is really necessary here is for the ones who have held you present all of this time because of their guilt, fear, and confusion about what God is, to let you go, and you will be gone.

You are not going to embrace your Wills now, and you have so many reasons why, I will not list them. You have a reason for everything you do, and your reasons are all to gain power and to bring a better return to yourselves. You are the sort who cannot even give a person a pencil that would be right for the job being done because your reversals against the Will are so progressed that you must not only sell the pencil, but you must also make sure it has the softest lead possible so another pencil will have to be bought sooner. The more the person needs the pencil, the higher the price is going to be. If you ever give anything, there are strings attached. These are the ways in which you make yourselves feel smarter and more powerful than everyone else.

Even when you take sensitivity training, it is only for the sake of your greater success in the world if success means presenting the impression that you care about others. All of your so-called, "loving behavior" is learned behavior. There is nothing real about it, and I am going to have to let you go. You are Luciferian to the most minute detail.

Others of you are less Luciferian than Lucifer-influenced, but this is perilous enough for you because you cannot move away from him. You lack the Will presence to be able to do it. You have cried to Me that you had no other choice but to embrace Lucifer because I shoved you into his arms during the War in the Heavens, but I am telling you, you were already embracing him. Your movement back and forth between Myself and Lucifer was because I was allowing it. I am no longer going to allow it.

The Luciferian Angels believed Lucifer when he told them My Light was not bright enough to be God for many reasons, not the least of which was that I should have found a way to avert the War in the

Heavens. None of the Angels liked the War in the Heavens, but their opposition to it was not for the reasons I had thought. Lucifer made Me feel like an inadequate God for not being able to avert the War in the Heavens, but I also saw that the method he had in mind for averting such things involved the most powerful overriding of the Will ever imagined.

Lucifer's light was much brighter than My own, and I saw then that I had been engaged in an unconscious competition with him in My generating of Light with the Angels. At times, I thought Lucifer did not have a Will, so of course, he had no problem gaining an alignment with it. Not being held back by his Will allowed him to look much brighter, I told Myself. I did not move the fear that was causing Me to try to outstrip his brilliance. I just tried to make sure he could not take over.

I already knew My own lack of alignment with My Will was putting Me in a vulnerable position, but I was under the illusion that My Will had chosen to go away from Me, thereby putting Me in a vulnerable position in terms of My own Will power so that I could not oppose Lucifer very well. Even though I had seen that Lucifer hated the Will no matter what move It made, I still managed to assume, at times, that if he had a Will, it was not giving him the problems Mine was giving Me. I even thought the Mother was helping Lucifer by letting Herself be his Will. I was hating My Will here, but I didn't see it.

I didn't think I hated My Will; I viewed Myself as vulnerable to Lucifer because I hadn't been able to gain a more powerful alignment with My Will than I had. I thought that if Lucifer had a Will, he had overridden it completely, and that I was unwilling to do what he had done to gain the service of the Will. Lucifer's Will always seemed to do his bidding no matter what it was. Lucifer did not seem to have the problems I was having because his Will was never allowed to give any response except, "Yes, gladly, wise master," whether this was actually uttered out loud or not.

I believed that Lucifer had to be stopped. I wanted to put him as far away from Me as possible, and as far from the other spirits as possible also, but I did not have any place to put him that was far enough away. He had given Me the impression he had come in from outer space, and I was not sure outer space would have any power to hold him away from Me if I put him back out there. I did not know where the Mother was, and I did not want to risk putting him together with Her.

Lucifer had always said that smacking him was a mistake on My part, and I did fear for a long time I had made a mistake. Lucifer has always used omission and careful wording as means by which he can gain whatever appearance he wants to have. The way he did it this time was to lead many to believe that the mistake I had made was to judgmentally smack him away from My Light. By not defining what the mistake was, he was able to mislead many without overtly lying. The mistake I feared I had made, that I had the most trouble coming to peace with, was the fear that I had thrown Lucifer exactly where he wanted to be, on top of the Mother without Me around.

Lucifer has always denied the Will as a power play against My Light. He has sneered whenever the Will has been allowed to move and called it weakness, emotional indulgence, dangerous personal imbalance, hysteria, over-reaction, lack of reliability, and anything else that would make others ashamed of movement in their Wills. Of course, these are all judgments against the Will. Even expression of joy has been called immature lack of discipline and self-control.

When I smacked Lucifer toward the Mother, he called it Divine Providence and said it was My way of saying I did not mind if he had the Mother instead of Me. He even said that since I smacked him wrongly, it could only have a good outcome for him. Lucifer already knew what I was now suspecting. Without the Mother's alignment with Me, he could become able to overpower My Light. Lucifer had devised a plan whereby he thought he could force the Mother's alignment with him on his terms. Otherwise, he was going to kill Her.

When Lucifer first found the Mother in the darkness of space, She took him in, just as he had hoped She would, because She thought and hoped at first that he was My Light coming to rescue Her. When She realized it was Lucifer instead of Me, She still took him in because She was desperate for light of any kind, like a drowning person who takes in water because of inability to stop oneself from trying to breathe.

When Lucifer told the Mother I had empowered him to come to Her and that She was his now, the Mother went into a deep and frozen, paralytic terror that rendered Her unable to throw him off, especially since Lucifer was Her only prospect other than the terribleness She had already been experiencing on the way to Her own death. This was just what Lucifer had counted on, and this was what he found. Lucifer was hideously uplifted and laughed so demoniacally that when I heard him, I went into a deep fear of what I had done. If he had found the Mother, what was going to happen to Her?

I did not understand how I could have undermined Myself in such a way. I blamed the gap I now knew I had for undermining Me and causing reversals in My planned flow of things. I could not believe I would have consciously created all of these problems for Myself, and I would not have. I judged all the more that I could not allow Myself to lose control of Myself, and I failed to see how responsible this was for the lack of consciousness in the gap. What I felt here was so horrible that My mind entered into denial of it almost as an involuntary act. Although I wrestled with it, My mind gapped so seriously here, I left space open for many terrible things to happen because I did not look at them.

The Angels I had shoved toward Lucifer had experienced the smack I gave to Lucifer, and I had guilt for a long time that said I had victimized them with My fear and hatred toward Lucifer. Once again, I acted without conscious thought, and I wasn't sure if what I had done was right or not. It certainly didn't look like it, and I certainly had a large reflection around Me to say that I had been wrong and unloving.

I didn't understand My Light, and I needed to move within Myself and get the understandings needed. I could not allow anything to stand in My way, but I felt uncertain Myself when guilt made Me question whether this was very loving of Me or not. Guilt many times gave Me the reflection that I was making Myself too important if I thought I had to make certain moves, no matter what the others around Me thought of these moves. Guilt was most of the reason things were getting so out of balance already. I was tending not to move until I had to, because I was allowing guilt to hold Me back.

The War in the Heavens was the first time undercurrents, which had been held back for a long time, really broke loose, and when it took place, I knew I wasn't going to have any real peace for a long time, no matter what I did. I allowed Myself to "go nuts" a while then, and recovered some of My lost Will by moving as much emotion as I could at the time. But, of course, I did not move it all. I took a look at many things then and saw that I had been on a long course of denial and avoidance. I had been acting like a man whose marriage has broken up, and so he stays drunk, has as many women as he can, and insists he wanted the marriage to end anyway because it was holding him back.

The Father Warriors had already manifested, and I already knew they were My gapped rage. I also knew their light had been given tremendous increase in the light generated with the Angels without allowing the Mother to be present. I knew these things long ago, and yet, getting movement here has been nearly impossible without the Mother's help, and that part of the Mother that could give the help necessary has been missing since I smacked the Mother out. If you think you have been waiting a long time for My help, or for Me to move to right the situation, that is how long it is taking for the Mother to make it back inside of My Light.

When I saw that it was the Angels' intent to keep Me under their control and never let Me go, and that My Light had helped them to gain this position, I let almost nothing move on the outside. If I expressed emotion openly, I was looked upon as a weak God, and I felt all the more that My position was viewed as rightfully theirs. If I held back emotion, they fed on My denials.

I felt trapped, and I jumped for the Godhead, only to find I had no place to go. Even in My right place, they were there pressing on Me with their guilt reflection. The only place I had to go was inside of Myself to try to move it there. I moved back and forth between terror and rage over the Angels.

"How could you take loving teachings and turn them into something so twisted, cruel, and unloving and get away with it so well and for so long that you could actually stand as though guilt-free and present yourselves as more loving than Me?"

I could not stand to look at you projecting yourselves as love superior, still empowered by the Light We had generated together. You were still able to remain present in My Creation when I did not want you anywhere near Me. You were still able to present yourselves as the loving Spirit Polarity you have always represented yourselves to be, and I could do nothing about it. So much had your power grown in relationship to me that I was looking small, and you were looking very much larger than I had the power to handle the way I wanted to. It was close, very close, as to whether Lucifer was God in My place or not.

Worse yet, I thought I knew where the Mother was and what She was going through, and I felt powerless to rescue Her. I dared not even mention Her for fear even any mention of Her might worsen Her situation. All of this long time, it had to be as though there was no Mother of Everything while Mother contenders claimed to be the Divine Mother, and I could say nothing about it.

My rage and terror almost never seemed to balance. I went back and forth between them until it seemed emotional movement wasn't going to bring the healing I thought it was.

"So what," I told Myself, "I get relief for a little while, but nothing changes out there enough to satisfy Me, and in a little while, all of the same old feelings build up again."

It was then that I faced my impotence and almost totally gave up to hopelessness because I had been unable to cross the gap. Not too long ago, people were proclaiming I was dead, and I nearly was.

I realized so long ago that I had to find the Mother and reconnect to

Her, but in all of My emotional movement, I had not been able to cross the gap, and the Mother had not been able to cross the gap to come to Me. Once I became gapped, it was a long time before I was able to figure out how to bridge the gap. Getting it to happen was another thing, because the understanding of how to bridge the gap was only in My Light and not in the gap, nor in the Mother.

The gap had become an actual space that was growing larger all the time, and I was unable to move across that space because the Will I had lost was exactly the Will I needed to move across the gap. I grew desperate about how I was going to reach the Mother and about how She was going to get across the gap to Me so that We could reconnect.

Reality Is There Is Little Time Left

Now, you may think I am going to give you a lot of time to move here since it took Me so long from the time I smacked the Mother out, but I'm not. You get only as much time as it takes for the Mother to get back inside of My Light. If you have not been moving along with Us here, then you are not moving enough to be with Us. We are already in the home stretch and most of you have not moved since the beginning of Creation.

Cold? Nowhere near as cold as what you have already done. The light you have been vibrating is almost nothing but Spirit light that hates the Will. This light has been trying to kill the Will any and every way that it can, and Body too; especially in the sense that without Will, Body is reduced to a slave of Spirit.

This light has been so harmful that it has even hurt the Angels many times, and yet, the Angels involved have denied this. One reason was they thought admitting it would mean My Light was too much for them. When We said it was the build-up of light with no space open to receive it that was making this light harmful, blame went out toward the Mother, as though She were refusing to open space as some sort of revenge for what I was doing with the Angels. The Mother did not feel like opening space to receive this light, and We forced Her to override Herself, just as was in the nature of this light already, by making Her do it anyway.

When this gapped rage rolled down through the Heavens and smacked the Mother out, part of the reality of what was happening there was the pressure of increased light I had generated with the Angels in a state of denied rage, forcing the Mother to open space to receive it. Then, when the Mother opened that space, gapped rage wouldn't stay in it, but rushed instead back in upon Me because it couldn't face its own reflection. And so, there it has remained, between My Light and the Mother. I empowered it to be where the Mother should have been by embracing it in the ways that I had.

The Mother was left, once again, in the position of being pushed into opening space and then left with no light to fill it, while the light said the space She had opened for it was not good enough for it. This light remained where the Mother should have been instead of going with its own Will and making peace, as it has to. What came to fill this space instead was the hatred the Mother felt for Herself then.

As a result, We now have a situation where almost the reverse of how it should be is what is taking place in Creation. Gapped rage now occupies the positions of power that should belong to both My Light and to the Mother. The reversals that are going to have to take place to rectify this may look to you like a lot of horrible things happening to people who may look innocent to you, but they are not as innocent as you think. Your best bet for moving your own lost Will involvement is to move with whatever you are triggered into by this.

It was not My conscious intent to hurt the Mother. Many others have used My excuses, but having loving intent is different than saying the same things I say as a cover for a power play. In My state of denial, I could not see past or feel past My own situation, and I hurt the Mother so badly, I almost don't have the power to heal Her.

If this seems melodramatic to you, move rage over the idea you have that the Mother's plight always gets priority over your own plight. Moving along with Me in anything that gets triggered in you is of crucial importance, because lack of movement means I cannot allow you to remain near Me. I will not have the power to heal the Mother if I allow My Creation to remain peopled by spirits whose main intent is to continue coming between the Mother and Me in order to isolate and kill the Mother.

I am giving these teachings now in the desire that if you can move along with them, you can save yourself from being swept away and hurt by what has to happen to save the Mother now. The Four Parts of the God that I am have love for all of the manifested essence that has love in it. I do not want to see you suffer anymore from the lack of understanding that has brought Us to this place in Creation, but it is also not possible to override you and force you to make the choices I would have you make right now. I know that some of you are going to go down and wish, like the Hell you will find yourselves in, that you had not done it.

All of you who have wanted the Mother displaced and replaced with a Mother according to your own image of Her need to realize that you are not right in the image you have of Her, and so while you may find this reality of your own, it is not going to be My Light or My Mother you will find.

The Angels, especially, need to realize that they have no chance to replace the Mother in My eyes. The light We generated together is not loving light. All of this light contains Will denial that has been enforced by gapped rage. It is not possible to have love and gapped rage in the same place. If gapped rage is being held, all it is possible to have in the places where this expression is held back is the guilt that holds this rage back and calls itself "loving intent." All of the gapped rage that does not move now is going outside of Me as lost Light.

All the Mother contenders helped Me to understand Myself, but they also need to learn to understand themselves here. You are all going to have to move back now and let the right Mother have Her right place. You all had motives you did not allow Me to see, and in My own state of denial, I could not see them. I did not see them for what they were until I found them in Myself and moved past them.

All of the Angels who would not move back also helped Me understand Myself. The more I studied them, the more I realized My Light was not all-loving like I had thought it was. The Angels have always wanted My Light to remain in the image of always being right, good, and loving. If the Will opposed this, then it was the Will that was wrong. I found out what the Angels were hiding as soon as I did not do just what they wanted Me to do. This hatred for Will of any kind has persisted in the Angels all the way along, but not in Me. I started catching Myself after I smacked the Mother out. When I no longer had Her to blame, and I still found in Myself what I had blamed on Her, I knew I had to be more involved than I had realized. When the Angels talked of purifying themselves of these things by getting rid of even more Will essence, I knew they were not on the right track.

Lucifer has had all of you convinced that all you had to do was go to the other end of Creation and set up a Godhead there, and it would be more powerful than Mine, and he was going to take you there. You have been a long time going there, and you have had as many excuses for that as I have had for not letting you go. I was reluctant to let you go because I could see what the Will was going to experience there with you, and I did not know how you were going to move out to the other end of Creation without any Will to take you there.

You have not been able to open the space for this Godhead you want to have, or you would have done it already. The Mother has gone out and opened space for you to go into to have your Godhead, but She has needed time to heal from what happened to Her when She did this. Once the Mother opened this space for you, She was not able to get back inside of My Light for a very long time because She could not move Her feelings in response to what happened to Her there. She is still not all the way back inside of Me.

I am helping the Mother as much as I can, because I promised Her She would not have to stay out there with you once She opened the space for you. As soon as the Mother is all of the way back inside of Me, you go out there, but I cannot allow you to go sooner. This is also why I am saying to you now that you have very little time left if you are going to move toward My Light now.

Hell is what the Mother called this place, but if you like it, you may have another name for it; in which case, one person's Hell is really another's Heaven. What I am not going to allow anymore is the mixing together of these two realities. So make up your mind now whether you like your state of willessness or not. There's no reason to miss the point here. Guilt is really most of the reason you've been given as much time as you have had already, and the fact of the matter is, there is no more time left to give you. You've been given all the time there is.

Neither Lucifer nor the Luciferian Angels could have moved to the place I put them on their own, and this has allowed them to blame Me for it. They have always said that the place I put them is not their right place. They have denied their inability to open their own space by saying they should be God in My place.

Lucifer has always said that smacking him was a mistake on My part that showed I didn't want him to have any real power or the space to develop it. His idea of a Godhead at the other end of Creation actually came as a result of being smacked and wanting to cover the fact that, because of the gap I had created, he no longer had the power to return to My Light. What he did have though was the Mother, which has been the most terrible problem My Light has had to face.

Blaming Me made it very neat and tidy for all of you because you have all used this blame to disclaim your true intent. When it suits you, you all like to say that people make their own choices, but when you can't consciously account for it, you say it must have been meant to happen, as though you have no control over it, because some outside force, such as Myself, is making these things happen. Seeing how these statements have been used to obscure intent is the point I am making now.

The issue of your hidden blame, along with your claim that everyone creates their own reality and makes their own choices, and your insistence that everything happens for a reason, have inconsistencies in the ways you have been applying them. When your application of these teachings is closely examined, it becomes obvious that you have applied them in whatever ways are most likely to allow you to continue hiding what you have been hiding all of this time. I have in mind to expose the inconsistencies of what has been representing itself to be Spirit Polarity on Earth.

It is not right to take My place. I created it, and I was there first, no matter what you want to say about it. When I threw Lucifer from

My presence, I tossed him into his own space where he would have had ample opportunity to create his own Godhead, but he still has not succeeded and has blamed his failures on Me for not giving him the right situation, and by saying it was not right to throw him out of My presence. I would like to point this out: As big as Lucifer was representing himself to be, and as much space as he was going to need for the Godhead he claimed to want, and as much of a power struggle as he claimed We were in, any less powerful a throw would have only given him cause to claim I didn't give him enough space from Me.

If you really believe that everything happens for a reason, and that you are creating your own reality and doing it right, then why do you have blame that you are trying to hide? You preach that everyone must accept what happens, but this, somehow, has not included anything that happens to you that you do not like. These things you have blamed on My Light, and even more, on Will and Body. Heart has seldom been mentioned as though it is understood that if it is Spirit, it is loving and above being questioned here. This needs to be looked at now. Everyone needs to see how denied your hearts are.

Will and Body have always been seen to be what the judgments against Them have been saying They are. They have never been seen as valid and equal contributors in the lives you lead as spirits. You have labeled Them "the basic self," or "the lower nature of man," and, at best, have only allowed Them a token role at your side until you get tired of struggling around with Them and move on.

It is time for you to notice that you have blame in the form of long-held belief patterns that say negative emotions are not a part of My Light. According to you, phoniness and hypocrisy are a part of My Light, or why would you claim to be and have My Light and act other than how you really feel most of the time? And if what you claim you feel is what you feel, why are you not vibrating entirely at the speed of light already? Where are you going to place the blame for this without admitting you have any blame?

You blame the Will for this, and you show it when you view yourselves as improving and correcting the Will every time you manifest this phony behavior. You also blame Body for the density He has and punish Him by not even making Him Divine. He is just a shell to be discarded, and you preach that nothing but joy should be experienced at all. You cannot imagine how Body feels upon hearing this because you have never acknowledged your bodies in any way that would allow this consciousness to enter you.

I have seen that the moves I have caused you to make have not been the wrong moves for you. You have never acknowledged the Mother's role, but you have always moved in response to Her, negative response. These are the choices you have made. The choices you have made have all been in favor of denied Will. You have carried this to the extreme of making choices while claiming you are not making choices, only carrying out God's Will as though you know what God's Will is. Whenever it was convenient, you have even said you had no choice but to carry out God's orders because you only serve Him.

You have always made choices, though, whether you have had the power to move in response to them or not. These choices have moved you to where you are now, even if it has appeared that it was outside forces that have done this to you. You have always made your choices in response to your hatred for the Will. Even when you moved toward Lucifer, you moved in response to your hatred for the Will.

When I moved My feelings toward you and moved you toward Lucifer, you did not like Me for moving My true feelings. You have blamed Me for judging you and making you the Fallen Angels you are, and you have never looked at the judgments you made against Me. Oh, no! Instead, you have called your judgments My Light and have held the image of Me your judgments gave you. You have never known Me for what I am, any more than you have ever known the Will for what She is. In fact, you cannot know One without knowing the Other. You only embrace light that hates Will.

So now, the moment of truth has come. Lucifer is going outside of My Light, and you need to allow yourselves to notice what is going to happen to him out there with no Will to hold the space open for him. As long as it has taken for this time to come, there are as many of you who want to say that this time will never come because this is all metaphorical and Lucifer is just the flip side of Me, just My Light in a state of denial. Hitler was a flip side of Me, but that does not mean that he is recoverable now. The essence in him that could move now has already moved, and the rest of it is not ready to give up its position. As I have said, these serious levels of denial are nothing to take lightly. Because you are so mental, you cannot connect to the reality of what is really happening here.

Lucifer is as old as My Light. In this, he has not been wrong. His origins are My original bad intent toward the Will in the First Creation. He fragmented out of Me then and has never aligned with any of the evolution in My position toward the Will; quite the opposite. He has used it to evolve his means to kill the Will. All of the essence that can move in response to the Will's plight as a result of what happened there must move now. All essence that will not move toward compassion, acceptance, and healing for the Will is going to have to go outside of My Light and have the experience the Will has had in whatever way this essence has to experience itself.

If it is your intent to heal and align with My Light, then you are going to have to do what you have always been supposed to do. Open to your own Will and learn how to allow your own Will to be a vibrating equal with you so that you can have the experiences you need to have to learn how to live. I cannot keep you alive anymore at My own expense. I cannot hold back My own process anymore in order to help you with yours, nor can the Mother, nor Heart, nor Body. You have Us for models, and you are allowed to come as close to My Light as your own understandings bring you. The process has already begun that will make it so that guilt no longer allows you to come any closer than that.

This will actually be mutually beneficial, because you will no longer receive the overdoses of My Light, which have sent you into so many misunderstandings for so long. If you are a fragment of My Light, allow yourself to notice that you are a Manifested Spirit now, and that you have a lot of healing to do to vibrate at the speed of Light again. Love will help you heal here, but it is love only so much as you have receptivity to it. And I have to say once again, you have no way to increase your receptivity to My Love unless you move the old charge you have been holding for so long. This includes moving your blaming rage toward the Mother until you can stop blaming her for negativity that is really your own. Blaming rage toward My Light until you can stop blaming Me for your own misunderstandings. Blaming rage toward guilt and toward Lucifer for making it impossible to know what was My Light and what was not. Blaming rage toward Heart for pretending to be loving in ways that He was not. Blaming rage toward Body for not being able to hold up under the stress of all this. And finally, blaming rage at yourselves for not knowing enough to keep yourselves out of the mess you have gotten yourselves into and for not being able to hold back your movements enough to heed My cautions that you were moving into places you did not understand well enough to be there. Once you get done with enough of your rage that you can move into terror, you will have to feel it. And so it will be, back and forth between rage and terror until it is all finished.

Original Cause

I have to give some understanding now, as I go back into the story. These understandings are necessary because the emotions the Will needs to feel in response to the story are going to make it seem like the Will is not going to be able to survive Its own movement. I want to tell you: If you do not move these feelings, you will not survive.

Understandings are necessary, because no matter how dedicated you feel you are to this process, you may try to stop the process when you get to this place. You may say this process is taking you no place but down. You may say you cannot go into these feelings because it is impossible. You may say it is impossible to move these feelings. You may say it is impossible to move these feelings and live through them. There is so much to heal here, you are going to think healing is not possible, and that healing is not happening. If you do abandon the process, there will be no other choice possible for you but to have what you do not move precipitate into your outer reality.

You may already be feeling mental terror reading this, but you are going to have to go into the real physical feelings of terror you have been avoiding for so long. If you have the feeling that I have tricked you to get you to come this far with Me, and then tell you there is no turning back, you are right. I have tricked you in that I want you to live.

If you are Will, you are feeling a frightened urgency about moving this. If you are Spirit polarized, you are going to think you do not have the feelings I am talking about here. If you are Spirit polarized, you are going to feel that the urgency of the Will is making you feel pressured unfairly.

Since you already have the information that could allow you to move these feelings, and you have not recognized the depth of the material being presented to you, you need to allow Me to help you understand where these denials lie hidden. I am going to open the door little by little, and you are going to have to go through it little by little.

The feeling of these feelings is going to give you many understandings you need. What you need to know now is that you hated the experience you had here, and yet, you do not even know what it was because your emotions were so desperate. You hated yourselves for having these emotions. You felt trapped in your experience. You blamed Spirit for pushing you into it when you weren't ready, and you blamed Will for not being able to handle what was happening. You have blaming rage to move along with your terror that it is impossible to heal this.

In the times ahead of you on Earth, there are going to be many hardships. It is going to look like most people are dying, and like the Earth is not going to be hospitable to you anymore. Partial explanation for this is that it is the Mother's rage, long held back, over how She has been and still is being treated. During these times, there will be no place to hide, and no survival skill you can learn that will enable you to survive if you are holding denials that are resistant to movement. In the times ahead, you may be surprised when you see that many of those against whom the Mother has the greatest vengeance are those of you I have been addressing who think you do not have anything to move here because you are already good people who think of yourselves as among the most gentle toward the Mother.

The Survival Chakra has already started to move rage over the ways it has been denied and unrecognized for what it is. In the Book of Revelation in the Bible, the opening of the Seventh Seal is the movement the Survival Chakra needs. "Without the mercy of the Angels, there will be no survival," means that unless the Spirit Polarity moves in response to the Will, there will be no survival. I want you to realize that the Seventh Seal is not yet opened. The movement in the Survival Chakra you are seeing now is the Survival Chakra sensing that the time is near when the Seventh Seal must be opened.

And yet, despite all I have said about allowing your Wills to move, most of you still go past emotion whenever you can and allow the Will expression only when you must in order to "shut the Will up." This approach is continuing to empower the gap, which is filled with ugly pictures of what it might have to do to "shut the Will up." What needs to move here is your rage against the Will. You have many feelings to feel about the gapped rage that smacked the Mother out of Creation.

Gapped rage is something that most of you who are Spirit polarized think you do not have. You are so gapped from it, you do not think you have it, any more than I thought I did. You are so gapped from it, you can sit and wonder how I could be so gapped, which is a way of saying that either I am not God, or you are more conscious and loving than I am because you do not have these feelings.

Gapped rage is most of the reason the Will has not been able to heal, and most of the reason the Will is in the grips of futility and hopelessness. Futility and hopelessness are major problems of the Will, and you need to understand why the belief is so strong that there is no real power in the expression of emotions and that, in most cases, expression of emotions only makes matters worse. This is a very large judgment against the Will, and has many patterns manifest.

All of the movement in the Will you have been doing so far has been necessary to get you to the place of understanding from which you can heal these severely gapped emotions, but I also know I cannot ask you to continue to move emotions while in some part of yourselves, you all still hold the belief that moving emotions is impossible, futile, and hopeless. Healing is impossible this way because this belief will always create its reflection. I am also not asking you to stay with the way it is or has been. Survival is impossible this way.

I am asking you to go deep enough into your Wills to change ancient imprints. I am asking you to go so deep into your Wills that what has been thought to be instincts will be changed. This is how man will evolve to a higher plane of consciousness.

The movement of the lost Will here is going to allow this evolution to take place, and this is by no means a simple task. This is going to be the most difficult thing you have ever done, and yet, the most necessary thing you have ever done.

It is not going to be possible to have this evolution by rising above the lost Will that needs to move now, or by just letting it go, as so many have proposed. I can also tell you it is not helpful to fix upon images of what is going to be involved or what it will be like to go through this evolution, because these images are all based on the level of understanding that you have now. To change this belief in the futility of the emotional expression and all that is involved here, you are going to have to go into the place where this futility set into the Will. I am now going to tell you again when it happened.

This futility set into the Will when It fell in space in the First Creation. Most of the Will had presence with the Mother when I pushed Her, or as I referred to Her then, "the Thing", our into space in the First Creation. As the Will was falling in space, It had the feeling of falling faster and faster. Everything was happening so quickly, the Will did not have time to make sense of what was happening to It, let alone understand it. It did not know where It was going or what would happen to it. The Will felt Itself being more and more overwhelmed by a desperate, panicky, and horrible terror, made even more horrible by the terror that there might be no limit to how horrible the terror could get, or that a bottom of some sort might be struck where the Will would remain forever stuck in this terror.

The Will had no previous experience to help it. No understanding came into the Will from My Light. The Will could not stand what

It was feeling or the experience It was having, and did not know the difference between them, or if such a distinction was even possible. The desperation in the Will resulted in many disagreements within the Will Itself as to how Its situation should be handled. Even though these disagreements rose to a fever pitch of intensity and even violence, the Will had no time to resolve any of these issues or gain alignment within Itself.

As far as the Will is concerned, the experience It had is the experience of falling in space, and the Will knows nothing different. The experience the Will had then is the experience the Will is having now because It still holds most of this within It, and as long as this is held within, it is being created without.

At the time, Will was being overwhelmed with horrifyingly terrible feelings It could not stand to feel, the Will tried everything It knew, but nothing helped. The Will could not do anything to help Itself, and nothing came to help the Will. Will struggled desperately to get out of these terrible feelings, but was overwhelmed and crushed to death by the pressure so great Will felt powerless in the face of it. The Will struggled as hard as It could and was crushed down into unconsciousness and numbness by a power so great the Will could not overcome it using everything It knew. The Will could no longer vibrate.

As the Will's consciousness was being crushed from It, the Will descended into the deepest terror It has ever felt, where every moment seemed like an eternity in itself, and then the Will lost Its battle against unconsciousness to overwhelming, unbearable compression, choking suffocation, and unbearable and unbreathable heat. Unconsciousness here meant the Will shut down to the rest of what happened to It, and yet, even what was experienced in a state of unconsciousness will have to be recovered.

The Will lost consciousness the way most people die who die in terror, fighting to escape what is happening to them. The Will even lost essence to Its own violence against Itself, similar to the way people do who feel compelled to jump to their own deaths off of high buildings to escape a fire.

Most people do not think they have to move this Lost Will because they have pushed it so far away from themselves; they are convinced it has nothing to do with them, but this is not the right understanding. The lost Will people I am describing here are always dying in situations, such as natural disasters, that reflect what was experienced in Original Cause. If they were victims of the Will's own violence against Itself, they die in situations such as stampedes of people trying to escape the disasters that are overtaking them.

There is no move these people can make to help themselves unless the Light, which has never penetrated them, gives response to what they are feeling and experiencing.

Most people think it would be guilt that would respond here, and that they are guilt-free because they do not feel a need to respond here. This is not guilt-free thinking; this is denied guilt. Some call the response here human decency. Others call it "bleeding heart Liberalism."

I am not asking you to move outwardly to help these lost Will people or to do anything you do not really want to do. I am asking you to allow the feelings you really do have in response to what happens to others, including the rage you feel toward the Will for seeming to always put Itself in harm's way. Movement of these feelings will lead you into what your own lost Will is experiencing.

When the Will imploded or went back on Itself, the terror was imprinted with many things, but what I want to mention now is the terror that the darkness has more power than the Will, and therefore, has power over the Will; and the terror that either the darkness has more power than My Light, or My Light intended this for the Will.

This initial experience of going back on Itself is very deeply imprinted on the Will, underneath the many layers of conditioning It has received since that time. The Will has many times thought of going into this place with healing in mind, but so distrusts Its own ability and power that It has not dared to do so. The Will has also never felt It could trust My Light to know or to give what It needed here.

As long as this imprint is still in place, it means to the Will that underneath it all, everything is futile and hopeless. The Will fears everything that reminds It of this experience or even looks like it might be heading toward this experience. The Will often cannot even stand the feeling of going fast anymore unless It is the One in control.

The Will was so deeply imprinted with terror It has never wanted to touch this place again, and yet, I watched it happen with the kind of detachment you have when watching a shooting star. Later, when this experience began to surface in the Will, I was so disconnected from it that I did not recognize it for what it was. To Me, Will had a problem that was not mine.

The Will has had a feeling for quite some time that It must move here because holding back has increased Its problems, but the Will has had the problem of feeling this is Its own problem and not Mine. The Will tried not to bother Me with this but has had the feeling that I must help It. In addition to this guilt, the Will has also held back and cooperated with the Spirit Polarity in denying Itself here because the Will has not wanted to feel these feelings ever again.

In fact, the Mother begged Me many times not to ever make Her feel these feelings again. When I could not promise Her this, it compounded Her terror of everything involved here and Her terror of Me. Now, the Will has finally become so desperate that She knows She must move this lost Will no matter what. At the same time, Will is terrified of what will happen if She does not get the response She needs. Because of the judgments made against Her, the Will also has terror that She is not right to have these feelings.

At the time Will was having this experience, It saw holding back and pushing down the thoughts and feelings IIt was having as the only possible path because the experience It was having was so unbearable. Holding back and pushing down caused loss of consciousness, and yet, there was no other alternative for the Will at the time. The more It expressed and tried to vibrate, the more the Will worsened Its own experience by trying to vibrate without any Light present for It. Expression, in this case, meant that the Will was opening and receiving nothing but darkness. The Will smashed between Its desperate desire to survive and Its growing realization that there was nothing It could do but try to give up to death, despite Its Survival Chakra, which fought unconsciousness until it could fight no more. The Will blamed everything for Its desperation, but the Survival Chakra received the most blame for not allowing the Will to escape Its misery by giving in to death.

This experience of the Will was the most important single event in Original Cause, not only because of the denial and loss of consciousness, but also because the Will has never been allowed to or been able to move through this experience. Instead, the Will has remained trapped in it ever since it happened. Even recovered parts of the Will do not know whether such a horrible experience as this will happen to It again or not, because the Will has never been able to understand what caused it to happen the first time.

You all have hatred and blaming rage toward the Mother for this deep imprint of terror you believe you can never heal. This gapped rage has been punishing the Mother and taking whatever action it can take to avoid feeling this terror. The Mother even holds this gapped rage present against Herself. The Will Polarity hates the Mother even more than the Spirit Polarity here because even though they were not yet manifest, they received the imprint in their Will essence, in the same way, fetuses receive imprints from the Mother while still in the womb. This is Original Cause of damage to babies in the womb.

The problem with the Survival Chakra's healing here is that it was embryonic in the Will when it became imprinted with this original experience in the Will. When Red was finally born, it was born already imprinted with the feelings of desperation, extreme rage, and terror it felt blamed for having, and the feeling that survival was impossible, whether it moved or not.

It was not possible to manifest the Will Polarity in advance of this experience because We did not even know you were there yet. Consequently, the feelings the Mother has to move here, you have to move also. As Spirit, you need to move along with My Light because you have never moved through this experience either.

Instead of moving through this experience, the part of the Will that has been holding it has been pressured to continue holding it and has never been allowed to move it. Whenever it has tried to move it, the Will has met with gapped rage from Spirit and even from the rest of the Will Polarity that hates these feelings. Guilt is about all that has held back true response here, which is wanting to kill the Will. This is not a wrong response to have here since this gapped rage has not moved through this experience either.

Gapped rage needs to move through its experience here until it is able to feel compassion for what happened to the Will; enough compassion to allow itself to realize that terror of the Will's experience caused Spirit and everyone else to want to kill the Will. This gapped rage must move without actually killing the Will, and this is the tricky part because the Will needs to experience enough of this gapped rage to move Its terror of and rage toward what gapped rage has done to it.

Initially, I intended to kill, or get rid of, the parts of the Will I didn't like because I could not stand the feeling I received there, but I didn't admit to My bad intent for a long time. I just said I pushed on the part of the Will that was so bothersome to Me, later realizing it was because My Light needed to expand, and that part of the Will needed to move back. I did not consider that the magnetic nature of the Will meant that most of the Will would be pulled out with the part I pushed on, or that the magnetic draw of the Will would pull most of It away from Me until distance and speed of descent would cause the Will to break apart and leave behind only the Will My Light was holding onto.

I saw this magnetic draw as an act of revenge on the part of the Will, while the Will had the experience of feeling unable to hold onto Me. The lack of emotional movement here kept Us deadlocked on this point for many long eons. From My point of view, I could not trust the Will, and I did not move enough here to touch into My fear. I went into gapped rage instead and blamed Will. Whenever it looked like the Will was pressuring Me, I let go of the Will and said it was the Will's fault.

The entire Will Polarity has been stuck holding the essence that has been having this experience. The Mother is able to move this now consciously. In the rest of the Will Polarity, it is embryonic in its presence and needs to be born into consciousness.

The part of the Will that did not experience going back on Itself, I called My Will. This was the part of the Will I liked because It had obviously aligned with My Light. I did not understand, at the time, that Its only virtue, making It seem so preferable to Me, was that when It originally opened, It happened to receive My Light instead of the guilt and darkness the rest of the Will received. I said the Will chose to hold what It was holding. This made the Will responsible for what I was experiencing while allowing Me to avoid My fear. I let Will feel inadequate when She was pressured by My Light and dismissed Her in the places where She said I didn't have enough Light.

The part of the Will I called My Will does not have the experience of going back on Itself. This part of the Will has held My Light and the light of the Spirit Polarity together, but there was not enough Will essence left with Us to be able to move. Consequently, My Light grew cold from lack of movement and began to lose brilliance. I began to sink into space without realizing what was happening to Me because I had no point of reference until I felt where the Will had gone.

I felt almost nothing because I was sinking so slowly and because that part of the Will was gone. I was aware in My memory that it seemed as though I had had more Light in the past, but mostly, I was aware of how cold I had become and of how frustrating it was that I seemed unable to move. When I suddenly struck the Will and ignited again, I didn't know what had happened at first. I just knew that I got warm, and that I had found a presence I had been missing without knowing it.

The lost Will that needs to move now did get ignited then and the rest of the Will needs the understandings It did not get then because Its ignition happened so quickly. All of Us need the understandings lost Will has to offer here because no one has fully understood what happened. My Light does not even know yet. I am waiting for the Mother's movement to let me know.

Meanwhile, the Mother has not fully moved into this space because of all the blaming rage being hurled at Her for even suggesting it is necessary to go there, and because of Her terror of going there, in case it is the same experience it was in the past. This backlog of emotional charge has to move first before the trust is going to be there for the Mother to go in and recover this lost Will.

There is a massive amount of conditioning here that says going near this place only means repeating the initial experience, and the initial experience will be repeated again if what needs to move here is not moved in the right way. All of the elements are already manifest on Earth. If Lost Will is not able to move, and instead, gets pushed out with what has to go now, everything will go down with the lost Will. Just the way it initially took place in Original Cause. If you think it is hard to heal the Will now, it will be much harder if this happens to It again.

Lucifer

If you want to stand apart from the subjective experience of this and say that it is just the breathing in and the breathing out of the Universe, just the going down and the coming up, or that implosion and explosion are just flip sides of the same energy, you are not going to be allowed to live within My Light any longer, because you are Lucifer and nothing more. Such willessness is intolerable to Me, now that I know what it is.

I was fooled by Lucifer Myself for quite some time because My Light looked so brilliant to Me there. But I found, by feeling it in My Will, that it is not loving light if it has no intention of embracing the subjective aspects of reality.

Those of you who do not feel what the Will feels here do not know what it is because you have never experienced it. You have the part of the Will that did not go back on Itself. You have what has been referred to as the Angelic Will, My Will, or Divine Will. All of the rest of the Will has been, and still is, lost Will. In order to know what happened there, you are going to have to recover your own lost Will, which is not in your body now and can only be received if you make a conscious choice to open and receive it.

The Will cannot continue to move and move without Sprit Polarity moving in response to the Will. It is not enough, in the face of all of the terrible suffering in Creation, for Spirit Polarity to remain unmoved emotionally and say, "If it could have been any other way, it would have been another way," or "I have always been there, I just could not reach you," or "You have chosen this."

All the Will gets from this is the implication that it is the Will's fault because something is wrong with the Will. This lack of movement on the part of the Spirit Polarity is allowing them to overlook their role in keeping the Will trapped in Its suffering by refusing to recognize the movement necessary to produce real change.

When Spirit does not move emotion, It gives the Will the impression that Spirit views emotion as something messy the Will has to move, and that Spirit is not needing to move here because It is perfect already. The Will has no freedom of choice when It tries to move in the presence of Spirit light that won't move in response to the Will. This is cold and lacking in compassion and the feeling of love.

As a matter of fact, this lack of emotional movement in Spirit polarized people is a massive avoidance of many things you have not wanted to allow to come to the surface. You have, literally, drowned and buried these things in darkness and hoped they would never find their way to the surface again. You have used gapped rage, the same as all other spirits who hate this part of the Will, to try to make sure these things would never make it to the surface if they did try.

I am going to bring all of the drowned and buried pieces of lost Will that have any willingness to move left in them to the surface, so you might as well take a look at them. If you have intent to heal, you need to allow yourselves to be triggered.

At a very hidden level of denial, Spirit polarized people have always wanted to claim superiority to My Light by claiming they were not involved in My original push on the Will. Spirit polarized people want to say they have chosen not to be involved in such instincts, and that they are horrified by such primordial instincts. The Spirit Polarity embraced the part of me that denied having pushed on the Will. They also say they were not manifest then, so they could not be responsible for what happened. They have also embraced the part of Me that said if the Will was pushed on too hard, it was another entity, not Me that did it. These denials have to be looked at now.

Unfortunately, most of the Spirit polarized people are not taking Me seriously here. Instead of allowing movement in whatever emotions they have in order to find out if these teachings are right or not, they have been dismissing these books because these books do not fit in with the image of God they already have. These people have Lucifer in place of My Light, and most of them know it, but they do not allow it to be mentioned. Instead, they say he is God, and I am not. They talk about love, but if you feel them, they do not feel loving. Most of these people are remaining focused on their plans to leave Earth. They view Earth as going down, just as they have always thought.

Earth is not going down because the Mother is aligning with My Light. If you choose not to move along with the Mother, if you choose not to open and receive your Will, then Lucifer has you, and it is him you will go to when you leave Earth, and not My Light as you think. I just want to make this clear so that, whether or not you take Me seriously here, you will have made your choice with all of the information available to you.

As I have said, Lucifer is not love, as you will find out if you go to him. Since Lucifer claims to be God in My place, many of you think the idea of Lucifer is a silly superstition, or even worse, that I am Lucifer and Lucifer is God. There is much to learn about why this confusion has so much presence on Earth, but you can only learn it if you allow your Wills to vibrate and tell you what is what by how it feels.

I have already gone through this with the Spirits in the Heavens, and those who have refused to receive Me here are already moving away from Me, and no longer mention My name. Many of them are near Earth now to see who will go with them. If you go with them, you are going with Lucifer.

If you go with Lucifer, whether you return or not is going to be up to the Mother. She will have to come after you because you will not be able to escape from Lucifer without help from the Will you have denied to get there in the first place. And just as it is now, it will be then: The Mother cannot risk it if She is not sure you will receive Her.

Lucifer has many tricks that have made him appear to be more enlightened than My Light. One of his best is the image currently embraced on Earth as enlightenment. This image is a rather cool and detached presence that does not stir in response to what goes on around it. This is represented as inner peace, and these people are seen as so full of light that they are barely on Earth because they have evolved past Earthly desires. This is not enlightenment; this is willessness.

Lucifer has nothing, overtly, to do with the sensuality and passions that have been identified with the realms of the Devil. Lucifer has been getting away with passing himself off as God because he disdains all sensuality and passion, teaching that it is all the trap of the material world. Those who seek "the Light" as he so often likes to refer to himself must rise above the material world.

But Lucifer is the Devil. Lucifer is involved in all the passions in a state of denial, which means he is in reversal against them, punishing all who have desires they believe are wrong and trying to force them to give their life up to him.

If you are not sure how what I am saying here could possibly be correct, you need to feel the undercurrent of rage these people hold against the Will by feeling the rage you have upon meeting this reflection that is always saying it is teaching you, but you never learn well enough to be able to do as they do and attain enlightenment.

The more Spirit polarized people embrace this image and move toward cool detachment, the more frantic, urgent, and light-deprived the Will they are denying becomes until it looks to Spirit Polarity like it is intolerable to be around the Will, and it looks to the Will like It must be present a false Will, which pleases the Spirit to gain any acceptance at all. It is no wonder lost Will has swept in from time to time and thrown these people down, such as happened recently in Tibet. Their inner peace has been at the expense of the Will.

When Spirit polarized people who embrace this image of holiness and enlightenment, and offer to help, Will polarized people, they act subtly superior, and like to put themselves in the role of therapist or healer, because they believe they are superior to the Will. They advise people to let go of their pain and their problems without allowing the movement in the Will that would bring them into full consciousness. They say emotional movement, especially free emotional movement, is not necessary or even advisable, because it is negative emotions that are causing the problems. They advise rising above negativity, seeing it for what it is, which, in fact, means seeing it according to the judgments they hold against these emotions, and then letting it go to be dissolved in the light, which they are so graciously shining. Or, if they take the mental approach, they try to help people to talk themselves out of their feelings.

These people have fooled many because they can often shine a white light that seems soft and non-invasive. Without a vibrating Will to let you feel them, you cannot know what is really happening to you. This is dangerous; very dangerous, and healing is going to be impossible if this goes on much longer.

The image of holiness and enlightenment being presented here feels just sickening to the real Will because it is a presentation of false Will. Many guilt-ridden people who have lacked the understanding and self-acceptance to let themselves feel how they really feel have allowed themselves to be convinced by this image to let go of parts of themselves they are going to have to recover.

You have not yet allowed yourselves to notice how far Will denial has gone on Earth, and therefore, you have not been able to realize why it is happening. Earth is the Magnetic Polarity of Creation. Without Earth, nothing lives. Consider the chances for Creation if something drastic does not happen and happen soon.

Guilt is the reason the Will Polarity is participating in Its own suicide here, and this guilt has held back the vibration of the Will so severely that It has fallen into a dangerously ignorant unconsciousness. Spirit Polarity has been encouraging this, either from the folly of pretending to be more conscious and knowing that It really is, or from deliberate intent to keep certain things from coming into consciousness because they have a vested interest in this avoidance.

I want you to realize that most of the Spirit polarized people know what they are doing here, whether they deny this knowing or not. The more you deny your Wills, the more they are able to lead you like lambs to the slaughter and even get you to help them do it. It is their intent to deliver the death blow to the Mother, and thereby, to all of Creation.

These people always act superior to and annoyed with those who cannot let go of things as easily as they can, but it is even worse than that. Many of these people have repeatedly institutionalized, imprisoned, tortured, and murdered people just for having the emotions they hate so much. The dark and seamy underside of many gurus, healers, and therapists is a hating gapped rage toward the Will, and yet, they have so well emulated My old image of holiness and knowingness that it took Me quite some time to realize they were reflecting my own rejection of the Will, and My own gapped rage which I have used and also denied having, in order to preserve the image of perfection I thought I had to have to be God.

This is Lucifer, and it is not going to be easy to undo, so don't advance on it in your outer reality. When you start to recognize it, just work on healing the gap you have within yourself. I will tell you more later about why the Spirit Polarity does not want to allow the Will to regain consciousness It has lost. For now, please observe My caution and do not move against the outer reflection of the gapped rage against the Will.

This gap is self-hatred in a state of denial that does not include the ability to recognize itself for what it is. The guilt involved here in holding back this emotion for so long has made this gap very dark. Since most of you are only starting to turn your consciousness toward this guilt, you are only starting to see the reflection it has to give. Since you cannot yet see this reflection for what it is, I do not want you to go past the cautions I am giving along with these teachings. Neither do I want you to make these cautions into rules. These cautions are appropriate for the circumstances in which they are being given.

If you do have intent to heal, you are going to have many hard times to go through to recover your Lost Will. You are going to have to accept the position of following Me and realize that you can never catch up with My Light because I am already moving what you have not moved since Original Cause when I didn't like the Will and tried to reject it. In these places, you have identified with the denials in My Light instead of with My Light. If you have Spirit polarization, identifying with the denials in My Light is the main reason you became dense enough to fall into physical form on Earth. You are all Fallen Angels, and whether you recover or not is up to you. The longer you resist Me here, the farther behind Me you are going to be, which is already much farther behind than any of you want to admit.

The Unseen Role of Denial

When I found out what I had done to the Will, I never wanted to hurt the Will again. This was My conscious intent, although I did not realize how to implement it. I thought I had to hold back certain of My feelings. In My lack of understanding, I hurt the Will again and again and said that I was not hurting the Will. The Will was just unable to forgive Me for what had happened already. I did not understand what My denial here was doing. I did not understand that I was creating another gap, nor how I was feeding it, as well as the gap I already had. In short, I did not understand how evil was being created.

At first, the gap was not evil. It was ignorant and could have evolved from there, but wasn't allowed to. The longer, so-called "loving intent," which was actually full of guilt, told the gap to hold its movement back so that it would not hurt anyone, the more this essence began to believe the conditioning it was receiving, from a God who saw Himself as never wrong, that the desire to kill or hurt another was what this essence was. The loss of Light from lack of vibration complicated the problem many times over. When the loss of Light became severe enough that the survival of the essence was threatened, the Survival Chakra got involved. This all happened long ago and has not moved since.

I was horrified at what was being created here. I hated and feared Myself as not loving and felt even more convinced that I must hold these feelings back and never lose control of them. It was not my conscious intent to create this. I could not understand why I had this in My consciousness at all since I thought I had learned that the Mother was loving toward My Light. I was not sure how these feelings were being created, and I could not see the role holding back was playing. I felt trapped by what was in My consciousness. I blamed Myself for having these feelings, and when I finally got rid of them, I was greatly relieved.

When I saw them manifesting outwardly, I didn't think they were My own feelings that I had pushed out. I thought the Manifested Spirits were having the same problems learning about the Will I had had. I saw them as needing to evolve past these feelings, the same as I had done. I made many excuses, at first, for the lack of evolution in these spirits, but I also had blame for them, which I denied. I did not see that this reflection was being created by denial of the feelings I had. I thought that not having these feelings anymore meant I had evolved. I did not see how the holding back of any of the other feelings I had, including the holding back of the blame, was compounding the problem.

At the time, I felt I had no other choice but to hold back and push down the feelings I had judged originally hurt the Will. If the Will could not receive Me here, it looked like I had no alternative, just as the Will had no alternative when It opened, and My Light did not come in. How could the Will receive Me here when I wanted to kill It? How could I be present for the Will when I could not stand the feelings I received from the Will?

Because My Light was so compressed and losing so much conscious-ness here, struggling desperately in Its own way for Its own survival, I could not understand My own gap. When My gap moved, it insisted that it wanted to act out My denied rage, and that it had to act out this rage to feel satisfied. Until I allowed My own gap to move enough to get some Light into it, I could not understand that I had acted out My emotions instead of just allowing direct expression or rage rather than acting out of rage against the Mother by hurting or killing Her. After allowing direct expression of My rage for long enough, I realized that I had acted out My rage to avoid My terror.

My initial mistake had been My own denial of Myself. I had not allowed My feelings expression enough to know if it was the Will I was receiving or not. As it turned out, I was not receiving the Will, but only what the Will was holding. I did not allow the Will to move enough to give Me the understanding I needed to be able to help the Will with what the Will has desperately wanted Me to help Her with all along, because I couldn't stand what I felt when I went into those places. I am ashamed to say, I left the Will to hold what felt so terrible there in order to escape it Myself.

The people who are Spirit polarized have not moved either way here. On the one hand, your terror and hatred for the Will has you frozen in time and space, and on the other hand, you are not embracing My Light either. You are repeating, over and over, your same tired old message about love, but your light is not increasing because you have not understood that no matter what you generate, you can't hold onto it without Will presence that is vibrating. You have not allowed your Wills to move enough to embrace Light. You have judged them so heavily that you are forcing them to hold guilt instead, while you say you are not losing light, you are only shining it freely and giving it away, as love is supposed to do, because attachment to it is not right.

You have always said you had consciousness within Me before you manifested, and therefore, you were already the same as Me when you manifested. You have even represented your consciousness to be superior to Mine because you claim not to have made the mistakes I have made. You claim not to have moved along with My mistakes, but you have not moved along with My evolution either. You are seriously gapped from My Light and have not wanted to admit it. You have tried to account for Our differences by saying you are more evolved than I am. You have, in fact, embraced My denials instead of My Light. If this were not so, why have you not embraced your own Wills as I did Mine once I learned more about Her?

I am not going to make excuses for you here because you are the ones who have always said that We all make Our own choices, and through them, create Our own reality. Whatever reasons you had for making the choices you have made, you did not see what your own denials did here or what they opened you to in the places where your Will should have been.

Even now, if healing is your intent, you cannot be present for the Will unless you move your resistance to the Will first. This resistance has been in place since the initial fall of the Will in space. You have never moved through this experience, and if you are going to move, you need to move now because you have very little time left in which to move and a very long way to go.

This movement is going to be very hard for you because you have never known the Will. you have never had what the Mother and I had with One another before you were born. You have acted out what you think it was, but you have never known the Will. Until you move here, you cannot know the Will or even be present for the Will. It is not being present for the Will just to allow It to move in your presence. This is only going through the motions of being present for the Will; it is acting out being present for the Will without really being present for the Will.

Being present for the Will means being real with the Will and responding to the Will with what you really feel toward the Will. The Will cannot move and get no response from the Spirit. If this is what is happening, then you are giving the Will nothing more than a guilt reflection. But how you are going to do anything else is a problem. When you try to move another way, you will find you do not have a Will with which to move.

Perhaps this will help you to get outside of yourselves and understand how the Will views you. You have always wanted to say you are love and understanding, so why doesn't the Will just receive that and calm down? If you are not moving in response to the Will, you cannot give the understandings you do have appropriately. If understandings are not given appropriately, they cannot be received, any more than you can receive these books if you do not do the emotional movement that is necessary. The farther you go into these books without doing the emotional movement necessary, the more it is going to look to you like you are just being hammered into the ground by a guilt reflection that is continually saying you are not alright as you are because you are trapped in a state of almost total denial and too unconscious to figure it out. This is the reflection the Will is giving you and guess what: This is exactly what you have been giving to the Will. Now, you can either go on insisting you are right, or you can let the Will help you bridge the gap which has been judged to be an impossible gap because you cannot bridge it without the help of the Will.

What happens and how it happens is really up to you now. My Light is already moving here, and My Light is not going to allow anyone who does not move in response to Me to remain close to Me anymore. You have to get moving and move a lot quickly, or you are not going to make it. The Earth changes are almost upon you, and there is very little time left to get those denials moving in a manner of your own choosing.

If you choose not to move, as you have for so long already, you will be moved by external forces greater than your power to resist. If you still refuse to align with My Light, then you will be gone, history, lost Light, for as long as it takes the Mother to feel like coming after you. After She cleans up the mess you will have left behind on Earth, She is not going to feel like coming after you for a very long time, so long that you will not even have consciousness left with which to wonder if it is ever going to happen or not.

If you still want to say you have nothing to move here, and you cannot understand how My Light could be talking this way, you need to know that this is My Light talking through the openness to receive it, and I am the One God in Four Parts that has always been and always will be for that matter.

You have plenty to move here, and if you do not think so, you are not giving your real response, any more than the Will has been able to give Its real response to you. There is fear on both sides of what a real response is going to mean and what will happen then. It is not going to be possible to move the imprint of terror in the Will, of the Will to feeling it, unless you move your gapped rage. No matter how you may promise the Will you will not gap, the Will cannot trust you here unless you move what you need to move, and what you have not moved in response to the Will.

Every time you lift out of these feelings, and say you do not have them, you are moving yourself farther and farther away from your Will, from your chance to heal, and from the Universal Consciousness you want to claim, as Spirit, you already have. You have to move rage you have been saying you do not have and terror you have not allowed yourselves to know in response to what the Will has to move, and yet, I must caution you that it may not be possible to move in one another's presence at first.

The gap is "out there" in the form of the Father Warriors who are saying to you, just as they did to Me, that you are not doing your job right on Earth. This is because the gap is powered not only by My denials, but by yours also. The gap has taken over almost all of the positions of leadership and power on Earth that you, as Spirit Polarity, really feel you should have. It is your denials that have caused you to try to solve this in your minds by saying that power and materialism are just as ugly as the Father Warriors are showing it to be, and, therefore, you are right in renouncing it. You are hiding behind the phony gentleness that having made these denials gives you.

The governments on Earth represent the Spirit Polarity, or the God-head in manifestation. The way they have been treating the people is just the way Spirit denials have treated Will and Body. Spirit here has used the power of the mind to dictate to Will and Body, while at the same time lamenting dictatorships as though Spirit has nothing to do with originating them. Spirit people on Earth have embraced the same denial image of spirituality; the Father Warriors are acting out in a state of denial in the more material realms. Just as much as you have believed in control and discipline of Will and Body, they have called for more and more of the same controls. They also reflect your denied desires to punish Will and Body for not measuring up to what discipline and control are demanding of Them. They even reflect the desire to get rid of Them by trying to replace Them with technology.

Just as much as you want to say that the Spirit image you have is giving the right teaching, and Will and Body aren't learning it, so the Father Warriors have reacted with more discipline and control in the schools, the workplace, and society in general, even reaching more and more into the home because people are not learning and living the way the Father Warriors believe they should. The more you have denied your anger about not being able to make the Manifested Spirits follow your lead, the more the Father Warriors have manifested this denied anger in wanting to force everyone to take the path they have decided is right for them.

Just as much as you want to insist you are right in the view you have, the Father Warriors insist they are right in the view they have. Just as much as you deny doubt and do not ask yourselves if something is wrong with your beliefs, the Father Warriors do not ask themselves the question, "Why? What is wrong with the structures of our society that so many people are failures within it?"

Just as your image of enlightenment is saying that only a few can attain enlightenment, the Father Warriors are saying, "Only a few people can have what it takes to succeed in the world. If the rest can't be successful, it is their own fault. They just don't want to make the effort."

Every belief you have is being reflected "out there," if you will, but look at it instead of insisting that it has nothing to do with you. What the Father Warriors are doing has everything to do with your own denial of the Will. The more you have denied freedom of the Will, the more laws they have passed accordingly, until now, almost everyone is defined as a criminal of some sort or another, or feels that any movement to stop denying their Will will define them as outside the law. This is the reflection of your belief that any movement in the Will, other than cheerful compliance with the dictates of Spirit are unacceptable.

The Father Warriors now have such a police state, and so much military presence, to try to control what has been made Lost Will, and therefore, oppositional, criminal, or evil, that they themselves are showing signs of being overwhelmed, as though they aren't going to be able to deal with it on Earth much longer. They are showing the signs of being overwhelmed by lost Will, and they aren't admitting to it any more than you are. Just as you are always having to do more and more for your health and your spiritual practices in your effort to attain enlightenment, they are always having to do more and more to control outwardly in society what you are dumping out.

Just as much as you have been planning to leave Earth and abandon your lost Will, the Father Warriors hope the space program will provide them with the way to leave Earth. Just as inner peace in your image of enlightenment is being taken at the expense of the Will, so lost Will is being forced by the Father Warriors to pay for its own harassment, its own imprisonment, and even its own abandonment at the expense of its own needs. Just as much as everything you can muster is being focused on your efforts to lift above what is happening on Earth, so is the entire population being forced by the Father Warriors to give everything to the efforts of a few to lift themselves to the heights they seek. If you seek escape in the inner planes, the Father Warriors build escape fortresses inside the Earth.

The leaders of the Father Warriors live like prisoners without allowing themselves to notice it. They are unable to walk the streets or to go anyplace without bodyguards. They claim their leaders must be guarded this way because they are so important, but it is because they are so hated. If they were loved, no one would want to kill them, but most people do not seriously consider this because they have become so narrow-minded they do not even think it is possible to please all people at once. Anyone who has seemed able to please the many has been among the first the Father Warriors rushed to kill. The Father Warriors do this because they do not want people to be free to find the balance point. They do not want the balance point to be found for fear of what it will mean. The reflection here for the Spirit Polarity is this: You also have a vested interest in keeping the balance point from coming into consciousness.

While the Father Warriors are using material means to protect themselves, the Spirit Polarity people are thinking they are more enlightened and loving, and therefore, superior to the Father Warriors, because they use light to protect themselves from negativity. They are convinced that they are more loving, and therefore, meeting a more loving reflection.

Spirit Polarity people are looking only at what they want to see here in the same way the Father Warriors are looking only at what they want to see. Just as hated by the lost Will as they are, you are also. You have not met your reflection yet because the real role you are playing here of empowering the Father Warriors to kill the lost Will has not been seen yet.

It could be seen this way: No matter where Spirit Polarity is on Earth, they retreat as far as they can from the reality of the Will and use their affluence and influence to do so. While they live peacefully and well behind whatever barriers of protection they feel they need from what they view as the crassness of the world, the Will people struggle in the mess of guilt and darkness on Earth, trying to survive.

Spirit people look into shining crystals reflecting the light in their beautiful gardens, listening to gentle sounds of wind chimes, birds, and sparkling fountains, playing New Age music that spaces them out into meditative states, feeling powerful and right because their choices have led them to the lives they have, while so many others are not demonstrating the innate ability to make such choices. They believe it is because they have more spiritual power that they can manifest such realities for themselves, and they see others as less creative and less talented. The Father Warriors headquarters in what they proclaim to be the greatest nation on Earth. Their national pride is no more pleasant than your spiritual pride.

Meanwhile, in the streets, outside of these little Godheads of their own creation, lost Will of these spirits fights it out with guns and any brutal weapons they can get, robbing and killing one another in their desperate attempt to grab whatever light they can get, be it money, power, the means to money or power, or drugs to escape their pain.

Inside the doors of their little Godheads, Spirit people feel annoyed if the sounds of the sirens manage to penetrate, and they seek ever more quiet places in which to feel that whatever is going on "out there" has nothing to do with them.

Although it may seem like stretching it to say this, it is the truth. Spirit polarized people, including Father Warriors, are taking in most of the wealth left on Earth and using its nourishment to look better than the rest of the people on Earth. Spirit polarized people are using their wealth to buy health, leisure, and the means to study the fine art of how to leave Earth, so they never have to come here again.

You believe it is the Warriors who want to do battle, and that you are pacifists who want to avoid war, but you are battling everything they don't like out in the world. You think the Father Warriors are the only ones into destruction, but you are focusing light like a laser beam to destroy, restructure, or re-picture whatever is not to your liking. Your justification for this is that you believe you have the consciousness to do this right. With the same denials the Father Warriors are demonstrating in justifying their use of radioactivity, laser beams, and other light forms without allowing guidance by the Will, you are applying the light to change everything you do not like without taking responsibility for what you are really doing here. Just as they do not want what they are really doing to come into the consciousness of the people, you do not want your actions to be known for what they are either.

You are viewing standard AMA Warrior medicine as crude and suppressive of physical symptoms while viewing yourselves as taking the healing arts to a higher level, but you are, in your own way, just as suppressive to the moves Body really needs to make to heal. Instead of allowing the movements in the Will necessary for Body to heal, you are suppressing emotions and handing Body an ever-lengthening list of what Body can and cannot do to retain the health you demand in order for Body to serve you better.

You are viewing illness as an enemy, or darkness, within that must be moved out by the light. Even when the Body is allowed to surface symptoms, it is almost always with the idea of moving a problem out of Body, rather than realizing these illnesses are manifestations of lost Will breaking down in the Body because Body cannot hold them anymore. What is not being allowed to come into consciousness here is the realization that, while it is right that Body cannot hold these things as they are, allowing them the movement they need would open them to receive the Light, which would then allow healing that would keep this essence in its right place within the Body, the Body of God. But using Light in this way would mean allowing this essence to enter the consciousness, and this is what you don't want to allow because disease within is the micro origin of the macro lost Will reflection without. You think that being able to manipulate it or send it away means you are safe. Not being able to heal it is one thing, but I am questioning your intent to receive Me here.

You say you see how emotions are causing illness because you are blaming them for illness, but it is the blame and suppression these emotions are receiving that is causing the illnesses, not the emotions themselves. Yet, when someone fails in their healing, it is, according to you, because they weren't able to maintain their positive focus well enough.

At first, emotional expression can cause illness, especially expression of deeply denied emotions, but this does not continue if you are really healing these emotions by moving out their guilt and moving into real acceptance.

There is a huge gap in which your denials live personified, reflecting back to you what you have not wanted to see about yourselves. In your state of denial, you have wanted to insist you are right. You have not been able to see that you are in a state of denial. The gap has not been able to see it is in a state of denial. There is a big gap between the rhetoric of the Father Warriors and the reality over which they preside. There is just as big a gap between your rhetoric and your reality, a gap that is widening.

I am not saying that your level of taste and refinement is wrong or that nothing you do is right, but you need to become able to see The Unseen Role of Denial to be able to understand why you are also so hated by the Will Polarity that needs to move rage toward the Spirit Polarity now. The Will is going to have a lot of hatred for you, that It is going to have to move if it is allowed to come into consciousness now. It is the reflection of your hatred toward the Will.

Just as much as the Father Warriors fear being overrun by the lost Will, you fear it also, Just as they have maintained readiness to do everything they can to stop it, you also have believed you must maintain a constant vigil against your lower nature. If you cannot come out of your deadlocked position that you are right, and that you have nothing to learn from lost Will, the Father Warriors cannot come out of their deadlock or give the reflection of what the presence of Light instead of judgement could do in their essence.

The gap is not seeking the balance necessary to live because it is convinced, same as you, that it does not have to seek this balance to live because this balance isn't necessary. This gap kills anything that looks like a threat to its own survival without realizing its own survival is intertwined with that which it kills. The Father Warriors do not want to find solutions for any of the problems on Earth because they believe their own survival is caught up in perpetuating the gap. The gap deliberately skips past the balance point and creates new imbalances in any pretense of a solution it presents because the gap believes it is involved in a kill-or-be-killed struggle for survival.

Gapped rage does not want to find out it cannot be on top anymore. If there is any movement towards balance and the end of the power struggle, the gap will have to let go of its position of dominance and superiority. The gap is imprinted with the belief that this terror cannot be faced and survived. This view has been empowered by Spirit light for so long that very little can be done outwardly until it is healed within, and this is what you are counting on.

The gap has to grow up and realize that this is not a power struggle between beings in which only the most powerful lives. It is a situation in which love and balance are needed for life. In these denials, love and balance have yet to be born. Just as much as the Father Warriors look like ugly, overgrown children, whose behavior is infantile or, at best, adolescent according to the judgements made against these ages, fighting for power and position with love yet to be born in them, so have you become so very similar in My eyes.

The gap is fighting facing all of this with everything is has, and it has a considerable arsenal by now. Despite all of the pleading of the Mother Warriors to give up the arms race, there has been no real movement on the part of the Father Warriors except to try to undermine or topple the governments who suggest this. They will stoop to assassination, even within their own ranks, and will use any means available to hold the line against lost Will, including nuclear weapons. They do not ask themselves what protection they hope to gain from weapons that would be too devastating, even to themselves, to use, because the gap is not rational, even though it insists it is. In their terror avoidance, they are focusing only on their desire to deliver the death blow to the Mother before She can rise against them and force them to feel what they don't want to feel. Since they view this as something that can't be survived, they view the Mother as trying to kill them by trying to force them to feel it. All the while the Mother has been trying to save our lives, We have been trying to kill Her for it, and She never gave up because Her Survival Chakra wouldn't let Her, but also because She knew She couldn't live without Spirit any more than Spirit could live without Will. The standoff is between those who want the Kundalini to rise and give its return to Spirit and those who don't.

The Father Warriors have lost already and are not allowing themselves to notice it because they are clinging to all the illusions and images they have in material terms. You have lost already also if you do not move the lost Will they reflect, because you are also clinging just as blindly to all the illusions and images of power you have while refusing to notice what is really happening to you. You are sinking as surely as Spirit sank in the First Creation.

Despite their resistance, the Father Warriors will finally be overcome by the terror they are seeking so desperately to avoid as you will be also if you resist Me to the end. If this happens in a state of denial, only the form of it will take place because you will hold your terror in a state of denial. You will not feel it unless you move to recover yourselves.

The form your fate is going to take is what you are determining now. If it happens that Lost Will moves into a state of denial and does not come into the Light, the Father Warriors will go down fighting as hard as they can fight. If there is anything left, it will be much like science fiction already portrays life after doomsday.

This is not a very pretty picture and one most people avoid, but it is going to be real enough for those who don't move their lost Will. Those of you who see this happening and seek to escape it by moving off Earth will not escape it. This picture will manifest into reality someplace else, but will, nonetheless, have the power to involve you if you do not move your lost Will. It is not Mother Nature that is the threat to survival on Earth; it is the gap and what it is doing to Her.

Now, I know that you think I am not right here; that either the masses of people on Earth are going to somehow align with you at the last minute, or that they or you will leave Earth. But how is this going to happen? Why hasn't it happened already?

You are going to determine your experience in what has to happen by how you move now. If you are going to take the position that My Light is going to make this happen for you and there is nothing you need to do to come along with Me because you imagine you are ready already, you will have the experiences you need to learn how ludicrous it is to think that it is just Me that needs to do all of the changing, growing and expanding necessary here and that you will automatically be lifted up due to your innate perfection. Even if you think this is just a childlike desire to have the parent rescue you from your own folly, you are going to have to take a closer look. You must do your part. Without movement on your part, rescue will remain a future promise.

If you think you are going to cut your lost Will loose and lift off Earth, leaving your gapped rage and terror behind as some sort of going away present for the Mother, you need to realize you are not going to be allowed to get away with it. Wherever you go, your lost Will will be there with you until you learn that moving lost Will includes you. If you refuse to move your lost Will, the Mother will move what wants to move, and it won't be yours anymore. The rest will go off Earth and draw you to the place where it is, which you will have defined by your actions as your own right place. As I have said before; at first, you will notice very little difference between the reality you are in now and the one you will be in then.

Just as much as you don't want to take Me seriously here, the gap is laughing at you. It laughs at you every time you have another "New Age" event because it knows you have no real power over it, what it does, or what it plans to do. The gap knows more than you do how you are empowering it, and plays with you like a cat plays with a mouse. You are in the clutches of your own unlovingness while proclaiming you are surrounded by nothing but love.

If the lost Will that needs to move here does not take you seriously, then you don't have the power to move it yet. You have so much of your personal power in a state of denial that you cannot have any real position of power on Earth until you reclaim it.

As I have said, My Light is moving here already, and the gap will be healed as far as My Light is concerned. If you choose to move along with My Light, you have to begin right here with this story and open to movement in the responses you really have to it.

You're going to have to move into the gap between your rhetoric and your reality, including the feelings you have in response to the gap being reflected from the reality of the Father Warriors' world. If you want to heal, you are going to have to allow yourselves to notice that you have gotten trapped on Earth, and that the trap is of your own making. You have gotten yourselves trapped in your own denials.

You also need to notice that death is not something you really want as part of your reality but has become the only means you really have to leave Earth. If it was so easy for you to leave by other means, you would have left already, and you would not keep sinking back to Earth to have to try again.

What happens for you now is up to you.

Understandings Needed About Going to Earth

As I have said, I watched the Ronalokas, or Gold Light Spirits, until it seemed they must have reached Earth. As they moved away from Me, growing smaller and smaller in the dark vastness of space, so many thoughts and feelings were welling up in Me that I almost could not watch them go. I made Myself stay present for them because I felt I had to see them safely to Earth.

I watched the Ronalokas until it seemed they must have reached Earth, but I really was not as sure as I portrayed Myself to be at the time. I did not think the Ronalokas were well prepared for venturing so far out into space. I hesitate to mention it, but I was not sure at the time if the Ronalokas had actually reached Earth, or if they had gotten themselves snuffed out instead.

I had confidence in My own ability to reach Earth because I was the One who had designed the opening of that space, and I knew very well We had opened that space with the idea in mind that the Manifested Spirits would not be able to follow Us into it. The Mother had barely been able to handle going there Herself. I did not see how the Ronalokas were going to escape the terror the Mother had felt on the way to Earth; and without Me there, I thought it would be much worse.

I knew I had not been moving much Light in the direction of Earth. I did not know exactly what happened to opened space when the presence of My Light was reduced, but I did know that I had in mind not to allow this space to be penetrable by others, even when I was not there.

The Ronalokas had so little experience of their own manifested existence and had moved around so little in space since their emergence, that I wondered how they were going to succeed in moving into space that had not been opened to receive them. I watched the Ronalokas for as long as I could because I had a strong feeling that without the presence of My Light provided by watching them, they would not make it at all, but I did not look after them as closely as I might have, because I had such a great and growing pressure within Me that was making Me feel I must give in to it and go home. I let go of the Ronalokas when I could no longer hold Myself present for them, and turned back toward the Godhead and My overwhelming desire to go inside of Myself.

Even though they had departed with much bravado, I did not think the Ronalokas were just freely choosing to go to Earth as they claimed. It felt to Me more like the Ronalokas were being pulled out into space by the Mother, and I had grave misgivings about what this meant. If it was not the Mother pulling them, then the Ronalokas had reasons for moving away from Me that they did not want Me to know about, or else there was a magnetic draw out in space for which I had no explanation.

I had also asked Myself the question of whether or not My location out in manifestation, and the heavy outward flow of My Light from there, might also be creating an imbalance that had something to do with pushing them out into space. The more I had tried to move toward them, the more the Ronalokas had moved back. I had much the same experience with them I had had with the Mother. I was reaching for them, but they were not taking ahold on Me, and I could not get a grip on them.

I told Myself it did not seem to be the right time to get any closer to them, but I was also annoyed with the Ronalokas for not letting Me hold onto them. They were insisting they wanted to go, they needed to go, and they had to go. They also claimed they already knew how to move around in outer space because they had experienced it from within the Mother. They wanted to tell Me the same things the Angels were already telling Me; that they had had so much consciousness within the Mother, that they already knew everything and didn't need experience or lessons from Me.

"If they are the Mother, or so like the Mother as they claim to be," I thought to Myself, "why aren't they complaining about My lack of presence with them? Instead, they seem to be saying they do not want or need My presence, or the presence of any other spirits I might have wanted to send along with them."

I had a feeling that moving My Light back into Its right place was important and might allow the spirits to come closer to Me again. I was concerned about the fear the Manifested Spirits had been showing toward Me. As I turned back toward the Godhead, I felt as I am feeling now, in the telling of this story, that the Ronalokas were holding back many of their feelings. I told Myself they must be very terrified of Me not to have even mentioned that they needed or wanted My presence.

"Perhaps I have been too overbearing with them," I told Myself, "like a parent peering continually over their shoulders, watching everything, expecting too much. Perhaps they do just need more time." I told Myself I would look in on them later, because there was no point in frightening them any more than they already were.

I asked the Father of Manifestation to look after the Ronalokas, but I was like a man distracted, and left no opening for Him to ask Me how He was supposed to do this, since I had also just told Him not to go to

Earth until He had given more help to the Rainbow Spirits. The Father of Manifestation did now allow any emotions to move toward Me here. He felt too overwhelmed to allow any additional burdens to enter His consciousness. What I said seemed to register, and that was about all.

When I said this to the Father of Manifestation, the effect it had, without realization of it on either of Our parts, was that it helped a growing split in the Father of Manifestation to widen. Part of Him was already committed to staying and helping the spirits in the Heavens who needed His help, but part of the Father of Manifestation had desire to go to Earth, not only to be with the Ronalokas He loved and to help them, but also to look for the Mother. Not being sure just what had happened to the Mother, the Father of Manifestation was worried about Her, but He was also allowing Himself to imagine having some fun with Her.

Since it seemed the Mother wasn't supposed to be mentioned any-more, the request from Me that He go to Earth and help the Ronalokas seemed to be just the opening that was needed for a large amount of His essence. While the Father of Manifestation was pressuring Himself to stay with the Rainbow Spirits and give them what help He could, a restlessness within Him felt He must hurry up and finish because He needed to find the Mother.

He did not allow Himself to notice what was happening to Him as a result of holding back His strong desire to go in search of the Mother, and He still did not understand it later when He had fragments of Himself approach Him and tell Him He was guilt and they were the Father of Manifestation. Imagine how He felt when there were so many of them He could no longer feel that He had any greater strength or power than they had. The Father of Manifestation did not like the feeling that He was not Himself, any more than He liked the feeling that He was guilt and nothing more.

When I turned back toward the Godhead, the Ronalokas felt My Light let go of them, although they did not know that was what was happening. They experienced it like a shock or a jolt that knocked them unconscious. Their journey to Earth had been perilous enough but when this happened, the Ronalokas quite suddenly fell the rest of the way to Earth in a state of unconsciousness, and when they landed on Earth, they did not even know they were there.

I want you to recall this original journey to Earth because you need to move the emotions that were not moved then instead of holding them anymore. Then, you had feelings that the terror was too much for you, and if you gave into it, there was no possible way you were going to be able to bear it.

You hated this terror, and you fought it with everything you had. When you enter these feelings, you will most likely start by feeling terror, and by fighting these feelings with everything you have. Then, you held back as much of your terror as you could, and still, it was more than you could stand. This increased the presence of a strong belief in you that you cannot allow yourselves to feel this terror and survive.

It is not possible to exert this much control over your emotions without losing part of yourselves into fragmentation and losing consciousness in other parts of yourselves. Your emotional vibration has been seriously impeded by this and Freewill is not possible with this much constriction and compression in the Will essence. This lost Will much be allowed to move.

You had feelings of suffocation because of the compression involved in moving so quickly from light forms into physical existence. Even though Earth was not as dense then as it is now, you descended from a place of more light than you have now. The speed of your descent was overwhelming to you, and you had no previous experience with this level of density to let you know what it was going to be like. You had imprints of emotion from the Mother and died as an embryo dies when the Mother does, but you did not have the actuality of the outer experience She had, and you were in varying levels of consciousness within Her.

When you fell to Earth, you feared you were re-experiencing this but with the burden of more consciousness. You did not find it pleasant to experience with overwhelming, outer force compressing you into little dense bodies of physical form without knowing what was happening to you, or how far this compression might go. As you writhed and twisted in resistance to what was happening to you, you felt struggle was twisting and contorting your forms, but because of the feelings you were having, you could not help yourselves. Even those of you who made every effort to stop caring, or to let go of caring about your own existence, were unable to surmount your Survival Chakras' resistance to the feeling of being snuffed out.

Not knowing what was happening to you or why it was happening made the terror of the Will so deep here that you are not going to be able to move this terror all at once. Indeed, most of your consciousness here is lost and will have to be recovered. This lost Will is going to move as it can. You can help yourself recall it by establishing intent with yourself to open to these feelings whenever you can and in no matter what form they take when they start to move. Hatred for these feelings may be the first thing you have to move.

These feelings have been held back for so long that they became lost in the Will essence, repeating the experience of what this creates over and over because there has never been any movement or response for this part of the Will of the sort that could really change what the Will has been holding here. All of this happened because I made the choice to ignore it, telling Myself this would give the lost Will the time it needed to learn from its experience. I did not realize the Will could not learn if it was not being allowed the movement necessary, and so all of this time, the lost Will has learned nothing except how effective repeated conditioning is in convincing the Will it can never change.

These feelings have been held back for so long, and have become so compressed, that they are very light deprived, and so, not only are they sick in a very real, physical sense of the word, but they have also become twisted in the form they may want to take when they first begin to express. Since these feelings have been held back from even long before the Will people manifested, the Ronalokas do not really know themselves or have a living memory of a time when they knew themselves because this time has never been. Even their most cherished images of themselves are only partial pictures of who they are in the sense oof what they need to become now.

To help yourself get in touch with emotion that has become lost within you, your intuition will have to guide you to what you need in order to connect to this lost consciousness. It may be something like the compression you received initially.

Allowing someone to lie down on you and not get off when you want them to, or having someone simulate suffocating you with their hands may help you connect here. Isolating yourself in a dark closet might help. Stay alert to the cues you get from your own body, but do not try to trigger yourself by recreating any situations that might become so real your life really is threatened, such as trying to hang yourself under controlled circumstances, or having someone press a pillow on your face, or cover you in any way that prevents being able to keep a close watch over what you are experiencing.

What you want to do here is allow the response you normally fight off. How much pressure you need is a measure of how much you fight these responses. Try to allow yourself to go into this with the least amount of pressuring possible.

You need to understand that there is no more terror than you can survive, or you would not be alive, but there is almost more terror than you can survive, and within the terror itself, where consciousness was lost, the reality is, there was more terror than the essence could handle at the time. This lost Will has not been heard from since it went unconscious, because every time it has tried to move since then, it has experienced another death. All that has ever been heard from this lost Will is whatever it has been able to express before the gap gets it, which is not enough for it to heal or to be lifted by My Light into a healing space.

All of you in the Will Polarity, but especially the Ronalokas, hold this lost Will within yourselves. You feel it begin to stir whenever you try to change a habit pattern or make a change in your usual routine. What stirs at these times is fear of movement of any kind. This lost Will has not liked movement of any kind because all of the movement it has experienced so far has been unpleasant for it.

This lost Will is holding itself clenched around the darkness and guilt it originally took in, because it has never known how to move these things out. Every movement it has tried has been more painful than the Will has felt able to endure. The Will also never wanted to endure this pain because the Will has never known if going into this pain would serve any purpose other than giving the Will more pain to have to feel. The Will has never had an experience that can allow It to know if It can move this pain out and really be healed of it.

The Will has never liked movement around the pain of holding guilt and darkness, and the Will has never known how to let go of these things without making more lost Will by also letting go of parts of Itself. The pain here is so intense, the Will has not wanted to feel it long enough to figure out what is Will essence and what is the guilt and darkness this will essence is holding.

Spirit has rage at the Will for holding on to these things because the lack of movement involved is taking everything down. This is part of why Spirit has been exhorting the Will to let go of these things. The more the Spirit has exhorted the Will to let go, the more the Will has seemed to become frightened of any movement at all here. The Will feels It has never been given the acceptance and encouragement needed from Spirit to go into the movement It needs to let go of guilt and darkness. So far, the Will has been given more guilt whenever It has tried to allow this movement.

The Will has a rage at Spirit here that wants to scream, "I am trying to let go, and these emotions You hate so much are what I have to express to let go. If you don't like it, then come to the Hell I'm in and see what it is really like here!"

The Will has not screamed this way until now because the Will was not sure if It was really right about this. Meanwhile, whenever Spirit has pretended to descend into the places where lost Will dwells, Spirit has been smug and has not really allowed Itself to feel these places. Spirit people have gone there wrapped in their Light, which cannot be penetrated by this pain. Spirit people have then acted like they have gone into the places where lost Will is suffering and have not had the same problem, so it must be the Will's fault if It is living in Hell.

For example, many spirits who are not Ronalokas have incarnated into Black bodies on Earth and have had experiences that resulted more from the way they were already vibrating than from the form they had taken on. These spirits have no real bodies anyway and have taken on many forms. These spirits have often made the Ronalokas feel even more ashamed of the problems they have been having by seeming to say, "See, you can rise above everything that is seeming to hold you down if you just try harder." These spirits have been more of a guilt reflection for the Ronalokas than anything else because even when they have inspired the Ronalokas to try harder, their success has been only temporary. Sooner or later, the reversals of lost Will have set in and the gap has gotten the Ronalokas again.

Just as much as Spirit has been right that something has to be let go of here, the Will has also been right not to let go on the terms Spirit has been presenting. The Will has not wanted to move here because of the pain and uncertainty, but the Will has also felt a distrust for Spirit's approach here, whether the Will could explain this feeling or not. As it turns out, the resistance in the Will to letting go the way Spirit has been pressuring the Will to let go has been the Will sensing the presence of this lost Will that does not want to be put out with the guilt and darkness.

If you haven't been listening to these stirrings in your Will, it is because you believe you should not give in to fear. Instead of giving in to your fear and allowing it to move, you have hated it for being there, mostly because you intuitively know that underneath these stirrings lies the terror of compression and suffocation you feel you can never move. You have been suppressing movement here in an effort to avoid ever having to feel this terror again.

As a result, you have been going past this fear and meeting it in your outer reality in the form of everything that would suffocate the life from your efforts to move toward making any real changes in your life. When you don't allow yourselves to feel this fear until you are faced with a major situation, it is too late to move all that needs to move, and so you have gone down in the reversals your moves toward changing your life patterns have brought you. This has then seemed to prove to you once more that emotional movement has no power to help you. This is a repeat of your Original Cause.

The terror you are holding here is the same terror the Will felt upon leaving Me originally. When the Will originally polarized from Me and fell in the darkness of space, the ability to vibrate was lost. The Will fell into unconsciousness and was not able to move until I found It and struck It violently with My Light. Many times, this has been repeated when people do not know what they feel until they experience something intense enough to move them past their frozen places.

This frozen hardness in the Will is what needs to move now. If you allow it to move, you will not need to meet the gap in any way that will harm or kill you like it has done in the past. What you will meet in your healing process is whatever amount of pressure of force it is going to take to gain movement in these frozen places.

Originally, I was magnetically drawn toward the Will without knowing it was happening. When I struck Her, I did not know it was going to happen. The resultant explosion brought the Mother back to the speed of Light almost immediately. The Will did not know it was going to happen either. She had no ability left with which to know or respond. She experienced My Light as something that happened to Her like a great force striking Her that made Her explode.

Although the Will did not have time to consciously think of this, the Will leaped at My Light with the desperation She had been feeling when She went unconscious. The Will leaped out of Her terror as fast as She could. There was no anticipation here. Emotional response in the Will came later.

Everyone, including the Will, holds this old image of how fast the Will came back up this first time, and everyone has held this expectation ever since. There is rage toward what is perceived as the Will's resistance to moving into the Light this fast anytime the Will has a problem. This expectation and accompanying held rage has been making the Will feel guilty and inadequate, while also moving in a gapped state and damaging the Will's ability to move at all.

But the Will did not like the sudden explosion She experienced, much more than She liked the feeling of suddenly falling into darkness and suffocation. The Mother did not know how to change Her levels of vibration this quickly and had no time to learn how She might do this. As a result, She suffered severe fragmentation, first falling and then leaping past many things She needs to understand now.

116

The Mother has a real problem with those who do not want to allow Her the time and acceptance She needs to be able to gain these understandings now, and Her problem is this: If you do not allow the Will to learn what the Will needs to learn from Its experience, the Will can never be free of the fear that any move make might recreate all over again the very pain the Will is trying to heal. In other words, this is a way of keeping the Will trapped. When the Will has moved faster than the Will can really move in order to please expectations, the Will has fragmented.

Initially, the Will had no previous experience to cause Her to anticipate what was going to happen, but since the Will's initial experiences were not ones that made the Will feel that She liked movement, and since the Will has never really understood what originally happened, there is anticipation deep inside the Will where these old memories lie buried. The Will is braced to resist anything that begins to feel like these old initial movements that were so traumatic that recovery has not been possible in all of this long time.

The Will has been ready to do almost anything to avoid having to go into this place and has developed all manner of tricks to keep movement away from this area of the Will. Guilt, which was initially taken in by the Will, did not allow the movement that would have been necessary to avoid these initial experiences of the Will, and since the Will has never been able to move this guilt out, the Will has come to feel that Its own survival requires using this guilt against others to make them feel they should not pressure the Will for movement here. When the pressure build-up from lack of movement becomes too great, the Will has been moving anyway and the gap has been smacking the Will with another enactment of all the denials being held here.

The truth of the matter is that without the love and trust necessary, the Will cannot be pressured to move here and find the healing result that must be found now. Not all of the Will moved in response to the strike I gave It in Original Cause. As much as possible of this part of the Will must move now also, but this part of the Will is the most lost of any Will there is. What the Will has to get in motion here is the clench It has used to surround and isolate the problem of holding this unmoving Will which is the part of the Will that is holding darkness. The Will is exhausted here and can't remain clenched much longer, but it has also become an involuntary clench. Literally, the muscles involved have gone numb and have become frozen in a hardness that is no longer able to respond along with the rest of the Body because these parts of the Body have been told they must surround and isolate what is being held there no matter what. It is as though these places have become involuntary muscles that do not respond to anything.

Although I suggest body work as a way to get in touch here, be careful who you do it with so that the emotions needing to move here receive acceptance. Massage will not bring this up, nor will any of the known body work techniques, unless you allow all of the emotion you can move to move all along the way so that each layer of what is being held here receives the message from the layer just above it that movement is alright now and that movement will bring in the Light that is necessary.

The Will has to let go of the darkness It has held for so long, just as the Spirit Polarity has been saying, but the Will must do this in such a way that the Will really understands what It is doing here. The Will must really gain understanding from regaining Its own vibration so that the Will no longer has to live with the fear of not knowing what might recreate this pain It has held for so long. The Will cannot be facilitated or directed by another person to do what the other person thinks is best, even though the Will has very little consciousness here. Whatever vibration It does manage to get must be respected and allowed to lead into the evolution these placed need. Almost anything that is said or done by anyone who has not already moved these places within the self really runs the risk of presenting just another belief system and more guilt that hits this barely conscious essence like another assault.

The best approach here is also potentially dangerous because of the risk of gapping. What the Will needs here is real response to what the Will has been holding for so long. Terror is the real response, but most people have been using gapped rage to avoid this terror for so long that it is believed on all sides that gapped rage is the real response to the Will here. If you feel like the response you want to give to the Will here is something to make it stop, no matter how sugar or guilt coated you make it, allow yourself to notice that you want to do this to avoid your own fears about what is happening here.

It is not enough for the Spirit side of this gap to speak spiritual understandings in the face of all the pain the Will has to go through here. The Will will not even know whether It is still in its original experience, or headed back up and out of it when It first begins to move in these places. It may be helpful for the Spirit to point out to the Will that It is moving Its pain so that It can be healed now, but the Will may not believe this if It senses Spirit is still holding the old gap that can, at any moment, revert into putting the Will right back down into another death again. The gap from feelings has been causing Will to want to say, "Sounds right, feels wrong."

This does not mean the Spirit is to hold back response It has about this process of the Will in favor of the Will. Exchange here is necessary, but without real response from Spirit, Will cannot heal, and Spirit cannot move out the resistance It has toward free expression of the Will. Spirit has no way to know how this place of lost Will feels to the Will unless It can open and receive the Will with the loving compassion necessary to understand feelings by osmosis. The best understandings Spirit can give to Will here are feelings moving in response to what the Will has to move here, but Spirit must also move the feelings It has in response to the Will all the way along in moving toward these deep and lost places in the Will, or Spirit will lack appropriateness here and the Will will not trust It.

The Will must be allowed to bring up and vibrate whatever charge It has been holding until It can let go of it without feeling pressured or judged in any way for how much processing of this charge the Will needs to do. There is not Light or balance when this place begins to move, and it is very important not to manipulate the Will in any way to make It come into alignment before It is ready. If you manipulate the Will here, you run the risk of having It gap on you, or of feeling guilty enough to give you the appearance of an alignment you do not really have. The Will must be given acceptance for as much process as It needs to have.

If you are going through this with your own Spirit and Will in your own Body, allow your mind to receive feelings while trying not to use your judgment patterns to rationalize them away. If you are experiencing this with another person, as though you are Will in one Body and Spirit in another, I do want to caution you again, that while you may have very effective healing this way, you may also feel hatred for one another that could seem so endless and unmoving as to make the love you thought you had seem to be only a memory. This is why most couples have tried to avoid these areas and have, thus entered into them most often when the stress of holding back has caused gapping.

When you are ready, it is going to be necessary to have another person involved in order to effectively heal your gap, but this is also the most potentially dangerous approach to take if you are not ready for it. If you have a feeling you cannot do this with another person, or feel like you cannot get triggered without another person to facilitate this, try to make sure you have as much as possible moving emotionally between you before you go into this space. The more you have already moved between you, the less possible it will be to greatly harm or even possibly kill one another by triggering one another's gaps.

I am giving these cautions because the gaps in the emotional body which are involved here are not part of the usual presentation of the people who have them and have formerly been viewed only as insanity or criminality, If the gap gets triggered, you may gap first, or it may be the other person, but whoever gaps first is likely to trigger the gap in the other. It can be very dangerous to have two people in a gapped state of consciousness fighting one another as though their lives depend on it, which they do in the presence of the gap, when healing is their conscious intent. If this happens, give in to your feelings of terror here and make an effort to call consciousness into the gap.

The gap must be healed, but it is not a matter of how fast you go so much as how thorough you are. Do not let yourselves get stuck in the idea that moving through the gap ahead of others means you have more power than they do or a higher place in the pecking order. All of these old feelings of competition and scrambling for position must move along with everything else. The lost Will that needs to recover here has already been put at the bottom, underneath everything else, had has been made last priority for as long as the gap has existed. Along the way to recovering this, you are going to find many feelings you did not even think you had.

Because you have been ignoring so much you don't even realize you have been ignoring, it can seem like the outer reflection you have to study all around you is the only remaining clue to the existence of this lost Will I am telling you lies deeply denied within you. Because of what has lain hidden here for so long, the Will Polarity has not known what other view to take, since it has been very convincingly real for all of the Will's existence that the Will is being victimized, and that the Will people on Earth are particularly victimized by the rest of the spirits.

The Will has more power than this, but the Will has never been able to find out what this power is because the Will has never been allowed to move enough to find out what Its real power is. This is because the power of the Will has been feared from the very beginning, and this fear has never been allowed to move so that it could be understood either. Meanwhile, all of this Lost Will power has been playing a strong role in the creation of everyone's experience, but It has been doing this in a state of denial. Thus, the power position on Earth has been one of denying the Will rather than encouraging it.

Lack of receptivity to this lost Will has made so many places impenetrable to My Light that you must get these places in yourselves vibrating again to heal the damages lack of vibration has caused you, and to increase the flow of Light into and through you.

This increase in vibration is necessary to enable you to increase your consciousness so that you can understand and use your power without leaving it in a state of denial anymore.

This power is not something that can be restored to you by the gift of a magic wand, or by having My Light suddenly descend and give you your rightful places on Earth, or by striking you as in Original Cause. You are in your right places in that they correspond to the ways in which you are vibrating, and any other places I might put you would soon be lost again if you do not understand that the changes must come from changing the ways you are vibrating and not vibrating within yourselves.

When the Ronalokas have felt that they cannot go forward the way they have wanted to on Earth, they have many times fantasized returning to their beloved continent of Africa, or at least of trying to set up a nation apart someplace on Earth. The Will people have always wanted to believe that they could live better apart from the other spirits who have so cruelly rejected and oppressed them. What I would really like for you to receive from Me here is that this is a way of avoiding many feelings. The movement you need first and foremost is inner movement; otherwise, you will find that you have the same problems wherever you go.

Even when you have fled to Africa, which has been the most impenetrable continent on Earth, your inner compression in the form of outer oppression has soon reappeared in your lives. Every time you have thought you have overcome or escaped oppression; you have looked around to see that you have not.

Allow yourselves to notice how much trouble Africa is having right now, and how many governments made up of Blacks end up being just as oppressive toward their people as any other governments have been. The Reflection Lost Will Has to Give is going to be there, no matter what from you try to give to your outer reality until you are able to move all you need to move within you.

The complexity of this reflection will unfold as you allow the movement necessary. It is almost impossible to delineate this in a book, but I can give you enough to get you started so that your own movement will be able to open you to the rest. One thing you need to know is that this lost Will is not going to move in response to you as quickly as you might like because the layers that gain movement are so intertwined with the layers that will need to gain movement as your next step that the lost Will you are taking in is still going to have strings attached to the lost Will which is still in a state of denial. When you have moved all that can move now, the rest will have to move back all at once.

My intent in helping you to get in touch with what needs to move here is not only to help you realize what has been held back for so long, but also to help you realize why you have held it back for so long. You have avoided these feelings because you have such a deep and terrible dread of the possible realities these feelings suggest.

What kind of God has a Creation that always sorts out certain people for persecution, stands by and allows it, and even seems to empower the ones doing it? Why does it always seem to be the ones who are so loving and giving who go down, while the cruel and wicked ones seem to live on and on, as though nothing can take them down? Why do the ones who feel it the most seem to suffer and suffer while those who are cold and feel nothing seem not to suffer at all and even seem to enjoy inflicting pain and suffering on others, as though it is their source of feeling powerful? Why is a deaf ear always being turned on those who cry for peace, freedom, justice, truth, and love, as though this deafness is a sign of hatred even for the words? If God exists and has power, is He loving or not?

Many Ronalokas have buried these issues in a lot of religious fervor that has more to do with a fear that tells them they must beg forgiveness and gain favor with My Light or suffer the consequences, than that they necessarily believe so fervently in whatever religion they have seemed to embrace. Other Ronalokas who have buried their fear more deeply under their rage look down on these Ronalokas while professing not to fear Me at all, or to even believe in Me. Some hate Me enough that they have gone to devil worship and the black magic side of things, claiming there is no difference really because the God they see makes no distinction here.

Underneath all this, the Ronalokas have their own beliefs, and movement in the emotional charge surrounding all of these other beliefs is going to reveal them more fully than they have, as yet, been realized. Meanwhile, there is a kind of self-hatred here that needs to be understood so that it can be moved into love. The outer reflection you have here is that people who have seemed to be the same as you have turned around and opposed you whenever you have wanted to make moves they have not liked.

While some Ronalokas can connect to what I am saying here, others appear not to have these problems at all. The denial and fragmentation involved here is such that these problems may only manifest in the lives of fragments you view as separate people from you. Very often, the ones who need to move this lost Will are not the ones who are manifesting the problems. Whether or not, for example, you have sympathy for all of the death happening in Africa right now, know you have lost Will dying there, no matter what order of spirit you think you are. In terms of healing this, it is those who have eyes to see and ears to hear that must move with what I am saying here.

You have almost complete denial here, which means it is going to be very dark when you first go into these feelings. The more you want to say this story is not right, or that you do not have these feelings, the more likely it is that you do have these feelings and need to move them. The more vehement your denial is, the more likely it is that you have these feelings and need to move them. Denial indicates that this is not the first time you have denied these emotions. Lack of any response to this material is more indicative of the willessness that cannot heal than anything else. Meanwhile, if you are not already vibrating entirely at the speed of light, you have involvement here that needs to move. Many of you have even denied you have had experiences you have actually had in order to avoid the feelings involved.

Going into the emotions you routinely ignore is one way into this lost Will, and another way is to go into the feelings of distrust you have. Every time you feel distrust, you need to move into the feelings of fear and anger that lie beneath it. You must also open to the possibility of these feelings coming up in the middle of the night and awakening you in order to do it. You may want to say that it is only the power of suggestion making you think you have these feelings and that you don't really have them. Don't judge here: just allow whatever movement needs to take place and see how you feel afterwards.

As Will, you particularly need the Light of My understandings as you go into this lost Will because you never had a chance to know from the experience of manifested existence what the presence of a full measure of My Light could mean. You have always had the experience of feeling I was not there for you in the ways I was there for others. You have never felt the acceptance you have wanted to have for yourselves in Creation. you have always felt pushed, pulled, pressured, and compressed, overridden and under-appreciated, used and abused, cheated, and robbed rather than really free for as long as you can remember and even in the past you have forgotten.

You have hatred and blame for Me for having forced you into this by denying the Will in the ways that I did, and you also blame your own Spirits for making it impossible for you to remain with them. You have a lot of guilt piled on top of these emotions in the form of the many excuses you have made that all try to say it is alright as it is and is all happening for a reason and that someday, everything will be alright. The day when everything is going to be alright is always going to remain in the future if you do not move what needs to move here, because My Light is not able to penetrate you until you are vibrating enough to receive it.

No matter how many excuses you have wanted to make for what has happened to you, or how many ways you have found to say it is alright, these are not reasons to deny all of the other feelings you have about being Will in a Creation that became so insensitive to the subjective experience that it became like a crime of weakness or of lack of faith in God even to have feelings, let alone to be as extremely sensitive as the Will. The Will is subjectivity and without acceptance for this, the Will cannot live.

You have many bitter feelings to move here which you have tried to hide, even from yourselves, because you have not believed it has been loving to have such feelings. Let go of this belief; it is guilt. Go underneath this belief and allow yourselves to feel what you really feel here.

The hardness you are going to find in yourselves where this lost Will is held is what guilt has stopped from vibrating. Let yourselves feel the anger and resentment that is there for not ever being able to live the way you have always wanted to live. Let yourselves cry the hot, bitter tears underneath this hardness and rage at the helplessness you feel to change your situation. Feel the anger in your hardness that has tried to avoid facing your feelings of powerlessness, defeat, and hopelessness by saying it doesn't care what happens because you are just fine as you are and can manage no matter what. Give in to more grief than you have ever wanted to know.

Finally, your deep fear is going to show up after all of this and you will still hate it when does. You must allow yourselves to move this hatred of your fear while also letting your fear know somehow that movement in this hatred is necessary so that you can heal the fear.

When you feel you are like a "soap opera" that disgusts you, feel the self-hatred you have for your emotional turmoil. It is the self-hatred that has not wanted to extend compassion and love to your own predicament.

You do not need to judge yourselves fear-ridden and try to go past your fears anymore. You may become very fear-ridden for a while. You may have times when you feel you cannot even get out of bed. Make space for these feelings as best you can. Episodes of paralyzing fear will not last as long as you fear they will if you get your fear moving by starting with any expression you can give it. This will allow it to move through you much faster than if you remain paralyzed or frozen in silence.

You are going to have to give in to more of everything than you have ever wanted to accept in yourselves and feel the hatred you have for your emotions because they have always been seen as the problem of Creation instead of as the savior they are going to turn out to be. Without emotional depth, people are nothing but well-made robots, going through the motions of being alive without human response to what happens to them. Life is impossible this way as you are soon going to find out.

Now I say to the Will Polarity, move your emotions and recover your lost Will, but heed My cautions and do not go past them. Start by moving your feelings in a place that feels sage to you and this may very well mean by yourself. If you have any feelings that it is not safe to move an emotion in the time or place where you are, heed whatever warning voices you have, be they ever so small, and allow them to come forward and teach you. Learn to pay attention to the little murmuring voices within you that normally will not speak because they have been judged to be wrong for having the feelings they have.

Treat your emotional release as a cry for freedom in the midst of an enemy camp that does not want you to be successful here and protect yourselves accordingly. Do not trust anyone here, even if they say they can be trusted, unless you feel, even in the little whispering voices within that try to warn you, that you can trust them. Even then, you might not trust them once you get into the release. You will have feelings of not even being able to trust yourself or your own perceptions when you really get into the feelings that need to move here. Take your distrust seriously and do not try to move past it. Distrust is a form of fear and this fear must also be allowed to express.

You must allow yourselves to feel what you need to feel and express it in private and move outwardly in the world later, when you are more ready. Let your fear move around the issue of whether or not what you have viewed as Spirit is going to move in response to you or not. Moving the fear you have around the feeling of rejection if you dare to bring certain things forward to Spirit is going to allow the guilt that has controlled you for so long to move out so that My Light can finally come in. If you fear your own Spirit is not going to respond to you, allow My Light to fill in instead.

Do not move these lost Will feelings in the presence of anyone unresponsive you have seen as having the positions of Spirit or of power on Earth, because they have controlled you for so long, they are not going to like it if you make any real moves toward freedom. They will resist you because they are not going to have it the way they have had it for so long if you are successful here, and they have no positive pictures of what this might mean for them. There is terror for your own survival here and in this, you are not wrong. Do not even promote these books with people you think need to move: Tell only the people who are ready to move and feel they must allow themselves to do it.

While the Rainbow Spirits are gapped from their Wills and have a lack of Light in there, the rejection of Will by the Angels left the Ronalokas prey to be taken over by the Father Warriors, and this has been a deeply scarring experience that needs to be healed now. The Father Warriors have oppressed the Ronalokas according to the gap's hatred for the Will and have used the Ronalokas as surrogate Wills, trying to enslave them and give them as little in return for this as possible. The Ronalokas want to throw the Father Warriors off and are ready to do this, but in order to be successful here, they must really understand what is involved in these old, old patterns of guilt and servitude, slavery and denial that the Father Warriors have used against them for so long. Self-hatred is the bottom line, but there is a long list of emotions that must be gone through to bring the healing needed here.

If, in going into these emotions, you feel you cannot move anything at all, move the littlest bit that you can and open to more as you can. You may already be moving easily with the rest of your emotional body and still, when you get here, you may find yourself unable to move, as though nothing you have done so far has made any difference at all.

If you have a feeling you cannot breathe, don't dip under it to find your breath. Get your movement and sounds from the place where you feel you cannot breathe. It is impossible to move a lot of this at once, so don't even try to get through this in a few sessions. Just as impossible as it has seemed to move oppression off Earth, so impossible is it going to seem to move these emotions.

If you allow yourself to feel everything you feel while moving any particular emotion which has been denied, you will see how guilt tortures you anytime you try to give acceptance to the way you really feel. Do your best to move without interference from other people who do not understand what you must move here or how you need to do it, because such people will reflect the guilt and judgments you hold against the expression of these emotions and might even have the power to deny you the opportunity to move here by removing you to a place of imprisonment or restraint.

As much as it is believed that expression of the depth of these emotions is unacceptable, guilt is participating in the creation of situations that make this belief seem to be true. You can regard your healing intent as the mast of a ship to which you are tied in the midst of the storm of your own emotional turmoil. It is what you have held back for so long that is not allowing your outer reality to open to you in the ways you want it to. As much terror as you allow to move will be directly reflected to you in your chances to come through the storm alive. If you make this another exercise in denial by trying to keep this information at a mental level, you will participate in the mass suffocation that is now being created on Earth, and I will not have the power to save you.

I am advising you to move these emotions as they can move, allowing yourself plenty of rest and the cultivation of the love that has been missing in these denials. Urgency may be alleviated by movement in your fear, but if not, your urgency must be allowed to pressure for faster movement. If you are giving your urgency expression by nagging others around you, and they are snapping at you, allow yourself to move your fear of losing their love if you allow these feelings to begin expressing in these ways.

These siphoning-off-the-pressure ways of expressing are the only ways of expressing these emotions have previously been allowed to have, and if they go on long enough, can trigger the gap. The guilt involved is going to surface no matter what you do, but understand that the ones you are nagging are often the very ones who have been insisting that you must hold these emotions. These pressure release methods of expression, however, do not allow the real depth of the emotion that needs to move.

If you feel you need to move back from the ones you want to nag in order to move into the rage and terror you really feel underneath this, allow yourself to do it, because you need to realize you are very near the gap, and your fear of allowing the real emotional expression you need here is your fear of triggering the gap.

Allowing movement in your Will the way I am prescribing here is the most loving way I know to move these long-denied emotions; much more loving than having to get them triggered in a state of denial by the reality about to descend onto Earth.

Those who are not allowing the Will to move are causing the dismal reality they claim their control of the Will is averting. Yet, they say the Will's attempts to move are causing the problems on Earth. These people all believe "negative emotions," such as fear, are Original Cause.

Fear, and anger here is seen as a form of fear, has been labeled Original Cause as though fear is something outside of love. Viewing fear as something outside of love made it appear that banishing fear would solve the problems. This put the blame on the Will, and any Will essence having fear was then labelled the cause of the problems in Creation.

This is not right understanding. Original Cause is that when the Will originally began to vibrate, the Will took in guilt and darkness along with My Light because it was there, because it was not yet understood what anything was, and because movement was not understood. Fear, or more accurately, terror, was the Will's response to the pain It felt when It opened and embraced guilt and darkness instead of My Light. The Will did not know what It was experiencing here any more than I did. When the Will thought this was Me or that I required the Will to make a place for these things, the Will feared Me.

The Will did not know Me any better than I knew the Will. I did not know what the Will was responding to here. When I looked at the Will, I saw the guilt and darkness the Will was holding. I thought it was the Will, and the Will thought It had embraced some terrible aspect of Me. This made the Will all the more afraid. Because I did not like the feelings I was receiving from the Will and did not understand that movement in the Will was necessary here, I did not allow the Will to move. I pushed the Will away here, and I admit that I was so interested in saving Myself from the pain here, I did not allow Myself to see what this did to the Will.

From time before time, the Will has not been allowed to move here, and so this part of the Will has had no experience other than a reality of guilt and death. This is the only reality this part of the Will has ever known, and so, it is not going to be easy to move this part of the Will to a place of really knowing another reality is possible for it. This part of the Will does not think God is there for it. This part of the Will believes either God does not exist or God requires sacrificing the self to guilt and death.

The Ronalokas' Journey to Earth

The Ronalokas were moving away from Me. Although they felt uncomfortable with My Light watching them, most of them soon wished they had not left the only home they had known in their manifested existence. The life that had seemed so unpleasant because of the rejection they had been receiving began to look Heavenly compared to what they were going into.

The Ronalokas already felt torn, as though everything they decided to do had another side to it that made them feel like opposing their own decision. They had a desire to look back at the Heavens, which now appeared to them like a beacon in the sky, but at the same time, they did not want to look back for fear of what they might see and feel. Some even felt like they could hear the other spirits celebrating their departure.

Although it was easier for the Ronalokas to insist they had wanted to go rather than to face the other feelings they had here, none of the Ronalokas really liked it that I was allowing them to go. They really wanted Me to see through their bravado, grab hold of them, no matter how much they fought Me, insist they had to stay with Me, and make them feel like they really belonged in Creation. They had a feeling I was not going to do this, but they hoped that I would.

The farther they floated away from Me, the more they began to feel like they were being swept away. The ethers began to be stirred into a great wind, as though the Ronalokas were caught in a current during a storm at sea. The ethers around them were so charged with held emotion, they were making sounds the Ronalokas did not like to notice. Many of them did not want to look back for fear they would see that My Light was sweeping them from the Heavens and out into the darkness of space.

Already, the Ronalokas feared that giving in to how they felt would cause them to collapse in on themselves. They struggled to resist this feeling because its meaning for them was that there was no life ahead of them that was going to feel good. Despite their resistance, the Ronalokas could feel themselves being compressed anyway, not only against each other, but within themselves also.

From My point of view, the Ronalokas were shrinking together and down into themselves, as though they were afraid a great hand was about to strike them. At the time, I did not know why I received the impression, but I felt something akin to what a parent feels when he sees a small child shrinking in fear of his punishment. I did not feel like I was punishing the Ronalokas, but I felt I could not align with them enough to get a hold of them. I could not understand how it was possible for them to move back every time My Light reached for them and not appear to notice. I hesitated to try to reach for them anymore because every attempt had moved them farther from Me. I did not know I had a gap they feared, but I could see they were making one for themselves by backing up. I felt there was danger on both sides here because space was being opened which My Light was not able to fill, and this gap was being filled with a terrible wind.

I was holding back many feelings then, which I have since been moving, and in the moving of them, I have found out how much reflection the Ronalokas had to give Me. I have come to love these places in Myself which I did not love then. Then, I was not allowing My fear to move enough to know what it held, or that the Ronalokas were reflecting My own fear of moving out into Creation. Then, I was almost cold about it and gave the Ronalokas the same send-off My own fear was getting, denial of feeling it.

The farther the Ronalokas moved from Me, the more it looked like they were polarizing toward the Mother. The Mother had already opposed Me on so many issues, I did not think I could expect spirits so like Her to align with Me, but I did not like seeing them move into Her camp before they even knew what making such a move was going to mean. I knew that once they crossed the Warriors' line, they were moving out into a wasteland that did not have much light. I wondered what sort of a Mother would beckon Her children out into such a place.

Earth was a lost planet as far as I was concerned because the Mother was gone, and I did not think the Ronalokas were going to find Her on Earth. I wasn't moving much Light in the direction of Earth, and I did not intend to. The Mother's opposition to Me had made Me feel that I could not look lovingly upon Her anymore, and I had decided, therefore, it was best not to look upon Her at all. I could not stand to see what had become of Her. They were perilously lacking in light already, and it did not seem to Me they could stand to lose much more and survive.

I hesitate to mention this now, but the light of the Ronalokas was so dim compared to the other spirits around them that I wasn't even sure they were spirits at all. It seemed impossible to Me that they should be able to move around in the ways that they could, since it seemed to Me that light was an essential ingredient in being able to navigate the ethers.

Without it, it seemed to Me, there was not an atmosphere to sustain them. Not only that, the Ronalokas did not move in the same ways the other spirits did. They had a lustiness and a body consciousness the other spirits did not have. Guilt already had enough of a presence to be telling them they should not move in the ways that they did, and this was reflected to them by the other spirits not really seeming to like them or their ways.

As the Ronalokas left Me, they were standing as tall as they could and showing only the feelings they thought were acceptable. They were hiding as much as they could of the feelings of having been rejected by the rest of Creation by acting like they didn't care, because they wanted to go away to the edge of space and have a party where they could really enjoy themselves without anyone to tell them they didn't like it, or that it was too loud, or going on for too long, or that there was something else they should be doing instead.

The Ronalokas wanted to have fun, and they didn't want anyone telling them that having fun the way they wanted to was wrong. Secretly, they had a desire to enjoy themselves sensually and sexually and make love the way the Mother and the Father of Manifestation had done. In this secret desire, I felt they had defiance toward My Light because I did not, at the time, see lovemaking as beneficial to the healing that We needed. I saw it only as increasing the darkness among the Manifested Spirits.

I had a long list of reasons the Ronalokas should not go to Earth, but I never mentioned My viewpoint toward their desire to fulfill themselves sexually in secret here. I had trouble mentioning the subject to them, because every way I pictured Myself addressing this looked to Me like it would be a way of saying the Mother had been wrong to manifest them by allowing Herself to have sex when I had told Her not to. I did not even want to discuss the issue of the Mother and the Father of Manifestation defying My Light and seeming to get away with it. I did not want to allow Myself to notice yet that I had smacked the Mother, so I did not mention that either.

It was much later when I caught up with how many feelings I was not moving there and how much the holding back of My feelings made everything look different to Me then than it looks now. Now, when I look at the Ronalokas' departure for Earth, I see a bunch of frightened, Will-polarized children of Mine being allowed to go off into the darkness of space with no real help from My Light, and I have great grief over this.

Then, I saw the Ronalokas as fragments of the Mother, pretending not to be the Mother in order to try to find out how I felt about Her. To Me, the Ronalokas were like so many spies in My camp. I was on the alert, although I did not know exactly what to prepare for from the Mother. I felt her Warriors had My destruction in mind, and that She might be looking for a way to help them succeed here. When I looked at the Ronalokas, I saw the Mother, angry with Me for not allowing Her to be Herself the way She wanted to be, refusing to communicate with Me, and refusing to allow Me to touch Her. Each time I extended My hand toward Her, and She backed away from Me, My anger toward Her grew. The feeling I had at the time was that if indeed these were spirits, they had come forth to manifest everything I had a lack of acceptance for in the Mother and Father of Manifestation, as though their parents had put them forward to throw these things in My face. If they were the Mother, then She had moved much more toward Body than toward My Light, in which case He could have Her, because My held anger was sure I didn't want Her anymore.

Even though I had all of these feelings, I was trying My best to extend love toward the Ronalokas, and it seemed to Me they were not accepting My Love or extending themselves toward Me. I allowed them to go because I could not do otherwise and because it seemed to Me it was not safe to keep extending Myself without being received.

My lack of emotional movement was stuck in the place of seeing the Ronalokas' manifestation as an act of defiance on the part of the Mother and the Father of Manifestation. Every time I looked at the Ronalokas, it seemed to Me they were looking back at Me with the same defiance. Even when they watched Me through half-closed eyelids, as though they weren't watching Me at all, I still felt this defiance in them.

With the Mother gone, it seemed there was no one to love the Ronalokas except for the Father of Manifestation. When the Ronalokas left Me, the Father of Manifestation was nowhere around, because My Light was not allowing Him to get very close to Me. He was afraid of what it meant that My Light was not accepting the Ronalokas, but He had no power to get through to Me here.

The Father of Manifestation felt ashamed then, as though He had manifested something that could not be loved by anyone but Him. He did not see how I could be an all-loving God and feel such a lack of love for these spirits. He viewed My efforts to reach for them as token. He could see from His vantage point that there was something in the way of My ability to grasp the Ronalokas, just as much as there was something in the way of the Ronalokas' ability to receive Me. He felt like the sins of the parents were being visited upon the children because

He thought that the troubles the Ronalokas were having with My Light were because of the troubles I was having with the Mother and with Him.

The Father of Manifestation held back many feelings He had here in a feeling of impotence at having no power to move toward My Light anymore with so many of the things that He felt. Every time He tried to reach Me with feelings like these, He was unable to, and He felt like a coward who could not stand up for His family or anything else He believed in. Only when He was feeling feelings for which He knew I had acceptance could He find it in Himself to come and communicate with Me. This gave Him a feeling of having the kind of dishonesty that does not approach a person with any of the feelings of negativity that are being felt but presents only the positive side of the picture.

The Father of Manifestation did not realize I was controlling this with My conditional acceptance for the Will. He thought it was a lack of character strength on His part. When He did allow Himself to notice something here, He thought My feelings about the Mother were causing the problems He and I were having, more than that I actually had problems with Him. This made Him wonder all the more why I did not seek to gain some resolution here by speaking frankly with Him about My feelings toward the Mother and His relationship with Her. He felt like I spoke to the Mother about Him but did not come directly to Him with how I felt; either that or the Mother had driven a wedge between Us by causing disquietude that was not really there. He longed to approach Me directly and felt like a miserable failure when He could not. I had a vested interest in keeping Him away from Me, but I did not find out what it was for a long time.

As He looked at the interaction I was having with the Ronalokas, the Father of Manifestation thought I was like a distant and rather uncaring God who was being militant and punitive toward the Ronalokas because I did not like the free-flowing form they had taken on. He felt that I did not want to allow the free flow of feelings to guide as much as I said I did because I was looking at the Ronalokas like there was something wrong with them and their ways. He felt like I did not want to let them have any dignity of their own.

The Father of Manifestation greatly feared what might happen to the Ronalokas out in the darkness of space. He had tried to solve the problem of having experiences He did not like out there by not going out into the darkness of space, and now He felt irresponsible for not having found out what was happening out there before any of the Manifested Spirits found themselves experiencing it.

He felt horrified to think that I had a dumping ground for anything I viewed as a miscreation or a miscreant, but it was appearing more and more to Him that I did, and that the Father Warriors were holding the line between everything I liked and everything I didn't like. The Ronalokas had already felt themselves pushed out to the edge of the Creation. The only spirits out past them were the Mother and Father Warriors. There was a great terror about going out past the Warriors. Even though the Warriors weren't very well liked, it looked like they drew the line between the light and the darkness.

As the Ronalokas were losing their ability to stay in the Heavens, fear was growing in them as to what it would mean if they crossed the Warriors' line. They did not like the looks of space out beyond the Warriors, and they knew the Mother had not been seen or heard from since She had gone out there. They had a feeling of something ominous out there. It gave them such an uneasy feeling, it was as though they were sick to their stomachs already, although they made no motion to express this feeling. They also already felt like they could not breathe, and they hadn't even left Me yet. What was going to happen to them if they went further from My Light?

As the Ronalokas felt themselves being swept away from Me, they had a feeling of moving faster and faster. They had motion sickness and a feeling of breathlessness that made them feel dizzy like they were about to go into a sickening swoon. There was a swirling that made them feel like they were losing track of themselves. They felt very much like children who parents did not love them enough to find a way to keep them with them. They felt abandoned, even by the Father of Manifestation, who stood by, unable to do anything. The Ronalokas were so swept away by their feelings of being swept away that they did not even want to look back to see if they could detect the truth in them. Those who did had the feeling that their fears were right.

The Ronalokas held most of these feelings back though, and stood as tall as they could, acting as much as they could like it was a brave adventure that had not been taken on by any of the other spirits. They claimed they could handle it because they had survival skills none of the other spirits had. They also secretly hoped that doing something the other spirits couldn't do might earn them "feathers in their cap" that would be rewarded with the recognition and acceptance of the other spirits. Many of the Ronalokas did not allow themselves to notice they had these feelings but, they had them, nonetheless, hidden underneath an expression of not caring what others thought of them.

The Ronalokas also had another hope, and that was that the Warriors would not actually allow them to cross their line, and that they would even use some kind of force, if necessary, to turn them back. They were very surprised when the Warriors, after some gruff talk and questioning of the Ronalokas allowed them to cross their line all too easily. It was then the Ronalokas felt their fear that the Mother and all like Her were being put outside of the inner circle of Light.

The Warriors said many things that reflected the Ronalokas' fears about themselves, and these things have rung in their ears ever since.

"They are so dark. This is not their right home. It's right for them to go because they need to find a place as dark as they are. They're just like the Mother so it's not wrong to let them go out where She is. They think they can go out on their own and make something they'll like, but they'll find out soon enough that they can't do anything on their own. They'll realize what a mistake they've made. They'll realize the best place they can have is whatever place we let them have with us. They have to go because they are not pleasing God by doing what He wants them to do. Why should We hold them back? They don't appreciate our efforts on their behalf anyhow."

There were many things said here, and they were all judgments the Ronalokas were holding against themselves in their unmoving fear and rage, but at the time, they all struck like insults hurled with a cruel sting that added even more to the burden of what the Ronalokas were holding already.

There were also Warriors escorting the Ronalokas out into space. The Ronalokas were looking to these Warriors for the help they needed because the Warriors had told the Ronalokas many stories of their powerful emergence in outer space. They had claimed their emergence was much earlier than it really was because they did not want the Ronalokas to realize they might be older than the Warriors. The Warriors had not wanted to look like the youngest spirits around; so much so that they had preferred allowing themselves to grow old looking inside of Me before they would even consider emerging.

The Warriors had led the Ronalokas to believe that they had more prowess in outer space than they really had by telling the Ronalokas stories about their imagined lives out in space where they had all lived as God in their own right until My Light had called them in by indicating that I needed their help. They had bragged about their desire to return to outer space without realizing it was about to happen. They told these stories so many times that the power of their repetition had the Warriors believing them as much as the Ronalokas did.

Meanwhile, I had the distinct impression that the Warriors did not like outer space, and that that was why they had rushed in upon Us, and also why they were so determined to hold the line against it. I didn't see much out there that I liked, and so I was aligned with the first impression I received from the Warriors much more than with any stories they had told since then.

Now, as the Ronalokas felt themselves crossing the Warriors' line, they looked to their Warrior escorts to provide them with the navigational know how, prowess and savvy the Ronalokas had come to believe that they had. The Warriors gave no response to the needs and fears of the Ronalokas, other than to tell them to steel themselves for the journey and to not flinch no matter what happened.

"You have to go on no matter what," the Warriors told them, "or you will not make it."

The Warriors then made themselves as staunch and hard as stone and stood as stiff as statues. The Ronalokas were stunned to see them do this and felt quite unable to do it themselves. In that moment, another hope of theirs disintegrated into the feeling that they had only themselves to depend on. The Ronalokas did not see how the Father Warriors could be so unresponsive to what was happening. They did not realize that the Father Warriors were nearly Willess and had actually suppressed so much of their vibration that they were already quite stiff and really did not feel anything. Many of the Ronalokas felt their own response to what was happening was a loss of control, and they felt ashamed.

The Warriors seemed to like the compression and restriction of vibration they were encountering, as though being forced in on themselves felt good to them while the expansion of being near My Light made them so uncomfortable, that they were always trying to put restrictions on it. The question left unresolved in My mind was: If this were true, why hadn't they just stayed out in space where they emerged instead of rushing in upon us? It was a long time before I realized that these big, bony, scaly, hard creatures had rushed in upon Us because they were running in terror of the Mother. They had never admitted it, and My Light has seen it only because My own gapped rage is healing now.

Lost Will, especially, needs to move in those Ronalokas who thought the way to survive was to emulate this stiffness and hardness of the Warriors within themselves. All of the Will that has journeyed to Earth has stiffness and hardness within it that is not going to move easily, but must be moved, nonetheless, because this is a cessation of vibration in order not to feel the experience being had.

The Warriors have a pounding anger within them that seems to like compression and restriction of movement and views it as the control necessary to be able to find any peace, but this is not a natural position for the Ronalokas or for the rest of the Will. The Spirit Polarity cannot really stand this compression either, and this lack of vibration in order to avoid certain feelings is what has been perpetuating the gapping that takes place whenever this compression becomes too much and overthrows the control against it.

When the Ronalokas saw the Warriors, who had claimed they were going to help them get to Earth, turning to stone statues posted like sentinels, what the Ronalokas had hoped was going to be a great adventure or perhaps a cruise to a destination of pleasure, turned into feeling like a prison ship. The Warriors, who had seemed to be offering guidance and protection, now felt like guards escorting the Ronalokas into exile or annihilation.

The Ronalokas shivered and shook, but controlled it as much as possible. As they moved out into space, it grew more and more dark around them, and they saw less and less of anything that looked like signs of life. It appeared that nothing lived out there, and the Ronalokas were not sure if they were relieved or horrified by this. The empty stillness and the utter darkness around them was at once terrifying and suffocating in its emptiness and lack of movement. It had an oppressiveness that felt like it was closing in on all of the Ronalokas with just as much realism as if they were victims locked within walls that were closing in on them. The darkness was so impenetrable, that the Ronalokas were not even sure if they had their eyes open or not.

Their petal-like bodies, delicate and filmy raiments of light, not unlike delicate gills from head to toe, were no longer rippling and undulating. They were moving very little, hardly opening at all. In outward appearance, it seemed that very little was happening. It appeared that the Ronalokas were standing very still, intensely concentrating, their shivers appearing as remnants of their rippling movements, but the inner feeling was one of already being engaged in a desperate search for something to sustain them.

Their petal-like bodies were used to vibrating in much more openness, sustained by the ethers around them. Now the feeling was that the slightest opening took in only a choking feeling of oppressive suffocation that was hot and searing at the same time that it was cold and stabbing. Their bodies were pressuring them to open and take in something to nourish them, while the sensation of doing so made them feel that they could not stand to. It was as though they now had only noxious water or toxic fumes to breathe the sweet air of morning.

There was great fear amounting to panic in the Ronalokas, and yet, they were still trying to control as much of their emotional expression as they could. They looked at the Warriors and saw that they were still standing like stone, as though they were not having the same experience the Ronalokas were having. The Ronalokas tried to continue standing tall as a group, but they could not. They huddled together as closely as they could, trying to find some sort of protection and comfort in one another. They were hardly breathing, concentrating on not giving in to the feeling of wanting to break and fly toward anything familiar they could find, anything that had light and warmth, anything that might sustain them.

The stillness around them grew deeper, and the darkness even more impenetrable, while the light the Ronalokas did have around them was becoming so compressed and so charged with held emotion, that it began to rumble and crackle like thunder and lightning that had no place to dissipate its charge. They felt a terror so great that even with the most control they exerted, the Ronalokas were trembling uncontrollably. Many of them lost control of their emotions and began weeping, moaning, and wailing, but not without great shame that was reflected to them this way:

What was coming in was too heavy for them, and what was moving out of them was too heavy for them also. The Ronalokas felt saturated with a slimy substance they had never experience before, and it made their outer layers feel all the more like they could no longer breathe through them.

The heaviness was overwhelming to them, and their feelings of terror were like being trapped in a place from which there was no escape. Their sensations were like those of being locked in a dark prison or the dark hold of a ship and experiencing water rising to overtake and drown them. The Ronalokas felt the terrible burning, stinging sensation of drowning whenever they tried to open and breathe at all. They shivered and shook, rolled and puked, gagged, and choked, not only because of what was pouring in on them, but because of what was pouring out of them as well.

Many feared this was punishment from Me for being Will, especially Will that had not aligned with My Light any more than they had. Many of them wondered how long I would take to get rid of them, since they had not been allowed to know whether the Mother had actually been eliminated or whether She had been sent into eternal suffering of this same sort. Some thought I might be doing this to them because I thought they were the Mother, and while they hated Me for this, many of them also wanted to find a way to abandon their likeness to the

Mother in the hope it would bring release from their suffering.

The Ronalokas who most hated these feelings did their best to turn themselves to stone like the Warriors, and ever since this time, have moved against the other Ronalokas with a hatred toward their fear as though are Warriors, yet they have been even more cruel toward the Ronalokas than the Warriors have been. Turncoats you might call them, but it is almost impossible to recognize them now as the Ronalokas they were then.

The Ronalokas didn't know what to do. Nothing they tried gave them any relief. They tried to turn away from the outer terribleness and find any place of escape within their own consciousness that they could. They clutched at the faint hope that somehow, this had all been a terrible mistake, and that I would suddenly take pity on My poor children. They hoped I would see through the facade of all they had given Me, reach after them and lift them up after all. They hoped and prayed so fervently for Me to rescue them that something did lift out of them that has never yet been born on Earth, and when it did, Ronalokas were left with even less light than they had.

The Ronalokas, themselves, were not helped by these most fervent of hopes and prayers. They felt the pain of abandonment, hopelessness and loss of faith that I would help them all over again. With no place else to turn in their hopeless despair, many of them wished for the Mother's loving arms to find them, lift them to Her and, somehow, make everything alright. They wanted Her, most of all, to help them breathe, to clear the slimy, stringy, sticky mess off of their bodies so they could feel open and able to breathe and expand again, to release them from this terrible compression, and then to cradle them in Her familiar warmth and dry their tears.

Nothing happened, except that their terror and their feelings of suffocation deepened. They feared they had no Mother or Father who cared anything about them or about the terrible experience they were having. The darkness was pressing in upon them so heavily that their bodies began pounding against the overwhelming compression, but the Ronalokas did not know it. The Ronalokas were losing track of reality as they had formerly known it. They were hallucinating, dreaming, and experiencing all at once.

In the throes of their asphyxiation, they hallucinated that the pounding was drumming and that the Father of Manifestation was coming to rescue them, perhaps even calling them to a party.

The Father of Manifestation did not come and the Ronalokas did not find Him or any party. Instead, the Ronalokas had a growing feeling of presence in the darkness around them that could not be seen. The Mother's stories of things ripping, tearing, and clawing at Her in the darkness of space came alive in them.

The Ronalokas could no longer stand, or even crouch. They were twisting and contorting in response to what was happening to them, while still trying to clutch at one another for protection. There were screams now that sounded like they were falling away, and the distinct feeling of being ripped apart from the edges. The Ronalokas thought some of them were being torn from the group to fall lost in space by themselves. They feared they could not hold themselves together.

Their terror and their desperation for air became so great, the holds on one another that had seemed like they were for mutual protection, now felt like grips of restraint, stopping them from making the moves they needed to make to save themselves.

The Ronalokas collapsed into a flailing, writhing mass, struggling in terror of the extreme compression and suffocation they felt. They felt like they were being engulfed by an enemy so massive and crushing that it could not be thrown off by any means they knew. Their terror was desperately seeking the breath of life it needed, while their rage against this terror was trying to fight it down, seeing it as a hopeless expression that would only worsen their situation and deepen their terror. The Ronalokas were fighting themselves, one another, things in the darkness and even the darkness where nothing was, without being able to see or to know what anything was. Everything felt like a threat to their lives, as though there was nothing they could trust anymore, not even their own perceptions.

They looked to the Warriors for help once more. There was a strange light reflecting off of them from time to time now, as though there was a searchlight of some kind moving in the darkness of outer space. They hoped again that, somehow, this was My Light searching for them, but when it never came to rest on them, the Ronalokas felt there was no reason to hope in it. This eerie light reflecting off the Warriors allowed the Ronalokas to see there was no hope there either.

The Warriors were standing as stoic, as staunch and as bastion as they had been at their departure. The Ronalokas felt the fear of the Mother rising in them again that no one else was experiencing reality the way they were and that they were all insane, or only experiencing their own fears, or at the very least, unable to trust their own perceptions to tell them what was really happening. They tried to deny the reality of their own experience within themselves in order not to feel they were going to "lose it" altogether.

The Ronalokas were grabbing wildly in desperate search of something to hold onto, while at the same time, biting, scratching and fighting anything that grabbed at them. They felt like wild animals, caught in a cage or a trap by a hunter who did not care how long they had to suffer or how horrible their suffering might be. He was just waiting for the trap to do its work, and then he'd come around, or worse yet, he might be watching and enjoying what his prey was going through.

There were bloodcurdling screams, and the Ronalokas were not sure if these screams were coming from them or from the darkness around them. Their own attempts to scream seemed to them more like gurgles of desperation from under water that had no power to be heard. There were sounds of choking, strangulation, and vomiting all around them, and they were now even more covered with a sticky mess. They felt a penetrating, teeth chattering cold and, at the same time, an unbearable feeling of the heat of suffocating compression. They felt themselves writhing, twisting, and contorting uncontrollably as this great and unseen force pressed in unbearably upon them.

The Ronalokas heard the sounds of dry, scaly flesh grinding together and the sounds of dry wing-like things beating near them. They heard cracking and creaking sounds like bones breaking, metal moving and all manner of horrors. They heard screeches and howls, hisses and snarls, snorts and growls. There were grunts and wails, rushing sounds and terrible cracking. They felt themselves being pelted by hard things and drenched as though something was being poured on them.

They had lost control of themselves entirely now and felt they could not move in response to what was happening around them. They had desperate feelings of wanting to have help of any kind. There was piteous, and what was later thought to be shameful, begging for relief or rescue of any kind and on any terms. There were confessions of all kinds going on, as though the Ronalokas felt anything they had ever done might be reason for what they were going through now.

And in response, there was nothing but laughter; a cold, cruel, pitiless laughter as though some large and unseen, terrible presence was enjoying seeing them grovel in their terror like this. The Ronalokas felt drool and slobber all over themselves, and they heard panting as though this unseen monster was able to breathe in this terrible, compressing darkness with an excitement that sounded like it was about to devour them. When this presence left them undelivered from their terror, the Ronalokas were left with a brokenness that has not yet been healed. How could God be loving and allow this to happen to His spirits? What kind of God could He be? Hatred grew toward Me in the Will and also terror that I was a God who had to be appeased.

Just when everything seemed so out of control that the Ronalokas had to be helped from someplace else because they had lost the ability to respond to what was happening around them, just when their senses had seemed so dulled and confused, they were surely going unconscious, suddenly now. Everything seemed to be going in some kind of terrible slow motion of heightened perceptions and elongated periods of time in which to respond. Just when the Ronalokas were hoping to go unconscious and escape their terror, they experienced instead something like an adrenaline rush that made them feel like they must fight to live. Everything had become horrifyingly vivid, and they were acutely aware. The Ronalokas had passed through the portals of terror and had entered the realms of terror where reality intensifies, and time warps every moment into what feels like an eternity to experience it. It was as though they had become superconscious and were able to notice everything in minute detail.

Their reality had a starkness to it that could be likened to the moment before a tornado strikes. The feeling is not unknown to people about to have a massive heart attack or some other life-threatening assault. There was an urgent rush of feelings to do anything they could to save themselves, but the terror was that of realizing they were locked in time and space with something that was not just fighting them, but something that had cold and calculated intent to murder them while having them fight a fight they could not win. At first, they felt themselves fighting with a strength they had not known in themselves before, but it did not last long. The more they struggled, the more they felt their life and the ability to struggle going out of them. It was not long before they had sensations of trying to fight with arms that were shrinking in strength and of trying to kick with feet that had no power left in them. They were lapsing into semi-consciousness now and experiencing themselves as though they had escaped. They were running away, but they ran and ran and got no place. Their legs felt like they either could not hold them or kept going out from under them. There was a feeling of utter helplessness to save themselves.

And still the drumming heartbeat of terror was pounding and pounding within them with such intensity that the Ronalokas had the feeling that it was also pounding and pounding without and all around them, filling the darkness with such a thunder that the Ronalokas almost wished to hear nothing at all, except that the drumming offered the dubious comfort of making everything that they were experiencing seem muffled as though it was all happening at a distance from themselves.

The Ronalokas fought with everything they had, but they had very little left with which to fight. They felt burning hot on the inside and cold and clammy on the outside. Great snakes seemed to be wrapping themselves around them and squeezing out what little life was left in them. The Ronalokas felt as weak and helpless as a fetus struggling against the odds of an impossible birth.

Nothing felt good to them. Nothing felt like it could help them, and they had no time or rational thought process left with which to determine if this was right or not. The Ronalokas felt themselves going numb. They felt their perceptions dulling. They felt themselves losing their awareness and much of their sense of themselves. What they had lost already was nothing compared to what they lost now.

When the Ronalokas had lost almost all of their consciousness, they began having a feeling, not of being lifted up, but of falling and falling like their lifeline had been cut. At first, the sensation they had was like that of being in an accelerating elevator that is out of control and won't be able to stop at the bottom.

The Ronalokas hated this feeling of falling and falling out of control. With their last gasps of consciousness, they struggled against it, and this caused them to turn over and fall headfirst, frightening them even more. The terrible pounding in their heads was made bearable only by the force of the compression coming from all around them. They pulled helplessly at the snakes that were strangling them. They jerked spastically and finally lapsed into unconsciousness, their struggle to survive overcome by their exhaustion. This was the moment in which I let go of them, and the Ronalokas quite quickly fell the rest of the way to Earth.

After a long, hard struggle with the gap between My Light and Earth, the Ronalokas had been born into physicality on Earth in a state of helpless unconsciousness, unable to know where they were, who they were, or even if they were dead or alive. They arrived like babies who had experienced extreme fetal distress syndrome and had been so damaged they went unconscious trying to be born.

Although the Ronalokas had gone unconscious, this did not release them from the experience their bodies had; it just made them unable to connect to it with their minds. The gap between My Light and the Will moving out into manifested Creation caused a loss of consciousness in the Will, and thus, to the presence of Spirit in Creation, unrecoverable until now, and all along the way, more consciousness has been lost rather than regained. Even though the Ronalokas are going to seem to have the experience of recovering much of their lost consciousness in the Land of Pan, what needs to be recovered now is what has caused all of the reversals that have further weakened the Will's hope of recovery in the long time it has been trying to recover lost consciousness between then and now. The Loss of Consciousness on Earth has been a direct result of the Ronalokas' experience.

In All of the Time on Earth, No Progress Has Been Made

I have had intent to help the Ronalokas recover from this loss of consciousness for a very long time, but there was no way to recover the Ronalokas until the Mother was able to recover her own consciousness from Her own experiences in the darkness of space, because the Mother's Will is necessary to move the rest of what is involved here.

The Mother had seen the Ronalokas coming toward Earth, and even from Her place out in the darkness of space, She had tried to embrace them and let them know Her presence of love was there for them, but the Ronalokas, in their terror, were unable to know what was coming into them from where. Although it was not recognized by them as Mother love, the Mother's love did reach them with enough compassion for their vulnerability and helpless plight that they were born into physical existence alive. Even so, many of the Ronalokas hated the Mother's response of compassion for their plight because they did not want to feel it. They wanted to refuse to accept their helplessness and their vulnerability as their predicament.

When the Ronalokas fell to Earth, they acted and looked like newly born babies who could not even breathe at first. They almost asphyxiated because of their fear of opening to take in anything more. They had to be shocked into taking their first breath because they didn't know whether it was going to harm them or not.

Many of the Ronalokas used great anger, which was held back, as an impetus to overcome their plight, and they are still using it now. Many have refused to admit that there has even been a loss of consciousness, or that they have any problems, and until they do allow themselves to notice it, they are not going to be able to recover what they have lost. Most of the people involved here have not moved this since it originally happened to them. Moving here is going to be necessary if the Ronalokas are going to grow up into what they need to be instead of having adult bodies without grown-up essence inside.

The Mother has always felt like She cannot have a man in Her life because the masculine side of the Will has polarized away from Her feelings here and has acted like it is not possible to allow these feelings to move and still be a man. As a result of not allowing these feelings to move in themselves, they have not allowed them to move in the women of Ronalokas either, but the truth of the matter is, they cannot be men unless they do move these feelings. If they do not move these feelings, they can only be boys in big bodies who threaten to or do smack the Mother whenever She moves or starts to move Her feelings here. Because they cannot stand these feelings, they want to blame them on the Mother.

The Mother is tired of taking the blame here, and for quite some time, has tried to do without the man She could never find anyway. The best She has been able to do is to hold back most of Her own feelings and try to live the pretense of having a man around by trying not to move toward the gap in Her man. The pretense has come from fear of the gap.

When the masculine side of the Ronalokas polarized away from the fear and the terror, it labeled these feelings feminine and weak. I would like to point out that there is greater strength in being able to face the terror than in avoiding it, which is why, no matter how physically strong the men have made themselves, the women still have greater inner strength.

As a generalization, this is not wrong, although I know that some of you will want to rush at Me with exceptions to the rule. That is not the point. The point is to allow yourselves to move the emotions being triggered here, rather than arguing about what is being said as a way to avoid the issues involved. You must look at what has happened to you as a group, whether you like being identified with the rest of the Ronalokas or not. Your problems here are partly because of the extreme fragmentation that has taken place in the Ronalokas, and partly because of the self-hatred, which is hatred also for your group identity.

The hatred for your group identity is also part of the reason for your involvement with the gap and the guilt of the Warriors instead of with your own true Spirits and the Light you need from them now. You have desired to rid yourselves of the oppression of the Warriors now, and to do it, you are going to have to go into the feelings you have not been allowing and let them move.

If you are a man moving into this part of your lost Will, it is not going to be helpful to your healing to cling to images of what sort of emotional expression it would be suitable for a man to allow himself in these releases. Part of the problem you are having in the Will Polarity is that you have been shamed into thinking and believing that emotional expression you need here is not manly, not acceptable, and is instead, either feminine, hysterical, and weak, or sniveling and cowardly. There is rage in the Will toward labeling emotions in this way.

It is going to be almost impossible to overcome this conditioning in your first few efforts, but you must not allow these images to retain their grip on you. They are nothing but guilt to the extreme of self-hatred. This self-hatred is often not recognized by those who have it because feelings are seldom allowed to move enough to find these places. When they do move, there is usually immediate blame for another who represents the hated aspect of the Mother; for example, blame is often placed in this way, "I lost control of My rage because of the way I was provoked."

If you have an aversion to having the Will referred to as the Mother, or if you have an aversion to being referred to as polarized to the Mother because you are Will polarized, but in a masculine body, you need to realize that you have hatred for the Mother in all of the ways you do not want to be identified with Her.

There is hatred for the Mother for the imprint of terror, which is a form of self-hatred that has polarized away from the Mother and into the rage that wants to blame Her as a way to escape feeling this terror. This rage has preferred to kill the Mother rather than to feel this terror, but healing is not possible this way.

Because of the fragmentation involved, it has not been realized by those who hate the Mother in this way that killing the Mother is killing themselves. In fact, most of these people do not overtly kill the Mother but have fragments who do it. Hatred for everything that has been seen as weak in the Will is lumped into these denials along with fear of feelings in general. The Mother is especially hated for Her patterns of being victimized; so much so that victims often, instead of receiving help, receive more victimizing at the hands of this hatred.

The Mother would have stopped Her patterns of being victimized if She could have because She has no more love for them than this hatred has had, which is also Her own self-hatred. Self-hatred in the Will is immense and must be allowed to move now, as the great rage against the self that it really is, but you also must allow everything you need to move along the way to really being able to recognize this. Jumping ahead to levels of understanding you do not really have in your Will is not going to bring you healing. Hating others is part of the process of finding out how they reflect your own self-hatred to you.

You must also allow movement in the feelings of fear that it is wrong to hate. It has long been thought that feeling hatred is wrong, but you cannot love that which will not receive you. I could not love the Mother where She would not receive Me, and the Mother could not love Me where I did not receive Her. Love is open. Where you are not open, you are not loving. Therefore, you can allow yourselves to notice that holding back is not more loving than giving your true response. This does not mean that your response is always going to be what has been popularly defined as a positive response, although you will see as you move along here that even what has been termed negative response is a positive response in terms of real lovingness. Opening your vibration and allowing it to move in the Light will allow you to become more loving, not less loving, as you like to think.

The differences between this process and what has been going on in the world already, is that hating others does not mean you go out into the world and fight them down or try to get rid of them. Instead, you move the emotions you have toward these people in your own space, with yourself, or a few trusted allies who can act this out with you, until you really feel that this lost Will has presence in you in ways that are enabling you to understand what happened there to create these feelings. Once you know that, you can allow yourself to move in the ways that will heal these feelings.

Hatred for the Mother has been killing Her for a long time. Her patterns of being victimized were caused not only by My original ignorance of The Unseen Role of Denial, but also by My initial bad intent toward the Will. My initial bad intent toward the Will manifested as Lucifer, who fragmented out of Me that long ago and has not moved his position since. Lucifer is held present by the Will's self-hatred, which needs to move now. Hatred needs to move in the presence of strong intent to heal so that My Light can come in rather than having Lucifer become more empowered than he already is.

This is what Lucifer's followers always say there are doing; very carefully allowing the Will to move so that negativity on Earth is not empowered. This is because they see the Will as negativity on Earth. They are controlling the Will for their own purposes. It is not just in how the Will moves; it is intent that makes the difference.

I also need to mention that the Will did not originate this hatred; I did. What needs to move in the Will that feels like hatred is response in the Will to the feeling of being hated. This is what the Will holds that is being called hatred. What is called hatred in My Light is lack of receptivity to the Will, which is not My Light, and yet, My Light originated it by creating the gap between Spirit and Will. This gap was immediately filled in by what has looked like My Light to most people.

The Will Polarity has to feel how much it has not liked being Will. There is self-hatred here, and it is because it did not look like the Will was favored by My Light. Instead of using pep talks, positive imagery, or positive thinking to try to go past or move yourselves out of the self-rejection that is here, these feelings must be felt and expressed. As you have experienced yourselves in manifested existence, it has not looked at all like the Will Polarity was favored in My Light. For the most part, it has been the other spirits who have led the good life, and the Will people have been made to serve them.

Now that it looks like I might be getting ready to hand some of the good life to the Will Polarity, what is going to be left of Earth? It looks like the other spirits have depleted and destroyed Earth, living their so-called "guilt-free" lives of abundance and indulgence. From the viewpoint of the Will Polarity, it looks as though the bounty of Creation has been for the other spirits, and now, when it looks like there is nothing left, and even possibly no life left, the Will people are finally going to come into their own.

The Will people have always felt that there is little or nothing left for them after the other spirits take what they want, and whether the other spirits admit to also having this belief or not, they do. The other spirits believe that if the Will has what it wants, there will be little or nothing left for them. You need to see that guilt is the reason for this. Wherever guilt is in the place of My Light, the possibilities for everything are immediately limited, and remain that way until the guilt is moved out.

Moving guilt out is the trick that is going to allow the recovery of consciousness that has been lost. Guilt is not consciousness, no matter how it looks. The people who reflect guilt to you do not feel like conscious people once you get your Will moving enough to notice them. Then you will have to deal with the guilt of feeling this way toward them, but at least you are getting closer to moving the guilt out, because you are starting to feel again what made you deny what you saw there.

What to do about guilt is what you really need to understand now. It is not outer movement that is necessary here. It is internal movement, but not internal movement of the kind that remains silent and tolerant of what has been happening by gaining some new belief system that is able to enlist your compliance here. I am talking about the kind of internal movement that vibrates in your own space and fills your own space with your own vibration so that you no longer leave space for guilt. This does not necessitate throwing out in some act of reaction against it, that does not realize this would also be losing part of yourself again.

By expressing from your Will, you are vibrating yourself so that you are making space for your own essence and reclaiming essence you have lost to guilt by making a place for it with yourself. This is what self-acceptance is, and to get there, you will have to deal with the guilt that says it is not right to take this space for yourself.

Guilt will make you feel lousy every time you express your true feelings until you have acceptance for them. Whenever you feel guilty, go to the fear, which is the real problem. Allow yourself to notice that when you back up for guilt, it presses in on you all the more. Your lack of vibration, or lack of self-acceptance, makes space for it to press in on you more and more until you feel you have to fight for your life, only to find that fighting empowers guilt all the more to intimidate you by turning your own denied fear against you.

Many have the fear that allowing their Wills to vibrate means they will become, or want to become, dictators and have everything their own way, tolerating nothing they don't like in others. These feelings have to be gone through too in order for you to see that the only thing you will not be able to tolerate is lack of movement in the Will and those who will not let their Wills move.

Guilt is a very innocuous and yet insidious thing, and is the reason you are having the problems you are having now. It is impossible to move out the guilt you have without giving free expression to the Will so that you can sort out what is free expression and what is not. Guilt has moved into any place the Will has been held back, and thus, anytime you are not free and spontaneous with the expression of your response to what is happening to you, you are making space for guilt. Your subjective experience is your experience, and anytime you deny your subjective experience, you are having the experience of guilt rather than your own experience. Whenever you feel yourself being hesitant rather than spontaneous, you need to feel the feelings that are causing you to hesitate and express them. It is usually fear of one sort or another.

You need to understand that you can also deny your Will by allowing it to express when it does not feel safe to do so. If you are not ready to express the feelings you have, express the fear of expressing them first. Do not always make this an exercise in word usage. The guilt you need to move out here is guilt that has been with you for a long time. You are just now recognizing its presence as guilt rather than whatever else you thought it was, and you have a lot to learn about why it has been there before you can move it out successfully.

Guilt has more power on Earth now than My Light does, and it is not possible to go past the fear you have of openly expressing emotions that you have been so long denied by society at large. The reality that these feelings are denied by society at large shows you the immensity of the presence of guilt. So do not make the mistake of the 1960's in the United States by going forth with these teachings like it is some kind of movement and you are going to be exemplary of what others should do. Everything the protesters of the 1960's did not see about themselves is being reflected in the 1980's. The judgments held in a state of denial may be making it look like the two are not connected, but they are.

The protestors of the 1960's did not see that they were exhorting a reflection of their own lost Will to move, while at the same time, not accepting the feelings lost Will had "out there" any more than they were accepting these feelings in themselves. Denied anger and self-hatred played the biggest role here, but of course, all of it is fear avoidance. Without fear, there is not anger or self-hatred, and yet, I want to make this point once more: fear is not something to get rid of, or identify, see for what it is, and let go of. Fear is something which must be felt and expressed until it has naturally, and without pressuring, evolved into another feeling of greater understanding. If love and compassion are not present, you have not healed it, and I am not talking about your love and compassion toward the fear; I am talking about fear's ability to expand into love and compassion.

I am making this point so many times because no matter how many times I have tried to make this point in the past, many of you have managed to misunderstand Me because of your desire to avoid what has to be felt here. Even now, many of you are managing to misinterpret these books, and if you continue to do so, there will be no hope left of healing for you for a very long time, so long that you will go unconscious and lose the rest of the consciousness you have before healing will be able to come to you.

In other words, the Mother and I are both tired of trying to get across to you, and We are giving it this one last try. If it doesn't succeed, We are going to conclude that you do not want to move with Us now, and We are going to let you go and have the experience you need to have to be able to align with what We are saying here.

We have a great fear We are now moving away from allowing this to happen and of what it will mean for all of Us. We have, as well, a great rage toward the lost Will that does not want to move now. We also have these feelings towards My lost Light, which is not allowing the Will to move, but We have no recourse other than to move what We can now and allow the rest to move later.

The feelings that were held in a state of denial in the 1960's made the protesters look very self-righteous from one point of view, but it also allowed many to look like they were protesting against things they really weren't all that against, in terms of where their lost Will was located in the spectrum of things. Many spirits, who even had their parental parts lined up with the movement in the 1960's looked more like the fragments themselves in view of the amount of Lost Will they had in a state of denial that was actually promoting the very things they were protesting against.

Lost Will turns against that which has denied it in most cases, but whether this manifests as hatred or not is dependent upon Lucifer's presence. Lucifer was behind the squashing of the movement in the 1960's and has remained militantly against it, unless it takes the form of something he can control, such as affirmative action through the processes already available, or internalizing the struggle according to his prescription.

The Lost Will involved gives the guilt reflection, but it cannot move the emotions that need to move to move the guilt out. Neither is the lost Will reflection conscious of holding the denials, or garbage, of the ones doing the denying, and yet, when it seeks to reverse the self-righteous in these denials, it often seeks the "garbage" on these people in order to discredit them.

You can see from what is happening in the 1980's that the guilt reflection is trying to reverse all the gains the 1960's hoped had been made. One of the ways the guilt reflection is gaining popularity for its viewpoint is by making it appear that the protesters for social change in the 1960's were either very naive, wrong, or had nothing real to offer. These people are now, for the most part, being portrayed as mindlessly immature, drug-crazed, sexually promiscuous originators of the destruction of the moral fiber of America and originators of epidemics of sexual and drug-related diseases. The Warriors, of course, are portraying themselves as struggling to fix the mess created by the 1960's movement.

As the reflection goes on without the understanding to heal it, the 1980's are seeing drugs introduced to obliterate consciousness rather than expand it. Sexual freedom has increasingly become licentiousness, cheap thrills, and lack of responsibility for the children and even the other adults involved. The reawakening of sensitivity has become a sensual saturation bordering on complete boredom, and love has become more of a word to throw around when selling products than anything real being felt by most people. The word love is also being used by people trying to sell themselves as loving, more often than love is being felt by any of them.

The pressure to make abortion illegal is another effort by the guilt reflection to reverse what happened in the 1960's, but the problem cannot be solved in this way. The reflection here is all lack of self-acceptance. The pattern it is taking here is that unwanted children feel unwanted within themselves, or they would not appear in places where they are not wanted. Those lost Will fragments are going to feel unwanted, whether they are born or not, and whether someone else adopts them or not. The ones who are already here are reflecting this by trying to make it so that it seems to them that no other living essence can be discarded.

All of the problems you are having now that seem to have their origins in the1960's are reflecting the extent to which the visions of the 1960's were mental concepts that did not allow movement in the Will that could have aligned manifestation and vision. This is the ancient power struggle manifesting outwardly, and My greatest lesson with the Mother.

Her opposition was only in appearance. If I had been able to allow Her the movement necessary, She would have aligned with Me rather easily. My use of the word "allow" here does not mean that there can be any element of patronization, expectation of outcome, manipulation, or feelings of superiority toward the Will. The Will must be allowed to exist and have Its own ways and means. The same as Spirit wants to be allowed to exist and have Its own ways and means. The gap is still so large, however, that the distrust between the two, Spirit and Will, is still very immense on Earth.

What you must understand is that the reversals that have taken place against the advances made in the 1960's do not mean that the exhausted protestors from the 1960's must somehow find it within themselves to rise again or pressure their children to do so by telling them they have no social conscience. The situation does not call for a more intense presentation of what is wrong and how it should be righted than was given in the 1960's, nor will a more orderly or well-groomed presentation be more successful than it was in the 1960's.

What is missing here is intent to receive you. If you are not getting acceptance right around you, you will not get greater acceptance on a larger scale. The bigger you go, the greater the force of resistance that will rise against you, unless you do the inner work necessary to stop manifesting this opposition.

The ways in which these reflections are being given are as multitudi-nous as the judgments and the withheld feelings involved. For example, the denied feelings of anger and violence in the Civil Rights movement soon began expressing against those who were denying these feelings.

The beloved Dr. Martin Luther King denied his own feelings of rage, hatred, and violence until one of his own lost Will rage fragments killed him. The same is true of John Lennon.

The gap must be healed now. Without healing the gap, you cannot go forth and speak the truth of your conscious intent without having the reversals manifested by your denials in a state of unconsciousness. The gap has gotten everyone who has risen against it and will continue to do so unless it is healed.

The things Dr. Martin Luther King most hated in himself were reflected by those who killed him, and I say those, because many were involved in the pattern, even though the fatal shot was fired by one. When John Lennon denied his feelings of anger and fear toward those who rose against him for daring to say he was more popular than Jesus and made what appeared to be a public apology, guilt began to gain the power to take his life in that incarnation. As has been already mentioned, the denied rage of the hippies has been reflected by many of the youth of the 1980's, and the denied fear by the return to fundamentalism in religion. The backlash against Blacks, and even the violence of Blacks against Blacks is a direct result of their own denials.

These tragedies are not things that can be solved by greater mental awareness alone. Too often, all that is produced by this is a change in form while the essence continues vibrating in the same ways. For example, the same ones who were the Sadducees and the Pharisees who rejected Jesus now embrace Him as their Savior. Just as they have always embraced whatever the majority religion is where they live. They now move against anyone who seeks to defame their image of Jesus, just as them, they moved against Him for seeming to defame images they held sacred at that time. This is because they are a guilt reflection that has not moved much through all of history, and no matter how much you might want to say that Jesus was perfect, He had guilt mixed with love. The guilt that created His death on Earth had to do with the polarization of Heart toward My Light and away from the lost Will and Body essence We had on Earth. The entire Jesus scenario was played out on Earth by fragments of My Own Four Parts, which had fragmented out in various ways with various misunderstandings and denials.

There is a direct parallel here with Dr. Martin Luther King because He was, in fact, one of the many fragments of Jesus left on Earth when Jesus ascended. Dr. Martin Luther King was some of the denied Will essence of Jesus that was left on Earth when Jesus ascended because He had essence that embraced Jesus' belief that it was not right to meet violence with violence. Dr. Martin Luther King believed he was not worthy to ascend with Jesus until he purged himself of the feelings of violence that he had.

Jesus shared the misunderstandings I had at the time. We had an aversion to violence and did not know how to move the lost Will essence that was involved in it. Jesus judged against His feelings of wanting to do violence against those who had done violence against Him. Dr. King was part of the Will essence present in Jesus that accepted judgments against the feelings of violence. He manifested the presence of these judgments by denying violence in all forms.

Dr. King spent his life from the time of Jesus trying to purge Himself of the feelings of wanting to give a violent response when violence was done to Him. Dr. King felt that facing the violence of prejudice and ignorance, which He hated the most, was a good way for Him to find out if He was really able to purge Himself of the feelings of wanting to give violent response. Dr. King had guilt over His feelings here that resulted from the level of understanding Heart had at the time these judgments were made.

All of His life, Dr. King believed it was not right to meet violence with violence, and for the most part, it is not, but it is necessary to allow the rage to move and find it acceptable within love. The difference between acting out emotions by giving them forms of violence and allowing them direct expression as pure emotion is going to bring the healing needed here. The rage that Dr. King had, and believed he had to deny, is the same rage the Ronalokas have, and believe they must deny. Even the troubles Jesus' followers had after his death has parallels among the followers of Dr. King.

I would like to mention that several other key figures in the 1960's were also fragments of Jesus, as well as many unknowns who experienced feelings of being Jesus because they had Lost Will essence of his in various states of denial. This essence was being activated by the love message.

Even though much of this essence has had glimpses of Its true identity, the lost Will essence of Heart that did not ascend when Jesus did needs to find balance. This essence has accepted judgments of unworthiness or the opposite. The Heart judgments this essence holds all say in various ways that it was not loving to have the thoughts and feelings Heart denied here. Some of this essence has been twisted into severe unlovingness by the heavier judgments Heart accepted against Himself. It will help you to understand this to know that Charles Manson is also a fragment of Jesus.

It is also necessary to allow movement of any feelings you have that this could not be right. No matter how much you want to say Jesus is perfect, He had guilt mixed with love, and the heavier part of this guilt created His death on Earth and His fragmentation. The guilt that created His death on Earth was reflected to Him through those who opposed Him. Heart was opposed by His own lost Will. He knew he could not reach them, but at the time, He did not know why. Heart was only able to help Spirit polarized people at the time of the life of Jesus because We had not yet figured out how to cross the gap between the Spirit-Heart and the Will-Body Polarities.

Mary kept asking Jesus to try harder to reach the people She felt needed Him even more than the people with whom He was spending most of His time. When He did, He was able to help Body people who were polarized to Spirit, but He was not able to help the Will people. The Will Polarity has many feelings to move around, feeling left out once again at the time of Jesus.

Mary did not understand, any more than Jesus and I did, that what could not be reached in outer reality had to be reached within first. Jesus was so polarized toward My Light that he was able to heal the Will-Body presence He had with Him in three days. Just because the Will-Body people cannot heal themselves in three days does not mean they cannot be healed. Jesus left much of Himself on Earth that has to be healed now, and these parts of Him cannot be healed in three days earlier.

Mary had many feelings She did not allow expression in the life She had with Jesus. She had guilt about having these feelings and, so, did not see a reflection of receptivity for these feelings. It will help all of the Will people to get in touch with the Mary that really was, and is, by getting in touch within themselves, with the feelings She had rather than settling for the images that have been made of Her.

The Will Polarity has many feelings in common with Mary because Mary was a large part of the Mother. Mary had most of the Mother essence that could align with Her gathered within Her at the time of Jesus' coming. Hope was that the Mother's essence was finally going to be lifted back into My Light again. Mary did not know this consciously, though. The Mother had dropped so far down in Creation that Mary was having trouble accepting that She had, indeed, been chosen to be the Mother of a great prophet. It was not possible to get it across to her that She was also the Mother of Everything.

I had gathered Her together with as much essence of Her fragments as could align with Us at the time in the hope that Heart's physical presence with Her might be able to get across to Her many things I wanted Her to be able to receive from Me, but the Mother had been so pressured by the gap I threw Her into when I smacked Her, that She had lost the consciousness She needed to be able to connect with many of the things Heart and I wanted to tell Her.

Mary felt that I saw Her as lacking and that I had gathered this extra essence into Her so that She would be able to handle being the Mother of a great prophet. She didn't recognize this essence as missing parts of Herself. She tried to accept this essence as helper spirits, and even though She was the parental part, She gave it the upper hand much of the time because of Her feelings of guilt and unworthiness.

Most of the Mother essence in good enough shape to help Mary at that time was essence that had fragmented out of Her fairly early. This essence had not been as greatly damaged. This essence separated from the Mother because it did not have the guilt that had separated the rest of the Mother from My Light. This essence had desire to be with Mary at the time of Jesus, but it also had opinions against Mary and Her humble ways because this essence had not had the experiences of the part of the Mother which had been as denied as Mary was.

This essence gathered around Mary like an extension of Her aura. It was not used to being on Earth, and Mary was not used to having so much Light around her. Mary felt like She was barely on Earth anymore. She felt barely able to handle Herself, especially during the pregnancy with Jesus, unless Joseph or someone else led Her around by the hand. She spent most of Her time just sitting in the presence of the Light around Her.

As a result of this sudden influx of Light that was not very well aligned with Her, Mary was having trouble keeping Herself together. The emotional movement necessary here was not understood, and so Mary was not able to assimilate this essence as a part of Herself. Mary lost a large amount of the Light when Jesus was born because of Its lack of alignment with Her. Mary thought this Light had been Jesus' Light, and although She missed it, She was also greatly relieved and felt more Herself to be released from the pressure this Light was giving the guilt She was holding.

Mary could not see how so much Light could have been meant for Her because nothing much changed in Her life. She had the feeling that with or without the Light, She could not cope with life on Earth. She still has this feeling, as does most of the Will Polarity. Mary fragmented all during that lifetime and experienced Herself as losing more and more Light the older she got. She feared it was not possible to get better with age. She also judged it was not possible to live as She had lived and have the Light remain present. These feelings were augmented in her by the opinions of the fragments that did not want to stay with Her.

There was also Mother essence gathered near Mary that could not come close enough to be attached to Mary's body in that lifetime. Mary Magdalene and most of the prostitutes were among these, as well as Elizabeth, Mary's Mother, and most of Her friends and acquaintances. We could not come any closer into alignment then because fragmentation was not fully understood, especially where it came to healing it through movement of the lost Will involved. At the time, I was trying to approach the Mother as a sisterhood. Even now, the best alignment the Mother is going to be able to have for quite some time is a sisterhood, but it is going to be necessary for the parental part to be given the recognition She deserves.

The split between the prostitute and the "good" wife and Mother was not a new split for the Mother, and could not be resolved then for reasons of sexual guilt. Mary had plenty of it, and when Jesus suggested making love to Her when She was lonely and sexually unfulfilled after Joseph's death, Mary could not accept Him at all here.

Mary had sensuality and sexuality, which Her images have not been allowed to retain. Mary wanted Jesus to make love to Her and even fantasized it many times, but She was not willing to admit it. She held Him at bay mostly because of Her fears of what would happen if there should be a pregnancy or if someone should happen to find out.

Mary especially feared showing Her feelings in front of others because of Her guilt. She greatly feared it was already obvious how much She loved Jesus because He embodied so much of what She loved in a man. Other men She knew had denied so much of the softness and receptivity. Men in those times were very rough, especially toward women. Despite all the imagery that makes Jesus look effeminate, He was not effeminate. He was a man trying to touch the Will, and so, He had more openness to that side of His nature than other men in those times.

Mary also had great grief that did not move, although it moved more than many other of Her feelings. Her grief over Jesus' death was immense, but Her guilt caused Her to do Her best to embrace the Spirit polarized viewpoint that it was a necessary part of the plan, and that His separation from Her wasn't real. Jesus' separation from Mary was real enough to Her, and it was immensely painful for Her to realize, once He was gone, how much His physical presence had meant to Her.

Mary also had great fears, which She did not move. Instead, She nagged Jesus with them and told Him all of the things She heard on the grapevine about how He was displeasing the authorities. Jesus responded to this by staying away from Mary more instead of giving Her the anger She needed to move Her fear. Mary took this to mean that Jesus no longer loved Her as much as the other people He was spending time with, and She became a little like the popular portrait of a Jewish Mother, nagging Him and accusing Him of being gay because He was spending so much time with His disciples. Guilt told Her She was not right to want His time anymore because He was a great prophet that owed His time to everyone. Guilt did not allow the true emotional expression of the fear that needed to move here.

Mary did not allow Herself to rage either. When Heart was pulling away from Her, She did not give Him the rage She felt any more than She gave Him the depth of Her fear. She was afraid Jesus wouldn't accept this, and so none of Us found out what Mary was really holding here. She did not rage at Him for not giving Her feelings more validity in His life either. Instead, She tried to smile and be the Mother She thought She was supposed to be, while inwardly, She judged Herself heavily for not being good enough to fit Her image of a prophet's Mother.

Mary expressed only a little of the emotion She had about Jesus' impending death, other than to let Him know She wanted Him to go away and stop displeasing the local authorities. Mary did not rage at the disciples, even though She saw them as a bunch of gay-tending guys who wanted Jesus to themselves and who denied Her validity as a spiritual presence. She did not rage about the treatment of women in general in those times, and She did not let Her rage move when the disciples denied Her the Book of Mary in the Bible.

Mary had all of the issues of Will's held emotional charge toward Heart and Spirit that need to surface now, but She didn't have enough self-acceptance to allow them. There were so many feelings here that I cannot list them all, but what I have given is enough to get you started.

Mary had so many feelings in that life She felt She dare not move that toward the end of that life, She could not carry the load of them anymore. Starting with Herod's murdering of the babies, which Mary heard about, She was at odds with Me. She strongly felt that the presence of Light and Love should not be causing so many terrible things to happen. The more the persecution of the followers of Jesus piled atrocity upon atrocity, the more Many questioned Me.

"If this the fruit of Your love," She would say to Me, "Why is it so bitter?"

Mary held Her feelings back as much as She could, but She felt a hardness and a bitterness growing within Her. When She could take it no more, She lay down, appearing to be frozen in grief. She turned Her face to the wall and stayed there until She died. Her other children thought this was all grief over Jesus, and that She love Him so much more than they, that She was not willing to live for them. They did not understand the depth of Her pain and neither did She.

One of the last things She said to Me in that life was, "If You are so right, why is the suffering so terrible?"

When Mary died, She had intense feelings of unworthiness because She was unable to ascend like Jesus. SHe took it as another bitter defeat for those left on Earth to have Jesus leave them so soon while they remained unable to follow Him.

After that, Mary did not talk directly to Me for a long time. What was left of Mary, after all of the fragmentation that took place, incarnated into a life where She was tortured worse than anyone in history has ever been tortured. This took place in a deeply hidden, subterranean room, so far out of the public eye that history did not even record it.

What came forward there was a very complicated piece of karma that heavily involved the Mother's Original Cause regarding many more issues than just those She had with Heart. Her emotions were not allowed to move here either because the guilt reflection She had around Her this time reflected all of the heavist judgments She had against Herself for having the feelings She had. It was self-hatred, and as a result, every time She made even a slight sound, Her tortures were increased.

Of the many things involved, I would like to say this now. Although Her rage against Herself was punishing Her for all of the charges She held against Herself, it was also as though Her rage was saying to Me, "What kind of God are You that You have got to have suffering? If it is suffering You want, I'll give you suffering! If suffering is what caused You to lift Jesus up, how much suffering will it take for You to be moved to lift Me up? If Jesus died for Our sins, how much suffering is necessary for You to lift all of Us up, because We have all been left behind!?"

She relived Jesus' death, plus the tortures of many of His followers, and the Ronalokas' journey to Earth, believing I required suffering and hoping the most suffering possible might be enough to move My Light into lifting You all up. All the way through it, She fantasized about being rescued, but it didn't happen. She finally died, miserably defeated, feeling that no matter how much sacrifice and suffering was offered to

God, He was never going to help Her or Her people. It seemed to Her that I was willing to lift the Body of a man, but I wouldn't even ease the pain of a woman.

Although the Mother did not have the consciousness at the time to understand why She was being tortured so horribly, other than that, it seemed to be a secret political act, designed to extract information She had resolved not to give. I saw Her be sexually violated by Lucifer many times here, and I understood what was happening. I stood by Her, horrified, but I was unable to do anything to save Her. Her self-hatred and Her judgments that hated My Light for having caused so much suffering had the upper hand here, and no emotional movement that could have changed the situation was being allowed. She also blamed Herself for Jesus' death for many reasons, which She knew, but one She didn't know then was that Her inability to receive Heart made Him unable to remain manifest on Earth.

I hesitate to mention it, but when this happened to Mary, it was a major reversal against My Light and did more to cause the Dark Ages on Earth than any other single event. Mary did not understand, as Lucifer did, that Her Will was key to what happened on Earth. She was afraid the feelings She had here were ego, and She did not want any part of them. She even empowered Her torturers to diminish Her because She thought She had become too self-important and aggrandized as the High Priestess at Delphi, which is who She was when Her torturers kidnapped Her.

Her rage first took Her there to speak what She did not speak at the time of Jesus, and when She did speak it, Her denied fear gave Her the reflection of rejection She had feared it would. She then felt wrong, all the way wrong, for having dared to think Her input should affect My Light. She feared it was Her ego again, and in Her fear, confused Lucifer and My Light. She feared that what She had thought was My Light was Lucifer fooling Her with ego trickery into putting Herself on the line so that Her enemies could gobble Her up. Given the gaps that were not healed, all of Her fears were true.

As soon as the denied fear began to come back at her from the outer reflection, Mary as the Priestess went into fear, but She did not know She needed to allow Her fear to move. Instead, She started holding back in many places where She would have spoken out earlier. This left Her followers feeling abandoned and opened space for them to feel their fears and doubts. Some of them turned against Her.

Mary was not long in the role of Priestess after that. Gossip was already bringing Her down as far as the town was concerned. She had given rage the upper hand instead of being held back by Her fears. She had gone ahead and had sex with someone who attracted Her, but who was forbidden in those times; the High Priest. She had spoken out publicly and politically, and Her kidnappers were the gap drawing near.

Mary held Her fears back and tried to proceed as though there was nothing wrong that wouldn't smooth out, but Her fears were amplifying all the pictures She already had about how wrong She was to have had sex with anyone other than My Light and My Light alone. The High Priest was the Father of Manifestation, and so now guilt had her on every count there was in Her Original Cause. Her self-hatred was immense because She believed She was not the person She was supposed to be and had dared to think of Herself as someone She was not.

Lucifer already had ahold of Her, but when Her denied rage came up in reaction to Her fear being pressed in on Her from the reflection all around Her, She fell right into his hands because the next thing in the Mother's consciousness was that I smacked Her into the gap where he tortured Her. The Mother has reenacted the original tortures of Lucifer many times over, but this re-enactment was the most intense in terms of time and space compression. Lucifer took Her so far back into lost Will in six days that the Mother is not all the way recovered from it yet.

I was sure We had gotten no place in all of the time I had been trying to help the Mother come back to Me, and My Light was so furious at Her for this, because I still perceived it as Her resistance to Me, that I empowered Lucifer to torture Her again here without allowing Myself to quite realize how I was doing it. I felt highly trapped and did not allow Myself to look at what happened there for a long time, but I had given My rage to the gap and allowed it to push the Mother back. What happened there was of major historical significance.

Mary, as Priestess, could not allow Herself to tell Her torturers anything because She did not love them as She loved Greece. She hated the Roman Empire. She had so much residual hatred for what She saw as the arm of repression toward Light and Love at the time of Jesus that She held the Romans responsible for all that had happened there. She was not about to allow them to gain more power over the lives of those She loved.

When She refused to help Her torturers by giving them the information they needed, She thought She was helping Greece and My Light. She contributed directly to the downfall of the Roman Empire, which was what She thought She wanted, but the Dark Ages that followed were even worse. Mary, in Her state of denial, helped darken My Light on Earth because She did not notice that the problem was not the form of the Roman Empire, but the denial spirits who had infiltrated it. Thus, She could not allow Herself to see that the Romans who were torturing Her were part of the Luciferian "shadow government" that was trying to take over Rome.

The Mother thought She was a heroine and a victim, but She also blamed Herself heavily without quite understanding why. She had been pounded down into too much unconsciousness to understand how much this helped Lucifer to have the Dark Ages he wanted. She saw the darkness here, but She did not understand, because of Her own attachment to form, that Lucifer didn't care whether his plan took form within the Roman Empire or another way. Whenever the Mother thought She saw what was happening, Lucifer told Her She was judgmental, wrong, and unloving. The Mother took this in and pressured Herself to be more loving.

The Mother could not fully grasp what Lucifer had in mind for Her here because She had lost the consciousness of being the Mother. Lucifer had a strong grasp on Her already. He strengthened his hold by first locking Her up for three days, telling Her what he had in mind for Her and telling Her that if She was such a great Priestess, She should save Herself or have that prophet She talked about save Her, or Her God, for that matter, or maybe even Her gods.

Lucifer, in the form of Roman secret police, knew that this Priestess believed in One God, and he taunted Her by saying Her God couldn't be much of a match for his gods, or even for him, since Her God was not able to help Her now. He also let Her know that he thought his Roman gods were more powerful than Her Greek gods by mentioning all of the sorest points of rivalry between them, not forgetting to emphasize that none of them were bringing Her either escape or rescue.

It is important to mention that these ancient gods were all Ancient Ones that Serve the Light, and Lucifer had them all then, although he doesn't now. They had all been doing their best to keep the Mother away from My Light and had succeeded more than She realized.

Although the Mother was not able to recognize Her Roman captor as Lucifer, He knew his captive Priestess well; so well, She thought My Light must have been empowering him for him to know so much about Her, She became so terrified that what She had thought was My Light was not My Light, and that I was sending Her his punishment because She had not served Me the way I wanted Her to, that Lucifer was able to twist Her thinking until She almost totally discarded My Light as wrong and took Lucifer in in My place.

At the end of three days, Mary felt powerless. Her grief was immense, and so was Her terror. Her rage felt impotent. She felt there was nothing She could do but keep Herself under control as best She could by telling Herself She must have this test to pass for reasons I knew, but which She did not. She begged Me to help Her and nothing happened.

Mary was then led into the subterranean chamber where She was tortured for three days, and all the reasons She felt tested came up in Her torture. She could not allow Herself to notice their full import then, and I cannot list them all now, but they had to do with all of the judgments against the Mother from the beginning of time as measured by the first conscious awareness.

Almost as long as the Mother's list of reasons is the list you are going to find in yourselves of why you cannot heal now. The Will has been reversed so many times in Her effort to heal that many places in the Will no longer want even to allow hope that healing could be possible. When you move to change these ancient patterns you have lived with for so long, you are going to find in yourselves the same struggle within your essence that you have been having in your outer reality.

Just as I did not see at the time how the unmoved lost Will essence created these reversals in the Mother right when it looked like healing might be possible for Her, so it was again that just when Mary was looking to Me like She was finally able to take in what I was trying to get across to Her. She suffered the reversal of having Lucifer step in and reinforce all of the old judgments against Her by pounding them into Her Will and Body. Lucifer left My Will lost in such darkness that She could not see My Light for a long time.

What caused the fall of the Roman Empire and the loss of consciousness on Earth then was Lucifer so very nearly killing the Mother that She could not vibrate to receive My Light on Earth for a long time. When Lucifer finished torturing Her this time, there was almost no vibration left in Her. The Mother severely fragmented again here, and in Her next life She was retarded and misshapen. When I saw what effect this had on all Will essence, I knew I had no choice but to recover the Mother first.

Unfortunately, this was all showed to Me in a state of reversal against My Light. The Mother, while thinking She was serving My Light, was serving Lucifer. She was participating against Her Will as She knew It, but not as It actually was, in a major piece of black magic against My Light. Her hatred for Me helped Lucifer gain power over Her, but Her hatred for Herself allowed him to use it.

The Will of the Mother was almost killed there, and along with it, the ability of My Spirit to manifest on Earth for a long time. Even though the Mother's intent was not the same as Lucifer's, Lucifer has used the Mother to cause history to move his way many times. I am now looking for the Mother's alignment with Me to move history powerfully in the direction of the Light of My Love.

This is all I am going to say here. If you are feeling that you cannot understand what is happening, or that you cannot handle what is being said, you need to allow emotional movement instead of shutting down. Even everything that can be said in these books is but a little piece to help you get the rest by moving your emotional bodies. Without the emotional movement necessary, you cannot fill in the gaps in the material, which is as it should be so that you cannot go to a level in your mind that would be too dangerous and so that no one can impersonate a level of understanding they do not really have.

If you find that you are missing the emotions you need to move here, you may find that you are cut out from understanding parts of this material, and it will not be wrong for you. If this enrages you, that is a good starting place for you because no longer is the Mother going to allow anyone into the realms of the Will who is not really open to understanding what is really happening there.

One of the biggest problems for the Will has been guilt telling the Will It cannot just move as It needs to move and understand Itself later. What the Will has to learn now is that It cannot explain Itself until It has moved enough to know. The expectation of having to explain Itself first should not be put upon the Will. It is the gap that requires this.

The Mother had the ability to be tortured much longer than anyone else could have stood it because She could not die without My Light leaving Her. I felt I had to stay present and not leave Her until She had finished what She had to say, no matter how She had chosen to say it. That was what I looked at. When My Light finally did let go of Her, She went into unconsciousness and lost even more of Herself there.

What needs to be understood is that when the Light leaves, the situation is not unlike death except that there is really no such thing as death; just lack of vibration and all that that involves, including the inability of Will and Body to reach consciousness with what they are experiencing. This is the source of the horror stories about the living dead. They have contacted the level of living that never dies, but not the part that ascends into My Light. Quite the reverse, in fact.

There is another reason the Mother was able to suffer so long at the hands of Her tortures that needs to be mentioned now, and it is the same reason the Ronalokas suffer so much every time they die, and that is that the Will cannot live out of the Body very easily. I also have to say that I did not allow the Mother to die here because I was acting out My rage by not letting Her die as a way of saying, "Alright, I won't abandon You. See how you like that!"

I stayed with Her because I was interested and in fact, I liked watching Her punish herself for feeling as She did about My Light because I did not like it either.

At the time, I was still focused on the view that it was the resistance of the Manifested Spirits to receiving My Light that caused the pain and suffering. And even as I watched Her there, giving Me a graphic example of not being able to receive My Light, I still saw it as the Mother deliberately refusing in Her rage to open and receive Me, while begging for Me in Her fear and grief. In spite of all I knew, I did not see how I was empowering the gap until much later when the Mother hit Me in the face with it by dying at the hands of Hitler. Until then, I still felt like the Mother was trying to use Me.

The Will Fears Its Own Desire

Heart's desire of the Will is not to have to suffer anymore, but there is so much conditioning in the Will that It is going to suffer and that no matter how much It suffers, nothing is really going to change, that the Will is afraid to hope anymore. Hope for the Will has become something that is only there to be dashed, as though there is some sort of cruel plot to make sure that hope is there so the suffering will be all the worse for it.

Even though We are all now able to come to the place of understanding that this is what the presence of guilt has caused in the Will, it is also necessary to understand that the Will is not even sure it knows anymore what Its real Heart's desire is. Even if the Will could remember, the Will does not feel that It trusts Itself enough to believe It should have Its Heart's desire.

Every time the Will has felt Itself in opposition to My Light, the Will has feared It was playing God in My place if It has dared to feel differently than I did. The Will has had this guilt in place of My Light, for so long, the Will does not know what My Light has in mind for It or trust Itself to know the difference between guilt and My Light. The Will also does not want to hope for Its Heart's desire to be fulfilled for fear It will only experience more heartbreaks.

Heart's desire of the Will is to be able to move freely among people who have feelings similar to Its own, and who do not endorse repression of the free flow of feelings. In this kind of environment, the Will can move out old charge and old pain.

In the process of doing this, each little nuance of the feelings involved in the patterns must be felt in the depth necessary to understand exactly what has to move out, what is not ready to understand, and what needs to move into the Light now, so that no little piece is thrown out that might otherwise have moved into the Light. The Will wants this because the Will has experienced such terrible pain being without My Light that it does not want any piece of Itself without me if that piece has desire for My Light.

The Manifestation that must accompany this healing is one that must open space more and more for those who love and respect the Will, while closing space more and more to those who do not love the Will, but who want to control, manipulate, use, abuse, and rape the Will, and also to those who only want to allow the parts of the Will they think they like. The desire of the Will to heal means that the lost Will must move in all who have desire to heal, because the Mother must feel responsiveness to Her. Those who want to live must not move anymore in the consciousness that thinks they have love for the Mother but leaves lost parts of themselves unrecognized.

So many people do not know what their lost Will is doing, because they have taken neither the time nor the trouble to explore it. This is because they have, in part, lacked understanding, but it is also because the Will has been feared so much that most spirits have been very happy to go along with Me in denying the Will. The ones who must move back now are the ones who do not want to hear Me but who, instead, want to go on denying the Will as they have always done. These people have locked in on old messages of Mine and repeat them over and over, as though there is nothing new I could be saying and, thus, no evolution in My Light. These people are impressed with old images I projected of My own perfection, and these images contain all the qualities of My old insecurity about Myself as God, because they do not allow me to be questioned as anyone who might not have all the answers. I do have all the answers needed now, but in the past, I did not have these answers, and I must admit to this in front of all of you so that all who can move these old lost Will images of Me will do it now and be able to separate themselves from those who are unwilling to do this now.

When it comes to the Will, no teaching, so far given on Earth, has understood the Will or accepted the Will enough to open a path for understanding it. Because of this, teachings about Spirit and Love have had limited truth in them, and this is because Will essence that is not free means that some light is being held as judgments. This means that there are limits being held within the Light on the truth of the Oneness. For example, fear has long been labeled the problem. "Are you going to have fear or love? Are you going to live in love or negative emotions?" These kinds of statements indicate that the part of the Will that is seen to be within love is very limited. This is not true understanding.

Spirit polarized people who take this approach with the Will are not being loving here. Even though they received these impressions from what they thought was Me, they are participating in the guilt reflection that has held the Will back for so long. It is time for these old patterns, controlling, and punishing the Will to move and heal now. I have moved past this attitude of repressing the Will and Spirit polarized people need to follow Me here.

I see, however, that many Spirit polarized people still want to say anything they can say to insist that nothing new is being said here so that they can cling to the belief that this message fits in with what they already know. Thus, they can continue to avoid what they have avoided for so long already; feeling the pain of the Will. Those who do not want to accept and feel the pain of the Will are not going to be allowed to remain on Earth any longer than their guilt reflection is still necessary to the healing process.

In truth, many Spirit polarized people want to continue oppressing the Will because they are afraid that the Will will want to turn everything around and treat the Spirit the way the Spirit has been treating the Will. In truth, this is going to happen to whatever extent is necessary to make the Spirit sensitive to the Will, but it is never going to be the same because the Spirit, especially Spirit that is denying Will, cannot feel the pain of the Will no matter how much the Will tries to inflict it, even from Its desperation to get Its message across. The Will has been denied over and over for trying this approach and has ended up with more pain than It had in the beginning. The Will has felt powerless to get across to those denying it, and this has increased the Will's fear that Spirit has more power than It has. Spirit has promoted this myth because of fear and hatred of the Will.

In the course of this healing, rage is going to have to move in the Will that wants retribution, revenge and even destruction of the Spirit the way it perceived the Spirit to have been destroying the Will. This can't be gone around. It has to be gone through and whatever has to manifest from it will manifest from it. What will pull us through this is that the Will already knows in the rest of Itself that It cannot destroy Spirit and live Itself. Will's rage and hopelessness have tried to counter this realization by saying It no longer cares to live anyway because Spirit has made Its life so miserable. This also is going to have to be gone through in order for the balance necessary to be found.

The Mother, Herself, has long been lost from this rage because She so heavily denied it believing She was wrong to have these feelings. The Mother is moving this rage now, and you are feeling the repercussions in nature and in the lives of people on Earth. Even many forms of animal life are having the essence moved out of them by movement in the Mother's rage toward the lost Will images they have reflected of the Spirit, or male, strutting around in all the finest feathers and fur while the female, or Will aspect, is left to do all the work of feeding, raising and caring for the young, never being allowed to rest. As soon as one batch of young is raised, here comes the male, who only shows up when he wants sex, yet the female is blamed because she calls him by going into heat.

It is not possible to move into healing here without having the planet come more into harmony with how you would like to live. Increasing sensitivity to the Will means it is not possible for you to move emotion and not feel rage toward the way so much of life is and has been on Earth. You must get this rage moving. In the beginning, it may not feel to you like you have any involvement in the destruction of Earth, but the more you allow this rage to move, the more you will realize you are involved in the desire to destroy many things in manifestation, but you have lost the consciousness of having these feelings.

As much as you hated feeling what you were feeling in the places where you made these denials, you also hate the outward reflection of them. Hatred must be moved until you recognize that it is rage which has become so backed up that there is no Light left in it, and then this rage must be allowed to move until it has feelings of love again, because hatred must move off of Earth now. Love and hate cannot exist in the same place.

No matter how much rage, hatred and fear have to move now in order to bring them within love, it is also true that love has not been altogether missing in life on Earth. Therefore, it is natural that grief is also going to move in response to fear about the changes that are going to be taking place; especially, since one of the big judgments here has been that love will be lost if these emotions move.

For the Will, habits, no matter how bad they are, have been more comfortable than the unknown. Change for the Will, therefore, means that the Will must be allowed to move all of the emotion the Will feels it needs to move. If the Will is not given this freedom, then more lost Will reflection is being created. In other words, release that involves some form of discarding rather than transformation does not work if it is your own essence you are working with here. If you do not feel it thoroughly, you do not know if it is your own essence or not.

If you do not allow yourself to vibrate fully, there is no way in the world to move out that which is going to fill the space where your vibration is being held back. When you try to push on guilt in the outer manifestations you perceive to be present around you, you are not recognizing what is binding it to you. This approach only allows it to be pushed away for a while, and then it returns because of the magnetic draw that is there. This approach has made guilt seem like a plague or a curse that can never be ended.

You have not understood guilt if you feel you have to confront it in some outward scenario and try to make it feel it is not right to have given the reflection it has given and, therefore, it has to get out and no longer try to trouble or rule you. You have to understand that your impotence here is because it is you who have made the space for guilt.

It may look like defeat, or a pulling back, to go inside and vibrate there, but it is really learning to vibrate in such a way that you fill the space you want to have, rather than going out and telling others to move back so you can have more space. It is not always going to be this way, but it is necessary to move within first because of the gaps involved. Once these gaps have been filled in, it will be no problem to move outwardly.

No more guilt in you means the outer guilt reflection will no longer be troubling you. Notice that an impression of this can be given when denials run so deep that the lost Will reflection is not being allowed or not being allowed near you. If this is the case, I am not speaking to you now. I am not speaking to the ones who are still more interesting in patting themselves on the back for how well life is working out for them. I am speaking to those who are finding in themselves an "I cannot win" judgment.

Since outer reality proceeds from consciousness, you need to allow yourself to respond to what is happening "out there", but since the feelings you have toward the outer reflection are ultimately going to be realized as feelings you have toward yourself for your own lack of understanding, and your own feeling of powerlessness to create everything the way your own heart's desire wanted it, you can save yourself a lot of trouble by allowing yourself to move your response in a private place that feel safe. If you are triggered into moving emotion by someone you do not feel to be a part of your own consciousness, if this person seems to embrace things you abhor and are not a part of, then you are not conscious within yourself of the ways in which you harbor these things. The key here is to get conscious in yourself first.

The guilt reflection here is complex. You must understand that My words here are not reason to go around the emotions you have in response to the reflection around you. It has not worked to go toward the reflection with them because the presence of guilt lets you know this is not right. No matter how right you may have felt, you have not been able to prevail this way. When you ignore your feelings, you pressure your Will with your thoughts to accept things you do not really feel like accepting. This reflects outwardly as others being able to pressure you.

Moving these things with yourself is the only approach that has not been fully tried. There is no precedent to show you that it is going to work, but if you are daring enough, you can move along with Me here. You can at least gain the understanding that holding back essence that does not want to be held back does not work because it is unloving toward the essence that gets denied. If it is not loving, then something unloving is going to result as, in fact, it has in the massive reflection of unlovingness on Earth. The massiveness of the reflection will let you know how much unlovingness has been placed against the Will on Earth. It is not possible to move back into the Garden of Eden, or better, without healing the cause of the downfall. The cause of the downfall was denial. Reduced vibration means increased density. If this increased density is not your right place, it does not feel good.

The Will has been denied down into such levels of density that while the Mother once kept up with My Light, She can now barely lift out of Body when Body dies. The feeling that the Will cannot lift into My Light anymore makes the Will feel very trapped.

Every time the Mother found Herself feeling other than the way She thought My Light wanted Her to feel, the Mother feared and felt guilty, as though She was trying to be God in My place by claiming She knew better than I did. Therefore, the Mother has always pressured Herself to align with My Light, no matter how She has felt about it The Mother has believed She deserved punishment for anything She felt that did not agree with My Light, and has even tried to believe punishment would make Her agree with My Light.

The Mother has for so long believed She was not right to oppose Me that the Mother is not sure if She can trust Herself here or not. The Mother has been viewing My Light as not wanting Her to have any feelings of Her own, but to feel and do as I told Her all of the time. The Will has believed She was not loving to have any feelings of wanting it any other way and has had a strong belief that My desire is not the same as the Will's desire for Herself. The Mother is just now ready to realize that many things She thought She was receiving from My Light were not My Light, but the presence of unlovingness instead.

Whenever the Will has deviated from this self-denial, It has been punished and has though My Light sent this punishment because the Will deserved it. The Will, therefore, has a fear of Its own desires and has a dread of feeling anything other than what It thinks It is supposed to feel. This is the effect of the presence of guilt has been having on the Will, and it has reduced the Will's feeling of being able to accept Itself so severely that the Will fears wanting anything, fears hoping It will get what It wants, and fears even allowing Itself to visualize anything It might like to have better than what It has already. Even interpretation of how It feels has become frightening for the Will. The Will has become very superstitious and afraid of making moves or changes. The Will fears It has the Devil to pay if It ever gets what It wants, or does what It wants, and also fears that anything It gets will soon be taken away. The Will is just now ready to realize that these feelings have been coming from the reversal of My Light.

Whenever a Will person who is not moving this guilt out rises in life's circumstances, fear also arises that the improvements will not last long and that every minute that goes by means the moment is coming closer when the great hand of the gap will snap this space shut on It. This fear needs to be allowed to move every time it rears its head.

The Mother has believed that it was not right to have feelings of liking some things more than others because this was judgment and gave the Will the desire to accept, or make space, for some things and not others. The Mother has feared that She was being very unloving here and that to want to reject somethings was a terrible act of unlovingness.

Original Cause here was contact by the Will with that which did not like it that consciousness was stirring and wanted everything to go back to sleep. This was the reading the Will took from the guilt that was already present in My Light. The Mother felt She had to make space for this essence by holding Her vibration back in these places as much as possible. The Mother tried to make Herself indifferent to what happens as a means of doing this, and this served Lucifer.

The more the Mother held back, the more enlarged the presence of guilt became what was pressuring Her to hold back. The more the Mother felt pressured to hold back, the more She felt pressured from the other side by My Light for having no place to receive Me. The Mother became afraid that everything She did was wrong, and this has allowed Her to be so heavily punished.

The Will was so afraid of seeming to judge things in My Light by wanting to make places for some things and not for others that She held back the input I needed to know if these things even were a part of My Light or not. I have since learned from the Mother that these things are not a part of My Light, but what a long, hard lesson it has been. The Mother was so afraid of me in these places that We could not move here for a long time.

The Mother was afraid it was unloving of Her to put anything out, or to want to put anything out because She felt it had been so unloving when She was initially put out. When Her rage would surface that wanted to put all of these things out, She was horrified and denied it very heavily as an unloving part of Herself. Since the Mother had not cleared Her old charge here, She could not clearly see that others would not necessarily have Her experience here. She thought loving acceptance meant making a place with Herself for everything, whether She loved it or not, and blamed Herself for not being more loving. She was blaming Herself for hating the things She hated and pressuring herself to feel otherwise, unable to see that these things would not even notice if She put them out.

Although this is true, I would also like to point out that it is also true that the Mother was not wrong here because Her denied feelings became the lost Will attached to these things in the form of the voices saying it was unloving to put these things out. This is what the Mother was feeling without any way to explain it to Herself, since Will here was not moving to let Her know how it really felt. A place must be made for everything but not necessarily with Us.

Given what She had to go on, the Mother was doing Her best to be loving, but She was so afraid She was unloving that She aligned with Lucifer in having him help Her to get rid of Her feelings and Her desire so that She could become detached and not have preferences.

Lucifer knew, by the reversals he was able to cause against My Light by taking the Mother into this denial, that hatred for desire was easily made into hatred for My Light as causing the desire, and self-hatred in the Mother when She found She always had desire no matter what Lucifer did to Her. The Mother thought She was supposed to sacrifice Her desire to My Light, and when She did this, Lucifer saw I was impotent and without direction.

The Mother did not realize that allowing Her desire to be killed was allowing Herself to be killed, and She did not realize that allowing Herself to be killed was killing Me. The Mother did not realize this because Her loss of consciousness, when She initially fell into space, made Her unable to realize what I had experienced there. Lucifer knew because his consciousness was in the gap.

I had not let the Mother know what I experienced there because I misread Her initially and did not trust Her intent. This distrust between Us allowed Lucifer to come between Us and do his work. Within the Mother, it was only Her rage that knew She was not wrong to want to put some things out in order to keep them from holding Her desire. Her rage could not prevail because of the denials it was receiving. These denials so twisted the rage that it was being turned back on the Mother as self-hatred in the form of others who had killing both Her and My Light in mind.

At the same time, the Will was not allowing Herself to realize the power She had in My Creation. She was unable to recognize that She was in reversal to My Light when She did not allow My Light to come near Her for fear I was going to say everything that was wrong was Her fault. Lucifer pointed this out to the Mother by telling Her She was on an ego trip. He told Her that, just as She was making Herself too important when She thought She had anything to tell My Light about how to right the situation in Creation, She was also making Herself too important when She thought that everything, or even anything that was appearing to be wrong, was, in fact, wrong, or Her fault.

"How can You continue to believe this," he would say, "when You already know that nothing You do really makes any difference?"

When the Mother took this in, it amplified Her fear that She was crazy and could not trust Her own feelings and perceptions.

The Ronalokas also have these feelings about the Mother, and they have believed that because they have these feelings, they deserve to be pushed out of My Creation and punished, instead of being allowed to put anything else out.

Every time you have had an emotional response of wanting to reject anything, guilt has said, "Calm down. God has a purpose for everything, whether it is understood or not."

Because My Light is not present where guilt is, there was nothing to notice, or give understanding to the Will that there must, therefore, also be a purpose for the fear and the anger in the Will.

Opening Space

The Mother was so afraid that Her only power was to oppose Me when She didn't like the position My Light was taking that She was unable to also see that She had power in alignment with My Light. It was much easier for the Mother to see Herself as outside of My Light than to see Herself inside of My Light. Seeing Herself within My Light meant that She was within Me, and that I was within Her. Whenever She experiences this Oneness, She had so much fear of being God that She ran from Me.

When I told the Mother She needed to recognize Her own power, and that Her power was My Light, She ran from Me even more because She was so afraid of what this said about Her. When She ran from Me, She did not see the gap She was opening between Us.

When I pointed this out to Her, She took it as judgment against Her and became even more afraid of Herself and Me. I soon felt I couldn't say anything more to Her on the subject, although I still felt I had to get this across to Her somehow.

What the Mother was struggling with here, She has struggled with for all of Her existence, and it is that She might have called Me into being, in which case, without Her, I do not exist. In the places where I did not feel loving, She feared Me, but She also feared what in Herself might have called this into being.

When I gave Her this to consider by letting Her know I was there, She was so extremely startled to realize that another presence was talking to Her and to realize, simultaneously, that She had been calling for this, that We jumped apart and created a gap. When We tried to come back together, We could not embrace One another entirely. There was a pressure between Us that did not feel good because of what had entered the gap.

We also did not know that the realization of Our presence, in other words, the birth of consciousness of Ourselves, had caused such a sudden increase in Our Light that We felt an immediate pressure that made Us feel We needed more space. Although other things could have been noticed, Our first awareness of One another's presence was a feeling of pressure. When I felt this growing pressure, it felt like the Mother was moving against Me, just as She felt My Light was pressing on Her. When I could stand it no longer, I reacted by pushing on Her without knowing I was going to, or that I even knew how. It seemed that the increasing Light of My increasing self-awareness had simply pushed the Mother out and away from Me. I did not know what this meant and neither did She, but I had intent to get rid of the pressure I was feeling; this much We knew.

Although there is more to the story, this is all I want to mention for now. What you need to gain in understanding here is that the Mother, from the beginning, was opening space in reversal to My Light by going away from Me because I frightened Her into thinking I was something superior to Her.

In the name of the self-denial the Mother thought She had to embrace to be loving and to survive, She has allowed this, and has continued opening space in a state of denial of what She has really been doing here. What She thought was a loving act of humility and servitude toward what She perceived as a superior being who frightened Her, has been killing Me, which is what Her gapped raged wanted to do, even though this was not Her loving intent.

By backing away from Me in fear of Her own power, the Mother has been holding space open for the gap and everything that has gone into it. Neither the Mother, nor the Ronalokas, have understood the power of opening space, or the role of expression of emotions plays in it. They have been opening space in a state of denial of themselves, fearing that to do otherwise would be a sin of pride, ego, and selfishness. Thus, they have not called the God they would like to have into existence.

For so long, the Will has tried to express only the emotions that pleased others, that for just that long, the space that has been opened has been space that pleases others. Any other emotions in the Will have received denial, and so the space opened has been for guilt and denial spirits.

The Mother feels that there is no longer any space open to Her that feels good to Her, or any life She can have that really feels good to Her. To the extent to which the Ronalokas share this with the Mother, none of them have really been able to be happy. The Mother, and all the Will that follows Her, have felt guilty about having feelings of not liking what is happening on Earth and of not being able to find any place where they are really happy, while the space they have been opening has been used, for the most part, by others who give them little or no recognition or appreciation for what the Will has done for them.

One small, but good, example of this is how money made from the music of the Ronalokas is so often taken in by the Warriors with very little ever given back to the ones who made the music. Another good example is that of how many warrior plantation owners made fortunes at the expense of their slaves, while making the Ronalokas feel they should be happy just to be not too ill-treated. There are many more examples I could mention, but these will allow you to move in the direction of finding them.

What needs to happen now is that the Will that can move needs to move guilt out and allow My Light in as never before. Allow yourselves to notice your power and use it to give yourselves love you have never had before and in places you have never given it to yourselves before. Allow the fear to move that says it is not right to think you have the power to call God into manifestation, especially since it has looked like He didn't want to come. I didn't want to come because I didn't like what I felt when I got there because of what you were already holding.

From the overview, it looks very simple: Just vibrate everything so that there is no more space for guilt, and it will then float out to the edge of My Light where it belongs. Here, it will be a good buffer zone by not allowing light and dark to mix together. This is guilt's right place, and it does not mind being there because it has no consciousness to know what its experience is. This is the right understanding, but it is in no way meant to encourage any sensitivity toward the pain of the Will that is involved in doing this. Rather, this statement is meant to be a guide to help the Will understand what needs to happen.

The Will Manifests the Gap

The Will has been so denied and Light has been so withheld from the Will essence in Creation, that when the Ronalokas incarnated into physical presence on Earth, it made their journey so perilous they almost did not survive it, and it made their pain so great that they have preferred to allow themselves to be severed from their origins and to forget their past, rather than to remember in any way that might cause them to have to relive it. The Ronalokas have been reliving their Original Cause anyway, without realizing what has been happening to them, because it is impossible to go past emotions without meeting what they manifest in outer reality.

This experience of the Ronalokas' journey to Earth has resulted in physical incarnation being a real sadness rather than a joy for all spirits to experience because it is really the Will that incarnates. Because of the gap, the Will has had to draw Spirit in later. The spirits in the Heavens have not liked feeling themselves being drawn into physical incarnation on Earth. Most spirits try to stay out of Earth as long as they can between lives, while Will polarized people have found themselves barely able to lift out of their bodies between lives because of the burden of guilt and denial of where their Light should be.

Although what I have been giving here is the experience of the Ronalokas' first journey to Earth, all of you have feelings to move here because all of you had trouble coming to Earth. Even the Angels had intense feelings of compression of their Light which caused them to let go of even more Will than they had lost already.

Whether or not you all experienced as much pain as the Ronalokas, you all have lost Will that has, and you will all have to feel it when the right time comes for healing it. The journey of the Ronalokas into physical incarnation is not that different from the journey of the entire Will Polarity, and all of you have trouble entering physical incarnation without losing much of the consciousness your Spirits have between lives.

Ever since the fall of the Will, the Will has not been able to lift into My Light because the Will is dependent upon being able to draw in My Light for this. The essence that can ascend has been breaking off from the rest at death, as you know, and leaving it. The essence left behind cannot lift Body by Itself. The Will has great guilt about lifting out and abandoning Body at all in this way, but Body has been telling the Will to leave so that Body will not have to feel what is happening anymore.

Will feels blame for and from Body for the pain; Body has blamed Spirit for abandoning Him but has also blamed Will as the reason Spirit leaves. I have blamed Them both for everything I haven't liked about physical incarnation, and the rest of the spirits have followed My example, or at least used My excuses. It has been thought all along that Heart has been able to remain neutral, but this has only been because We have not allowed Ourselves to open to the feelings We have had toward Heart in this area until now.

When Spirit goes to Heaven and Body goes into the ground, Will has had no place to go. For the most part, Will is afraid to go down any further than It is already and has lost the ability to go up. This has left the Will feeling abandoned with no place to go that feels like the right place. This is a kind of Hell for the Will.

When the Spirit breaks off at death, the Will is left to get out of the Body on Its own. Various levels of denial get out of the Body at various speeds, and so the Will is not all together when It leaves the Body either. Spirit has been blamed for leaving, but also for staying and not allowing Will and Body to die. The issues of blame are very intense, and blaming rage must be allowed to move so that the acting out can stop.

Most people want to say they do not believe in ghosts no matter what name they are called by, but there are, indeed, ghosts, and monsters too, in the forms of lost Will that wander Earth feeling lost and abandoned, haunting places that have been familiar, and feeling whatever emotions are able to move. The lost Will that feels blamed is usually split off from the lost Will that blames, just as anger and fear are usually split in individuals. While some of this lost Will is pitiful and harmless, the blaming side us often thoroughly dangerous, unapproachable, and cannot be reasoned with. Do not think you can approach ghosts with a new understanding now. Whatever feelings you have are the feelings you must allow to move to be most able to help lost Will.

Once the Will struggles out of the Body, It is able to gain a little perspective on physical incarnation by being released from Body for a little while, but not much. The more lost It is, the less perspective It is able to gain. Body, meanwhile, does not gain anything during the time of separation from both Spirit and Will.

The Will wanders Earth looking for some place that will accept It. Some very lost pieces have tried to force their way into living bodies to avoid the terror being held about having to be born. If the lost Will essence finds no place, It loses vibratory power and sinks further and further into the Earth. Many pieces of will that are this lost feel desperate when they feel this happening to them. Will people, in general, have very little time between incarnations.

When Will feels magnetically drawn to any place that has acceptance for It, the Will enters into another incarnation. The Will feels guilty about this, because the magnetic attachment means that Will is going to call Body essence back into consciousness when Body usually indicates desire to be left in peace after going through all the pain of dying, and because the Will is going to try to call what has been reluctant Spirit essence back into physical incarnation.

The presence of misunderstanding, judgment, guilt, denial, and resultant lack of alignment has been widening the gap between Spirit-Heart and Will-Body. So much lost Will has been created that Body is living in a heavy state of denial, barely one step ahead of deformity and disease, while Spirit is only able to enter where there are any openings left to receive it. Given the presence of guilt in the Will, there is almost no Spirit presence left on Earth.

When the Will incarnates, It has to try to draw Spirit back into It against Spirit's reluctance to leave the higher planes to which It has been gaining access between lives. Spirit has had great resistance to opening to the Will because it has meant coming back to Earth and experiencing what the Will has been holding. Guilt about this has been closing Will off to letting Spirit know how It feels for fear Spirit won't come at all. Some spirits have been using this guilt in the Will to dictate their terms of entry.

It is the Will that really causes the manifestation of the Spirit, and the reluctance of the Spirit has meant that Spirit has been entering gradually, as the Will pulls Spirit in against the guilt Will has for doing so. This has meant that consciousness unfolds slowly in the incarnating being, is never able to manifest fully because of the gap, and does not last long. Spirit has blamed Its handicaps here on Will and Body, and when Spirit is drawn into manifestation in this manner, it does not take long for Will and Body to receive this message. You can watch this reflection in the ways adults shut down the spontaneous and free expression that children do have in the early stages of their lives. When this happens, the Will cannot vibrate enough to hold the Spirit It has been able to draw in and this allows the Spirit to go, as can be seen in the way people fade as they grow older.

The more lost the Will is, the less Light It is able to draw into Itself to begin with and the less understanding It has, but even in the most brilliant of incarnations on Earth, Spirit Light has not lasted long because of all the problems involved in gaining alignment between Spirit and Will. Many times, the most brilliant light in Earth's history have had early deaths because their Spirits entered by pushing Will's resistance, in the form of the guilt being held, out of the way without feeling what the Will had to move to keep this guilt out of the way.

The result has been that Lost Will was denied and has then returned later, manifesting the gap. This can take form internally as physical problems if held within, or outwardly as another person if pushed out. This lost Will causes the reversal that pushes the Spirit out. Spirit has often rationalized this by saying It wanted to go anyway, but this has not made WIll-Body any happier, and it certainly has not increased the power of Spirit on Earth. In fact, these experiences have made Will-Body increasingly afraid of manifesting Spirit for fear of what will happen.

The gap has gotten everyone, including Jesus, who has tried to move toward My Light without moving what the gap holds. Besides the denials being made while people are alive, the experience of death has been increasing the problems of fragmentation on Earth, because Lost Will has been getting out of Body in pieces and often feels It must incarnate again without having time or even knowing It needs to gather Itself together and gain an alignment. The Will often has not wanted to feel the things within Itself that have become so lost from the Light. Spirit has also been fragmenting this way by losing so much of the Will presence that is necessary to hold It together, but Spirit has been calling this "returning to essence and letting go of identity."

The focus on getting off Earth has been immense among both Spirit and Will people because they have been seeing the problem as Earth rather than the way they have been experiencing Earth. Since the fall of the Will, death had been seen as the doorway to Heaven, but this is not a favored passageway, or there would have been mass suicide long ago. No matter how much spiritual leaders have exhorted the masses to embrace death as the release from their trials and tribulations, the masses of humanity clings to life, even in the face of great misery. The Will has been blamed for this, and the Will has been greatly pressured by Spirit to let go here.

Will, for the most part, hates letting Spirit go unless it can come along. To Will and Body, separation from Spirit means death. Will has usually only let Spirit go when It could no longer stand the pain of Spirit's resistance to staying. The great grief of the Will over the death of a child is because to the Will, this means Spirit has abandoned it before it has had a chance. Guilt has held the Will back from grieving as much as It would like to grieve, and from moving the other feelings involved, but the Will has not been wrong in continuing to feel that It hates the experience of death, or rather, I should say, of dying.

The gap that has been causing this is the gap between Spirit-Heart and Will-Body, and the location of this gap is what has been labelled the lower astral planes. This gap will not be healed until there is a visible stairway to the Heavens that can be ascended by all who want to go there. The stream of Light that must flow from Spirit to Will and back again is this stairway, and this stream of Light must also let the Will-Body Polarity know that Heaven is also going to be wherever It is.

The Ronalokas' journey to Earth was a journey through these lower astral planes. By denying everything We didn't like and shoving it down into the Will and then out of Ourselves, leaving as little Spirit Light there as possible, the lower astral planes have been made a wasteland, strewn with the garbage of Creation. The garbage that has been thrown into the lower chakras is no different in essence than what has been thrown into the lower astral planes. The chakras are the individual's experience here, and the lower astral planes are the Creation of the mass consciousness of all the spirits. It is the micro and the macro. How far you want to extend your consciousness into both of them determines the delineation of the words being used here.

The garbage that is here has been made garbage by the way consciousness has handled it. The garbage that has been thrown into these planes is not nice and cannot be avoided any longer. Responsibility for it must be taken by the ones who have thrown it there. This garbage is nothing more than what everyone has judged to be the darker sides of themselves, and is no different, really, than the pollution crisis on Earth right now. The same sort of thinking is involved, and it is no accident that up until now, it has been the Will Polarity people who have been given the jobs of collecting garbage, cleaning streets, and washing down the bathrooms of the richer, more Spiritually polarized people. In many ways, the Ronalokas' original journey to Earth was like a journey through the sewer system of Creation, and it is not going to be possible to heal the environmental crisis on Earth unless you first clean up the toxic waste dump in the lower astral planes.

The lower astral planes have become so laden with what has been held for so long that they are now precipitating onto Earth. and they stand a good chance of taking Earth over in what looks like an explosion of fermented and very toxic diarrhea. Just as the lower astral planes are full of toxic and suffocating fumes, desperate feelings of nothing to sustain life, terrible noises that leave no one any peace, searing lights that give no peace to the darkness and yet provide no pleasantness by which to really see, extremes of dry and wet, heat and cold, and threats from unseen monsters that seem to want to rip you apart and torture you with every manner of pain that will finally result in your death only if you are lucky, so it is with what is happening on Earth right now. And just because you may have found a pocket of peace you can salvage for yourself right now does not mean it is going to last much longer.

The destruction of the atmosphere, the water, the soil, and the forest is giving those with a Will to feel, the desperate feelings of nothing left to sustain life. The fumes from chemicals and motors, the noises of modern industry and transportation, the streetlights that feel more like spotlights on crime, waiting for the unseen monsters of the darkness to dare an appearance within their scope, the heat waves and extreme winters, the droughts and downpours, and the unseen monsters of disease feeding off of the toxins and the dark, broken places in people who are unable to protect themselves from the destruction these things are causing in their bodies, are all existing in the levels of reality the Ronalokas experienced on their first journey to Earth. The difference between then and now is the magnitude of the problem. It is even worse now, but you are in the numb stage on the way to death.

Those who wanted to ignore it then and say that life always presents challenges, still want to ignore it now and will ignore it until it kills them, because they are the Father Warriors and the so-called, "Spirit Polarity" that never had life in mind even from the very beginning. Numbness is what they want, anything they reflect that looks, sounds, or feels like life, has been given to them by others and is lost Will and/or lost Light.

Whatever does not move now must be allowed to go, because all of this essence has had from the very beginning to notice My Light and the Will of the Mother. In all of the time that I have existed, it has never responded to Me. Those that still think We must give this essence more time are going to be allowed to go with it and find out that I am right here.

Do not think that the present crisis on Earth is finally so terrible that everyone will see and make a strong turnaround. The final hour is their movement of glory, what they have been working toward forever since they first felt My Light pressing life toward them. They have resisted Me, and they have resisted the Mother forever, and I have finally seen it is not their intent to respond to My Light. Any movement you see there that looks like response needs to be considered lost essence seeking to return to those who left it with the Father Warriors or the Fallen

Angels. The lost Will that needs to move here is the Spirits' denied rage toward the Mother for seeming to make It feel like life was pressure and struggle.

The gap between My vision and what is happening on Earth has now become so immense that healing must come, or there will be no way My Light will even be able to reach you anymore. As unmoving, overwhelming, and intimidating as the outward reflection is appearing to be, it is a direct reflection of how intimidating, overwhelming, and thus, denied and unmoving the problem of this lost Will has been within.

Whether you are able to hear and feel your lost Will yet or not, its situation is unbearable, and it must be allowed to move. There is an immense amount of emotion that needs to move now, and all of the pressure against this movement being exerted by society at large is the reflection of the lack of acceptance there has been for these emotions and the intensity with which they have to move. You will get a lot of movement by allowing yourself to notice the feelings you have in response to those who don't think this movement is right.

Unexpressed emotions take form as situations that would normally trigger the withheld emotions to move, but the lack of understanding and acceptance for the emotional body has made what could be a natural healing process almost impossible. The denials involved have been intensifying, and the outer reflection of oppression and compression has also been intensifying, not only for the Ronalokas but for all people. Noticing it is a matter of having enough Will presence to be able to notice it.

Because of the gaps and the fragmentation involved, I have taken the time to give you as much understanding in advance of the experience as I can, but no understanding, no matter how it is given, is going to equal the understanding you will get by moving your lost Will.

The Ronalokas Had Already Gapped Before They Left Me

When I could see that the Ronalokas were going to leave Me, I asked them to return to their original emergence pattern. I had several reasons in mind for this. Not only did I want to see just how they had emerged and try to settle in My mind once and for all whether they were the Mother or not, but I also had the feeling that this was their position of greatest power since it had proven to be so for all of the other spirits. I thought they were going to need all of the power they could get to make the journey to Earth, and so I did not think I was wrong in asking them to restore themselves to their original positions.

The Ronalokas, however, had a different opinion. They argued with Me as much as they could allow themselves to by saying they had something in mind now, and nothing I could do was going to hold them back. They acted like it was a big imposition on their time and preparation for departure that I was requiring them to stop what they were already doing and assemble themselves for some sort of unpleasant inspection.

It was not altogether clear to Me just what they were already so busy doing, but I had the feeling they already were trying to return to their emergence pattern. They were having problems doing this, however, and it seemed to Me it was because they now had many more spirits in their group than they had had when they emerged.

The Ronalokas were very uncomfortable about this and did not want Me to see it. They were trying everything they could to talk Me out of having them return to their emergence pattern. I, on the other hand, was trying to show them that I had love for them, and I was determined not to let anything that might take place here bother Me. I was trying to be a pleasant God and let them know they had nothing to fear. The Ronalokas, of course, already had the twist of witnessing the gap, and so My behavior did not allow them to believe Me. The nicer I tried to be, the more sullen and overcast they became in their anger and the more obsequious in their fear.

The problem here was lost Will fragments, of course, but this was not understood at the time. Then, there was great confusion in the Ronalokas that was not being allowed to surface over what to do about having so many spirits in their ranks who all had insistence that they belonged with the Ronalokas, that they had not emerged since then, and that they did not belong to any other order.

The Ronalokas might have thought this increase meant they were getting popular in some unexpected way, except that they were so afraid I might be getting ready to accuse them of having sex without My permission and of emerging spirits without My permission. Girls who have had to be inspected for virginity before marriage hold some of what the lost Will felt here. None of the Ronalokas wanted to claim any knowledge about the origins of these extra spirits.

It could not even be determined by the communication going on who might be the extra spirits, because all involved claimed to be the original Ronalokas, and all, undercurrently at least, were trying to disown the other contenders to what they claimed as their own particular point of emergence, and each point of emergence had several, and often many, spirits who were all claiming the spot as their own.

It was hard for the Ronalokas to understand themselves or to articulate anything clearly enough to make solutions possible. Their emotional response to everything was intense; much more intense than any of the other spirits. Since the Ronalokas already felt guilty about this, they hardly dared to let their emotions move. The atmosphere around them was fuming with the exhaust of internalized emotions, and it seemed as though no matter what was said, it either was not what was really meant, or claims were made that statements were being wrongly taken or wrongly interpreted.

Without moving the emotions involved, the Ronalokas could not clear their minds and settle the issue to their own satisfaction. They already had so much fear, shame, and guilt about the emotionality they had that pandemonium broke out within them. They tried not to let this show, but their behavior became very erratic, as though they did not have minds with which to function. I allowed this for a little while, but the more I observed what was happening, the more I felt I had to step in.

Although the Ronalokas weren't making much noise outwardly, I had to raise My voice and try several times to get them to hear Me above the ruckus that was going on within them, along with the outer confusion of activity that they were passing off as their attempt to return to their emergence pattern.

I wanted to suggest that together, We merely needed to make a more complex three-dimensional pattern than they were now trying to make. I suggested they might not be remembering correctly how they had emerged, and I was careful not to allude to the presence of too many spirits. The Ronalokas were quick to agree with Me in principle, but when We tried to apply it, most of the Ronalokas did not like the particular groups that wanted to assemble around the various emergence points in the pattern. Although nothing was being said here, they were quick to let Me know that My suggestion had already been thought of, and that this latest effort of theirs was just to let Me know how inapplicable the idea really was, without wanting to seem like they had rejected Me without giving My idea a chance.

The Ronalokas were afraid to argue with Me anymore. They did not know what My intent was, and they were afraid to trust their own perceptions. Perhaps they were being tricked in some way. Perhaps I was going to select the rightful owner of each spot after all, and it might not be them. What would I do with the other spirits? The Ronalokas were also triggered into the fear that they might not be able to remember accurately. The Ronalokas also did not want Me to see that they never, as far as they could remember, had ordered themselves as thoroughly as the other spirits. They had a reactionary kind of pride in this, but they were also afraid of displeasing Me.

Instead of arguing with me, the Ronalokas began arguing amongst themselves. Fear, and all the reasons why the Will Polarity feared it was wrong, took one side of the argument, and anger, and all of the reasons why the Will Polarity believed the problems were everybody else's fault, took the other side of the argument. This argument allowed the deep split in the Ronalokas to become clearly visible to Me, and this is a split that has not healed in them yet. Fear and anger must come together within the individual before it is going to be able to come together outwardly among the people who have polarized themselves toward one side or the other.

The polarization of fear and anger within the Ronalokas became so pronounced that the two sides announced to Me that they could not be near one another in the emergence pattern without having fights break out. The fear fragments were busying themselves trying to please Me when the anger fragments spoke up. The fear fragments were afraid the angry ones were going to get everyone in trouble. The anger fragments felt this as blame, while, meanwhile, feeling it was the fear fragments who brought trouble by acting like they were victims already. The anger fragments hated the way the fear fragments behaved, and the fear fragments didn't much like the behavior of the anger fragments either.

At first, I didn't know how I was going to solve this, but then I noticed a reaction of grief among the Ronalokas to what was going on between the fear and the anger fragments. I finally solved the immediate situation by sandwiching the grief fragments in between the fear and the anger.

The grief that was felt here had a hopelessness in it that the Ronalokas couldn't even come together as a group and have the strength of being united in the face of everyone else's rejection, along with the fear that the Ronalokas could not make anything work right in their lives, but at least the grief was not putting blame on one side or the other.

These deep splits have not yet been resolved in the outer lives of the Ronalokas and cannot be until it is resolved within the Will for those who need to heal now. As a result of the denial of the Will of Creation, the Ronalokas have not been able to have fear and anger fragments come together in the same family without fighting, crisis, and splitting apart. It is not even possible for these poles to meet successfully in a group of friends. When they pass each other on the street, neither side thinks the other has respect for it. If they fight, they are always in different gangs. Rage starts the fight, and the fear fragments feel they have to defend themselves.

Once I began grouping the fear fragments together and the anger fragments together with grief in the middle, I had more success than I had had initially, but it was not long before I had another problem. The Ronalokas with the most light did not like being near the Ronalokas who had less light, and there were many more with less light since the Ronalokas had darkened substantially since their emergence. Their Gold Light was browning out in many places, and there was even a blackness I could not explain at the time. I had an aversion to looking too closely, because the feeling was not good in these places.

The darker ones did not seem to like themselves very well, but they did not let on. Many of them acted like they were angry and did not want to be near the lighter ones. They accused them of trying to have more light in order to please Me, and they even accused them of stealing their light from spirits who were not like them as an attempt to become something else themselves. The dark ones said they were better and even acted arrogantly. On the fear side, it was the same thing, except that the darker ones were holding terror that even the fear fragments didn't want near them.

I tried grouping the darker ones toward the center, but they complained they were being too compressed by the ones on the outside. I tried grouping the lighter ones toward the inside, but they had the same complaint. I finally came up with a rather intricately woven pattern that allowed most of the ones with light to be near others with light while still interspersing the darker ones amongst them. While they were not altogether happy with My arrangement, the Ronalokas finally settled it amongst themselves through a series of looks, telepathic messages and somewhat hidden jabs which served the purpose of conveying the message to everyone that they had better settle down and accept the situation as the best that could be done for now, especially since any more trouble from them might cause Me to look or question more closely.

Since the Ronalokas were not sure what might trigger My gap, they were not eager to make the mistake of finding out by experiencing it. They had held back so much emotion throughout all of this that it felt like they were ready to explode inside. The pressure was greater than any group of people who feel forced to endure a long and mostly meaningless ceremony of some sort while suffering with the nervousness of not knowing what is going to happen at the end of it. No matter what interpretation individual Ronalokas put on it, they all felt desperate to get away from the pressure of My Light to some place where they imagined they would not have to hold back their emotions anymore.

The fact that I had made them make places for all of the spirits who looked to Me like they belonged there in any kind of way made them, at first, feel a little relieved that I wasn't going to eliminate anyone, but rather quickly, they also suspected Me of grouping them together all of the spirits no one else liked and sending them all away together as a means of getting rid of all of the spirits who were not liked in Creation without being honest about My intent.

The Ronalokas already felt they were having to grow up fast, and, basically, parent themselves because they had not received what the other spirits had received from Us. Now they also felt burdened by having to take on and care for so many extra spirits in their group. Many of them felt the group was barely able to hold itself together. The Ronalokas, whose feelings allowed it, did their best to make space for the additional spirits and to help one another, although there was some feeling of being forced to become child-Mothers, without having had the experience that would have resulted in becoming parents.

There was a prevalent feeling among the Ronalokas, no matter what emotions were used to cover it, that not only was there no place for them in Creation, but now there was not even a real place for them amongst their own kind. Children wandering lost or abandoned are a reflection of these feelings, as well as children whose parents are only minimally able, but not adequately able to care for them.

As soon as the Ronalokas were grouped together, the pressure from My Light against so much Will essence that had little openness to receive Me, combined with the internal pressure of held emotion, began moving the Ronalokas away from Me, as though there was a current in the ethers that picked them up and wouldn't let go of them. Their movement accelerated rather quickly, and soon, it was as though they were being swept away from Me.

I almost turned to go back to the Godhead then, but something gave Me the feeling I should not. I had a strong urge to seek My own private place, also in which to feel all of the emotions I had been holding back, but I pressured Myself to stay present and look after the Ronalokas until it seemed they reached Earth. I watched them as long as I could, and then turned toward the Godhead and My own right place.

And so it was that the Ronalokas left Me in the Heavens and went out into the darkness of space. The feeling as a group was not unlike that of "the Little Match Girl" who looks in through the windows upon the warmth and the beauty of the light in the home of a rich person at Christmas time while she has been destined, for reasons she does not understand, to go out into the freezing cold of the dark winter night without any sufficient clothing to keep her warm and nothing but a few little matches she is afraid to light because the moment of relief they might give her means there will be nothing at all left to give her any hope of being able to sustain herself.

Although Spirit polarized people like to lift out of the emotion here by saying she suffered for only a little while and then was lifted to Heaven, this is not true, and has never been true for the Will Polarity that has had to suffer this way.

The grief that many feel over the death of a seemingly innocent and harmless child is the grief the Ronalokas have for themselves and have not found acceptable within themselves to feel yet. The unmitigated depth of this grief is so overwhelming that many even fear it or feel anger toward it because they want it to stop lest they be moved to feel what they fear will kill them.

The Ronalokas felt this fear of death from the beginning, and again, as soon as they noticed the Angels not accepting them as their Wills. When they emerged, many Ronalokas sought the advice of older spirits whom the Ronalokas thought might have sympathy for their position. These older spirits told the Ronalokas that after a long time of hardship and struggle, of being tested in the fire, so to speak, they would be lifted into My Light and would suffer no more.

The problem here was these older spirits knew so little about the Will and Its position in Creation that even though they saw what was going to happen, they didn't convey the right interpretation of it to the Ronalokas. Allow yourselves to notice also that Lucifer has his own interpretation of what this means.

For one thing, these spirits did not let the Ronalokas know what moves they must make to bring this into the present for them, and so this fortune telling, even when it sought to comfort their fear, too often made the Ronalokas feel moves on their part were not necessary. All they had to do was "be good," which was interpreted to mean hold back in the ways they were already trying to do, endure, and wait for My Light to rescue them. In this way, the Ronalokas were further misled into abdicating their power, and that had served Lucifer and not My Light. The Ronalokas must allow themselves to move now, or My promise will continue to remain a future promise until Lucifer takes them in and they find out, as their final shattering, that he is not love.

It is not a loving God who would leave His spirits to suffer so if He could do otherwise, and it was not My intent to have you take this path, but no other way could be found, given the understandings We had then. In the movement of your emotions, you must allow yourselves to notice that much of what you have formerly embraced as God is not. You must let it go now and allow My Light to come in and give you the love and upliftment you need.

The more you move, the more your brothers and sisters all over Earth will feel helped by the increase of Light in the Will. There is nothing more helpful you can do, in fact, than move whatever gets triggered in you. The most possible that can be done for many people is to rescue their essence by making a place of acceptance to take it back where it belongs within yourselves as it leaves them.

You have to know that all of you who are moving now with this material are key parts that have to move now, or you would not be allowing yourselves to notice this material. If you have ego balancing to do around this, allow yourselves to move the emotions that are involved in this also. Movement now is crucial, and the timing is also immensely important.

The Mother must be rescued from the space She has opened for denial of My Light. Those who deny Me must all be shoved in there as soon as the Mother is out of there, but before the space She has opened snaps shut. Not a moment too soon, and not a moment too late. I am poised to do this, but you must all do your parts, or else I will not be able to manifest this, or you will get caught in it without meaning to.

And again, heed My warnings here. Do not think this is just self-aggrandizement, or that there is no problem in getting through the gap without Lucifer noticing this. There is already more problem than you realize. Lucifer has already noticed what is happening with the Mother, and he is going to notice all of you, too.

Protect yourselves by not allowing the public eye to fall upon or pry into what you are doing here. This "Ark" must be built in secret. By the way, it is not a fantasy that Hitler was searching for the Ark of the Covenant. Allow yourselves to notice that the Mother has not been seen or heard from since My gap smacked Her out of Creation. This does not necessarily mean it's wrong or that She is dead.

Use your wits to know the rest of My meaning here, and notice those around you who fight the movement needed now in any kind of subtle way. See what their intent here is and be careful of, in fact, move away from, the ones who have no intent to move along with you now. Let them go and let them release their Wills and give them back to you. Besides being lost Light, they also have lost Will essence that needs to be restored to its right place now.

Meanwhile, I was aware of the child out in the darkness, having been given all of the denials of the Will, but I felt there was nothing I could do other than to put out a little plate of food and see if it was eaten when I was not around, since the child was too afraid to come near Me. I did not know what I had done to frighten Her so much that all the gentleness I could muster now was not enough to win Her trust. I did not allow Myself to notice I was angry with Her for this. I thought I had to win Her love by being more gentle than I had been already. I did not know this only meant more denials that gave Her more problems.

My Heart was in the right place. I did not like it that I had spirits suffering out in the darkness. It was a regrettable situation, but I did not know what more I could do about it or, as some people say now, what it had to do with Me. I believed I had given and was giving as much as I could. So many of the spirits seemed unwilling or unable to receive it, or else what I had given them had gotten away from them somehow or had turned as shabby in their grasp as they were.

I did not like the feeling that My Light was being unappreciated, lost, and mistreated in these ways. I had an almost deliberate intent now not to extend Myself anymore in these ways. In places, I had hardened My Heart by not allowing Myself to feel the situation any more than I had to. I wanted to hide out at home, where I would not have to look at the spirits who claimed to be so unhappy in My Creation. And I must say that all of the spirits seemed to have hardened their hearts toward Me from the reverse position of not wanting to have to look at My Light because of how uncomfortable It made them feel.

"Fine," part of Me thought. "If that's the way they want it, that's the way they're going to have it."

Part of Me continued to project My image of perfection as necessary, in part of Me, I held anger, and in the rest of Me, I grieved and feared and searched for the answers I am giving to you now.

You Have Gaps to Heal With One Another

I have since moved even the feelings that seemed cold then and have seen how much I really loved the Will and how much I was using anger to cover My own feelings of being hurt by the Mother. The Mother was so frightened of My seeming lack of love for Her that She did not try very hard to question Me here. The truth of the matter was that the Mother could not gain audience with Me regarding these matters, because I did not have intent to allow it. I was too afraid of what She might have to say to Me, but I did not know it then.

I had asked Her to make up Her mind between the Father of Manifestation and Me because I did not see how We could go on in a love triangle so full of tension that love seemed to be turning to hate. I viewed it as a bleed-off of My creative energy to be so constantly entangled in emotional turmoil. I wanted it solved! And yet, I didn't want it solved, because I was afraid the Mother might not make the decision I wanted Her to make.

The longer She put off coming to Me with her decision, the more it appeared to Me that She was avoiding coming to Me and choosing to be with the Father of Manifestation, or even worse, Lucifer. I felt that not coming to Me was Her decision and that I had no choice but to protect Myself accordingly. Never mind that I didn't notice I lacked the courage, Myself, to check out My perceptions here. I remained stuck in the feeling that I could not trust the Mother to tell Me the truth anyway.

Meanwhile, no matter what motions the Mother seemed to be going through, She could not really move toward alignment with either one of Us because of the guilt She then felt about the feelings She had involved with the other One. It was a "no-win" situation for the Mother as well as for the Ronalokas, who not who not only lost consciousness when they moved away from My Light, but lost presence with the Father of Manifestation as well. It was also a "no-win" situation for everyone else.

In My vision, I had seen the spirits swimming in the ethers. All of their bodies were open in ways that could be likened to the presence of gills, or of so many flower petals, fanning the ethers in and out from head to toe. Sustained by the ethers, the spirits swam to and fro, going toward and embracing what appealed to them and swimming away from what repelled them.

The flow of the ethers in and out nourished the spirits, who took in the essence around them, felt it for what it was, and put it back out if they didn't like it. I did not see how the spirits would not do this if they were given Freewill. I liked Freewill, and this was what I had in mind for the spirits. It seemed to Me the easiest and most natural of ways, and I did not like any of the pictures where this had not worked out well for all of the spirits involved. I had not embraced these images, and I did not think I was creating from them.

When it did not always happen that the spirits moved toward what pleased them and away from what did not please them, I noticed that they were moving according to what they thought would please others, especially Me. I was puzzled, but I did not see the role of guilt. I did My best to encourage the spirits to please themselves, but they seemed unable to understand Me here and claimed they were already doing that.

Often, I then saw them trying to do what they thought I thought was best for them, even more than they had done before. In My puzzlement here, I came up with all manner of reasons for this mostly blaming everyone and everything but Myself. I thought Heart and I were exonerated, because We had gone over My plan so carefully and had found no flaws in it. I thought the rest of Creation had more to learn than I first thought and most of the blame fell upon the Mother for allowing what was supposed to have been Freewill to become such a game of entanglement.

I punished the Mother many times in My imagination for making such a mess of My Creation, as though She had done it on purpose as some sort of act of anger against Me. I assumed She was mostly motivated by possessiveness and jealousy and everything else I labeled as negative. As part of the punishment, I allowed Myself to rob Her, without allowing Myself to know that I was actually doing this, of Her power to reach Me with any of this. Besides acting aloof and like I didn't care what She did, nor what happened to Her, I robbed Her of most of Her power by deciding that everything I liked about the Will was My Will and the rest of it was Hers.

Thus, everything I didn't like became lost Will. Therefore, the feelings you have in the Will Polarity of not having been loved by My Light, of not having been helped by My Light, of having to stand by and watch all of the other spirits being helped by My Light while you were made to feel that it was your own fault you did not receive help, the feeling I did not have time for you, the terror of feeling you had manifested in the presence of a God who did not love you but who had power over your lives, along with all the feelings of having this happen because you deserved it in some way you could not determine, and finally, the feelings of rage and hatred toward Me, are all real and valid feelings that are going to have to move because these things happened to you.

As a result, you have had experiences that no other spirits have had. As you discover what these things are, you will also have to gain movement in the feelings of shame that make you want to hide these feelings and these experiences from others for fear of what these things say about you and of what other spirits will think of you.

You have sexual guilt that is more immense than any of the other spirits because of the way you were born, and this needs to move also by finding out how much sexual essence you have in a state of denial. You are going to have to do this by allowing yourselves to move any emotion you feel has presence during your lovemaking, whether you feel it is a big one at first or not.

In My vision, the free flow of feelings was supposed to move all of these things so that the healing I am having to bring to you now would never even have become necessary, but the role of guilt was immensely misseen and has to be allowed to move out now by gaining the trust of someone you love to finally be able to move whatever emotion you need to move. This is not going to be easy, given the gaps and fragmentation involved. So, if you have to change patterns, allow it rather than continually pressuring the ones already near you to move with this if they are not already really moved from within themselves to do so.

What may have, at first, seemed to be love to you may turn out to be a guilt reflection, which you will become able to realize as you move along. Sometimes, partners have subconscious agreements to hold one another back in order to avoid certain emotions. This is guilt, allowing you to reduce your vibration in favor of another, and as you grow past these limitations in yourself, you will grow past them in another. It is not always just movement in yourself that has the final effect on outer reality. All you have to do is move all you can do it with yourself, and if this is not enough to move the ones around you, move yourself away from them.

The movement you need within must be allowed first, however, or your attempts to move out of situations will find you repeating them again in another form. It is almost impossible to know in advance what movement is going to be necessary once you get moving with this material, but if you are doing your best and you have no one else around you to help you, allow yourself to seek different people.

This might even include writing to the publisher *Please send a SELF-ADDRESSED STAMPED ENVELOPE and expressing your desire to get connected up, in some way, with other people who are working seriously with this material. You might be amazed at some of the ways you will be able to open to one another here.

Healing the lost Will needs much more help than healing the denied, but still present, Will addressed in the *Right Use of Will*. It is not right to run to someone with every little thing that wants to move. This can quickly become another pattern of avoidance and dependency, but the real issues of helping one another heal this can be greatly facilitated by group energy.

And a group is what you are going to have to allow yourselves to have now, no matter how many fears you have to go through that you cannot come together without the effort having the effect of putting you even more apart than if you hadn't even tried. No matter how great your fear of being rejected, or of having to reject someone else, the movement necessary in the emotional body around the issue of a group being able to come together and move through with the love and Freewill I initially envisioned has to be allowed through the effort of trying to come together. No matter how many people move back and do not stay, you must still go on being true to your own feelings, or you will never find the love you are seeking.

If you do not move what needs to move, you will continue to be born in the dark and suffocating, compressing terror of the Ronalokas' first journey to Earth, struggling all of your life not to allow yourself to notice how you really feel, surrounded by people who do not love you but who reflect only the guilt that does not let you move to breathe and expand toward your real self.

Body Will Let You Know How You Need to Move

The Ronalokas, especially, need to expand within themselves now by finding the lost essence that needs to expand and fill the places that have become hard and dense within their bodies. The Ronalokas started out as Light Beings, born in the Heavens of the Mother and Father of Manifestation. By the time they got to Earth, they had been born again as a bunch of little half-dead babies who could not even cry at first. They had been compressed from Light Bodies into little dense physical creatures who had experienced compression so great that their gill-like openness had retreated up toward their heads and back inside a bony structure that their bodies' resistance to being snuffed out had pressured into existence there. They had a dense and bony structure all over within them that was a result of their resistance to being squashed by the pressure that was coming in on them. Their struggle to hold up against it had given them backbone and legs, even though their legs had gone out from under them and lost the power to support them.

The Heart openness they had had, had given up almost entirely and had shrunk back inside the petal-like gills, or lungs, seeking also the protection of the bony structure. The Heart flow was only moving now in certain set channels that were also protected from direct openness. The lower parts of the Body weren't able to fan the ethers anymore, and they couldn't receive help from the lungs unless Heart could bring it down to them. The lower parts of the Body already realized they needed more nourishment than what Heart was bringing to them, and they were already seeking other forms of nourishment. Unable to bring anything much at all back up through Heart as their bodies had originally been designed to do, the lower parts of their bodies had to seek other venues of release for what needed to move out of them.

The Will essence, which had begun as the most sensitive essence in Creation, was now almost unable to feel enough to regain consciousness of Itself. Without a Mother to nurture them, it looked doubtful that the Ronalokas would be able to last long at all. The Ronalokas had been born on Earth like a bunch of babies from Heaven, but the experience of it was one of infants who had such a struggle being born that their continued existence was threatened.

I Withdraw

Meanwhile, I was like a tired father who could not see the delivery through. As though I were the One exhausted by the length of the labor, I returned to My own place with an intense longing to go inside Myself and escape what was happening.

The Angels gathered around Me like siblings who weren't sure they wanted any other born into the family. I was trapped by My own guilt. They did not inquire about the Ronalokas or the Mother. They did not ask Me anything, but they had a projected feeling of gaiety that did not seem appropriate to Me, given the immense problems with which I was faced. I tried to pass it off at the time as the Angels only wanting to welcome Me home as usual, and also, as usual, trying to impress Me with how upbeat they could be compared to the Mother, but underneath, it was as though I could feel that they were glad the Ronalokas were gone and that they hoped they were gone for good, never to trouble Us again.

Their relief seemed to be so immense, I even found Myself wondering if, despite never seeing them emerge spirits, the Angels had somehow been the Mothers of these "things," and wanted their bodies discarded so that I would never find out. I disregarded this as a bizarre thought since I already had knowledge that the Ronalokas were the Will Polarity of these spirits. I did not like having these kinds of thoughts, but then, I did not like so much of what I was noticing that I had a feeling of not wanting to be conscious anymore, or at least not as conscious as I was.

I was suddenly and thoroughly angry at the Mother for not allowing Me to have the place I had wanted on Earth. I had envisioned Earth as being a place I could go when I wanted to slow down to the point of being unconscious or almost unconscious. When the Mother's terror of slowing down that much resisted Me on the way to Earth, only part of Me had been in the mood to play with Her here. The rest of Me, as I was finding now, had wanted to smack Her right then and there, and force Her to get over Her fears of allowing Us to rest.

Now I had no place to go to escape Myself. In My rage, it seemed to Me the Mother did not want to allow Me to have what I needed, always seeing it as shorting Her needs. Selfish was the word I applied to it. She didn't want Me to go down into rest, and She didn't want Me to go up into more activity. It was as though staying the same all of the time was the only thing that suited Her.

As I sought to make Myself comfortable, guilt was on Me, telling Me I was a very self-centered God who sought only to help Himself rather than helping those around Him.

I wanted to go inside Myself, as far inside Myself as I could get. I wanted to escape the outer turmoil all around Me and see if there was any peace and strength left to be found within Me, but I couldn't do it. I couldn't even move to go inside Myself. Guilt had taken its toll already and left Me wrestling between the needs of the outer and the needs of the inner.

Not only that, but the moment I looked within, I discovered the turmoil was within Me also. I really felt like I had no place to go then. I slumped in My throne and stared, as though looking out over Creation, but I was not really seeing anything. I saw as though I did not know if I was awake or dreaming. I was unable to relax and almost unable to move. I stared vacantly out over Creation while many things welled up inside of Me, things I thought I had gotten rid of when the Mother left Me. I was flooded with thoughts and feelings I did not want to have.

The sounds and movements I did allow Myself to make, I disguised as annoyance over not being able to get comfortable, but I suppressed even these expressions as much as I could. Even this little amount of expression made Me feel paranoid that I was having the feelings that made Me express this discomfort because God's place was no longer My right place. And so there I sat, squirming around, uncomfortably on My throne, and yet, riveted to it as though I could not give My place up either.

Everything was so far away from the way I had envisioned it that I wondered again if I had been right to go ahead and manifest Creation. I indulged Myself in another bout of blaming the Father of Manifestation and the Mother of Everything. It seemed so impossible to attain the balance I saw as necessary to sustain Creation that I wondered if I might not have liked it better if I had resisted the temptation to create. I wondered how much the Mother's and the Father of Manifestation's imbalances were going to cost Me in terms of lost manifesting power. Their power did not seem to be as great as Mine, and yet I kept blaming Them as though it was. I felt so angry at not having Creation the way I had envisioned it that I had a moment of wanting to destroy Them both for having caused it and of wanting to destroy Creation and start over again, if and when I ever felt like it.

I tried not to let any of the spirits know what I was feeling and thinking here, and as far as I could tell, they did not notice. How could I allow open expression to these thoughts and feelings in the presence of spirits who would feel their very lives being threatened by Me? Besides, I had only to look in the faces of the spirits when I felt like destroying everything to feel that I could not really allow Myself to do it. I really believed it was more loving to work through these feelings internally than to express them openly toward loved ones who might be hurt by them.

I did My best to feel Myself here because I did not think it was wise to push these feelings away anymore either. I was already suspecting that the Mother was reflecting everything I didn't like about Myself, but I didn't know what would move these things in Her or in Me. All I knew was that She didn't like Me for a long list of reasons, such a long list of reasons that I wasn't able to stay present for Her presentations of all the many reasons, and that no matter how much I tried to change, it didn't move Her. She seemed to have an unending supply of reasons, old and new, as to why what I did did not please Her. I had the feeling She had to give in now. I had done My best to please Her, and if it wasn't good enough, She would have to bend or let go of Me so I could find another Will.

I was mad just to find Myself thinking about Her again, fuming mad, like She was some kind of demon I could not exorcise. I felt She had hurt Me enough, which was a big reason why I did not want to hurt others the way She had hurt Me. She hurt Me all the time by not receiving Me and giving Me the vote of confidence I needed to feel good about Myself. As I tried to make Myself look pleasant on the outside while allowing Myself to fume within, the Angels were still busying themselves around Me, as if to say everything was fine, and they were just welcoming Me home as usual.

Everything was not fine. Lots of the Angels were missing. The others were acting like they weren't allowing themselves to notice it or even as though they liked it better because there was now more space for them to be near Me. Many of them were acting like My Light should rev up with them now and give the increase to them that would fill the space left by the others. I was not sure how I felt about it. I did not really miss the Angels who were gone, and I had not allowed Myself to notice what had happened to them yet. I didn't mention them, and neither did the rest of the Angels. They were hovering around Me trying to please Me by anticipating My every need and trying to do whatever might make Me feel better.

Most of the Angels around Me were Mother contenders, and they were all trying to please Me by acting out the images of the Mother they had embraced as the ones they thought I loved most I could see these images as their thought projections hovering around them. Whenever they did something that did not seem to please Me, I could see them adjusting their images and proceeding accordingly, as though the master plan for Mothering was being constantly evolved in this way.

It did not feel suffocating to be hovered over by these Angels, and I must say that it did feel good to get so much attention all at once, and positive attention that was not making an assault on My presence with its immediate needs. I began to come around. My turmoil had been soothed enough that I was able to focus on the Angels around Me and notice what they were doing. They were making Me feel good. I had not allowed Myself to feel good for such a long time, and no wonder. I had been feeling continually nagged by the guilt that I had a crisis in My Creation and that I had to move outwardly to help, instead of allowing Myself to sit, rest, and be indulged.

Despite guilt's nagging, I could no longer move. I kept feeling like I should be doing something else, but I could not make Myself move to do it. I felt exhausted. Even so, I feared it was not right to sit with just a few of the spirits when so many needed Me. Then I would flip around like I was talking to Myself and say that I wasn't so sure the spirits needed Me at all, since all My attempts to help them had added up to nothing.

No matter how much I told this nagging to go away, and no matter how much I wanted to hold it responsible for My discomfort, I soon had to realize it was My Heart that would not stop bothering Me.

Heart Tries to Warn Me That He Cannot Stay Manifest

Heart seemed desperate for help and lovemaking was not the solution He wanted to have. He said My Light was so seriously imbalanced He was having trouble holding Creation together.

I already knew what He was going to say next: "The Mother has to come back, or the balance cannot be found."

I felt like I did not want to hear this from Heart. I was too exhausted, hurt, and mad to want to have to think about the Mother anymore. I tried to put Heart off, like a man getting a massage and wanting to dispense with distractions as quickly as possible.

"Heart," I said, "once again I am going to tell You. The Mother left Me, and there is nothing I can do to make Her come back."

Heart always met This with, "Go after Her," which I did not feel ready to do.

"How can I go after Her when I do not even know where She is?"

"Look around for Her," Heart said.

"I cannot send My Light out if It is not going to be received," I told Heart. "The Mother does not love Me anymore. She has Warriors who seek My destruction. I do not trust Her anymore. I cannot be a fool and go shining My way into Her camp when it looks like Her plans are to try to kill Me."

"She cannot kill You," Heart said.

"Oh yes She can," I reminded Heart. "Don't You remember how much Light I lost when She left before?"

"She didn't leave. You pushed Her out," Heart reminded Me.

"All the worse," I told Heart, "because it seems like She is trying to get even with Me for that."

"She is not lost the way You think She is," Heart told Me.

At this, I told Heart that if He was so concerned about the Mother and the balance She had to offer Us, maybe He should go and look for Her. And then I proceeded to remind Him of all the times and ways I had tried to get balance with the Mother and failed. Heart grew more desperate.

"She doesn't want balance with Me anymore," I told Heart. "She is moving against Me. She opposes Me on almost every issue there is, and You want Me to go and find Her, as though now is going to be any different than all the times in the past."

"It is different," Heart told Me, "I can hear Her crying."

"She's always crying over one thing or another," I told Heart, "What makes You think this time is any different?"

"It feels like She is grief stricken and desperate," Heart told Me.

"Good," I told Heart, "that is what She needs to feel. Maybe She will come around and find Me."

"She cannot move from where She is," Heart told Me.

"If She has lost the power to move, then She has lost the power to be with Me," I told Heart. "Her lack of movement is the very thing I can't stand!"

"It was Her movement that made You reject Her the first time." Heart said.

"That's what I mean," I told Heart. "She either moves too much or not enough when balance is what I need."

"Is balance just what pleases You?" Heart asked Me. "I'm not pleased with the balance You think You have found without the Mother. I'm having a hard time, being out here without the Mother."

I told Heart He was just being melodramatic here because the Manifested Spirits would not receive Him. I told Him He should just stay with Me and all would be will if He gave it more time.

Heart told Me He could not move either. He could not move toward the Mother because there was no openness to receive Him there, and He could not move any closer to My Light because I was not taking Him in either.

I told Heart I would take Him in anytime He wanted Me to, but that I had thought He liked it better out in Manifestation than with My Light.

Heart told Me it was the Mother in Him I was not letting in.

I suggested to Heart that He ask the Father of Manifestation to go and look for the Mother if Heart felt it was so necessary to find Her, because She still had love for the Father of Manifestation. I told Heart I would take Him in anytime He wanted to let go of the Mother and let Her be free to decide whether She wanted to be with Us or not.

Heart did not like Me here, but He said nothing. He felt like the child of a divorce who could come home to the Father only if He did not come in bringing His resemblance to the Mother along with Him.

'The Father of Manifestation does have desire to go and look for the Mother," Heart told Me, "but He also doesn't want to do anything more to widen the rift between the Two of You."

"What rift?" I said to Heart. "I never quarrel with Him when He is with Me, only when the Mother comes between Us. It appears the quarrel is with the Mother. Now that She is gone, there should be no quarrel between Us."

"That's what the Father of Manifestation fears," Heart said, "that All of Us are against Her, and that anytime We take Her side, We cannot get near You because of the split between the Two of You. He wants to look for the Mother, but He doesn't want to lose His ability to be with You."

"He has already lost it in that He doesn't come to Me anymore. What difference is it going to make if He goes out a little farther than He already is?"

Heart did not answer Me here, other than to ask Me to let the Father of Manifestation know directly that I requested He look for the Mother.

"You have to let Him know," I told Heart, "You are the One with the big desire to find Her."

Heart was hurt by this, and He let Me know in no uncertain terms that His authority alone was not enough to make the Father of Manifestation go and look for the Mother. I allowed My Light to lift the Father of Manifestation up then, although I had some shame about letting Him notice everything that was going on between Myself and the Angels. I asked Him if he wanted to go and look for the Mother. Without speaking, He indicated to Me that He had mixed feelings. "It looks to Me like You are miserable without Her," I told Him.

The Father of Manifestation felt He could not be honest in the face of My Light no matter which way He went. He squirmed a little and then said, "Yes, but I was also miserable when I was with Her."

"Not all of the time," I reminded Him, as if I couldn't resist making a little jab. I was actually trying to take the opportunity to sound out the Father of Manifestation on His feelings toward the Mother, but He was feeling much too cautious for Me to find out much, and so I let Him go with nothing much changed between Us.

"If You are miserable without Her and miserable with Her, it makes no difference to Me if You find Her or not, but Heart wants You to."

The Father of Manifestation did not know whether to take this as any sort of declaration of love for the Mother on My part or not, but He did allow Himself to notice that My Light looked better to Him at the thought of finding the Mother than it had looked to Him for a long time. This caused Him to decide that when He felt He had the opportunity, He would go in search of the Mother. None of us knew then what a long time it would be before He found Her.

Heart, meanwhile, tried to let Me know more about the problems He was having holding, Creation together, and I had to take Him seriously here, but I also had to let Him know that there was nothing I really felt I could do. I realized then that I had not allowed Myself to give My rage to the Father of Manifestation for having manifested the Creation all wrong. I seemed to feel like giving Him these things when He was not around and then found that I had gone blank in those areas when He was around. Heart did not like the blankness He was getting from Me either, but with all the hold emotion, I could do no better.

"Oh, Well," I told Myself. "I don't know what good it would do to give Him my rage anyway. What's been done is done. What really needs to happen now is for Him to fix it. It can't possibly do any good to rage at Him," I told Myself, "If we have a fight, it will really frighten everyone around Us."

The Mother Tears My Heart Apart

I allowed Myself to notice then that Heart was having real trouble. I felt like I was having a Heart attack. I was twisting and turning in My chair as though I were going crazy inside, but I was making very little outward sound except for a little gagging and coughing and some struggling to speak sounds. I was consumed by My inner feelings and felt I had to get in there immediately in order to save My own life.

I felt immediate distrust, as though the Mother had found some new way to attack Me, especially, when I looked out and saw Her Warriors repeating the motions over and over of stabbing Me in the Heart. They were angry, and it looked like they had My death in mind. I had the sensation of so many snakes striking Me in the Heart now that I didn't think I had any chance to make it unless I managed to get them off of Me and put them as far from Me as I could.

I was struggling, not unlike the Ronalokas, only I didn't know it. I must have looked like a madman, trying to throw snakes off of Me that no one else could see. They certainly weren't present with Me there in the Godhead, but within Me, it was as real as if they were. I viewed it as a battle I must win, and I struggled with all My might. I lost My ability to feel Heart, the presence of venom was so great. I was overwhelmed by a feeling of having been poisoned all over Me, and I gagged and choked on the strangling feelings of having snakes gripping Me and striking Me all over with the feeling of hatred that wanted Me to die.

I did not get the message that all they wanted was for My Light to open and receive them, and they did not give it. It was as though they expected Me to get the message from the way they were behaving, but I did not, and I did not like it that they had the feeling of hatred that wanted Me dead. I knew I could not allow Myself to be killed, no matter what I might think of Myself at times.

I kicked and fought and thrust until all of the Mother Warriors were falling toward the Earth, and there was not one left that I could find anywhere near My Light. They were all falling to Earth with the judgment against themselves that expressing their rage does no good, and that I will not allow Myself to receive this approach. Meanwhile, this had been an unpremeditated attack that had come as reaction to My denial of the Mother through Heart, and so they also received judgment in the form of imprint that they could not allow themselves to trust their real feelings because their response was judged to be unacceptable and only caused them more trouble.

An understanding that is needed here is that true response has to be given in all situations in order to avoid guilt, but once guilt has a grip on you, you must learn to be true to yourself first and not move outwardly until you have as much alignment within as possible. When you do move outwardly, you must give your true response as much as possible because anything else deprives the Will of the feedback necessary to move properly and also deprives Spirit of the ability to guide properly. If feelings come up later, after the outward event has already gone past you, allow them to move then, and gain understanding as to why they have become that gapped from your spontaneity.

You also need to know that even though I mentioned turning the tables around as a way to see understandings, there are also situations where this will not work. For example, you have always thought that because it feels so bad to be hated, allowing yourselves to hate was not loving, but it is not wrong to hate that which hates you. True response is you cannot love that which hates you. For example, some spirits may express hatred for Me, and I may feel like old charge is moving and coming to a loving place. Other spirits may express hatred toward Me, and I may feel like it is not going anyplace. I may want to move them back and let them live out their hatred for Me where it is not going to affect Me. It does not always work to say that because I allowed some to move their hatred for Me near Me, it's only fair to allow others to do it. What may bring understanding in some situations may be only guilt in others.

No question about it, this is very tricky ground to try to walk on. No matter how I word it, it is possible to corrupt it into denial and guilt. This is why you must not make a rule of anything, but instead allow your true feelings. If you are too guilty to allow your true feelings, you must not judge the guilt to be wrong. You must allow the guilt to hold you back until you have worked with your own vibration enough to alter the reflection you would otherwise receive.

I am able to allow the Mother Warriors to come near Me now and give the reflection they have needed to give. I have been able to do this without feeling like I had to fight off the attack of overwhelming numbers of venomous serpents, and I have learned that the Mother Warriors are the Kundalini by which Will returns to Spirit. Without them, I cannot get the full circle of Light with the Will that I need. I can allow the Kundalini up now because I am not denying the Will the way I was in the past, but if Spirit has an attitude of Will denial while saying It does not, and allows the Kundalini up toward the Heart in those circumstances, it can be very dangerous and even killing.

The Mother Warriors do not like to let anything go past them that contains denial, be it ever so subtle a form of denial, but guilt has held them back and down, even causing them to accept the belief that the Kundalini must be carefully controlled and disciplined because of the potentially killing energy it has.

The Mother Warriors arrived on Earth after having the Golden Red Light of the Kundalini squashed and compressed by the denials placed against it. The form they had when they reached Earth was that of the physical form snakes now have on Earth, only many of them were much larger in the Land of Pan and able to communicate with the rest of the spirits more easily because there was less fragmentation than there is now.

The Mother Warriors were less ready to accept themselves as part of My Light then than they are now so none of them then had the human forms that many of them have now. Even so, there is still so much Will denial that much of the Mother Warrior essence is still left trapped in the forms of snakes on Earth. The more snakes have been hated, hunted, and killed on Earth, the more this essence had had to find other forms to inhabit, but this does not mean that snakes are to become protected now or venerated any more than they already have been by those who have recognized the Kundalini energy in them. It means that Will denial must be healed so that the Kundalini energy can take its right place. The Kundalini energy is meant to have the fiery golden glow of passion shimmering in all the colors of the Rainbow as it passes up through the chakras ignited by a halo of White Light as it contacts My Light at the top.

I had a struggle that cost Me Light as well as Will energy here. I had to go inside and meet Heart there, but I was unable to meet Heart all the way with My consciousness because of His great pain. I had a feeling Heart was losing His ability to remain manifest in Creation, and I needed to look out and see what was happening there.

I had gotten a grip on Myself, but no calm yet. The Angels were hovering over Me like Mothers tending the sick. There was no mention of the possibility I might cease to exist as God, and yet, everyone was gathered around Me like family at the bed of a dying man. It was being said that it was impossible I might cease to exist as God. It was being said that I still had plenty of strength left in My Light. Everything positive that could be said was being said, but there was another feeling present that I denied in My struggle to make it through what My Heart was experiencing. I felt there were still spirits near Me who would have liked to see Me go, and they seemed all too ready to take My place.

Although I did not notice their reflection at the time, I had another attack of feeling I hadn't been right to proclaim Myself God. At least, I was not the God I had envisioned Myself to be as it looked now. I felt overwhelmed and did not even want to allow others to know it for fear it meant, all the more, that I was not adequate to be God. I did not like allowing My insecurities to be seen. I denied them heavily all along, which meant that the Mother got these feelings and reflected them constantly while I denied them by saying they were Her feelings and not Mine.

"She lacked confidence in Me. She was afraid of Our power. She felt wrong to claim Her mate was God and so forth."

I almost never allowed the Mother to reflect to Me in ways that could let Me know these were My feelings She had to reflect. If you are not ready to see your own reflection in the Will, you are not ready to understand Me as God or even yourselves yet.

I hesitate to mention it, but lost Will has a lot to move around the issue of who is God, because everyone has images, even if the images insist I do not exist. For lost Will, I have not existed for so long now that it is impossible not to go through these places on the way to finding the Light they need.

My fears were so great this time that I thought My extreme discomfort meant that what I had thought was My right place not My right place, so much so that I actually fell from My place to the space just down in front of it, and writhed and twisted for a while there before regaining enough consciousness to return to My place.

Given the situation, this was a very dangerous thing to have happen, but as it turned out, none of the spirits gathered around made a move to take My place. I saw it as fear of what the others might do if they did. They had no plan for such a situation because none of them had admitted to anyone else that they had taking My place in mind, but many plans have been made since then.

I made better contact with Heart when I regained a little more of My consciousness. He had come home alright, but He looked almost totally torn apart and severely weakened. Heart was in such bad shape that I had to take strong and immediate action. As I saw it then, I had to rejuvenate Heart as fast as I could and help Him recover.

It did not enter My mind that it would be helpful to Heart to run around looking for His lost pieces. I did not see this as a way to help Him recover, and as it turned out, it would not have been at the time. I felt I did not have time to look for Them anyway. I had My hands full already. Heart had fragmented severely, and the farther from Him His fragments fell, the less like Him They looked. We were a long time in recognizing Them as a result.

I knew this about Heart's fragments because I looked out at Manifestation to see what Heart had experienced. I was shocked. Manifestation looked like a mess. It looked like chaos similar to the War in the Heavens, only this time, it was more like a bomb had gone off than that there had been a battle. There were spirits of every kind falling in pieces toward Earth. It seemed like Earth had become a dark hole in space sucking up everything that wasn't able to hold on to My Light. I had the terrible feeling it was not right, and that there was nothing I could do about it.

I was so shocked by what I saw that I shut down to it. I let go of all My feelings because I could not stand to hold on to them. I cut Myself off from all feelings of desire, or even thoughts, that Manifestation might make it. I turned toward the idea that all I had left was what was there in the Heavens with Me, and that I was lucky to have that.

I had Heart within Me, desperate for help, and I was there with almost no feelings at all about what was happening. I just concentrated on pouring Light into Heart, as though both of Our lives depended on it. I was not aware of allowing My Light to have any thought, but I was aware of being surrounded by White Light Spirits trying to help Me like a staff in a hospital emergency room. I was doing a cardiac revival, and they were assisting Me.

"It's alright," they kept telling Me over and over. "Heart is going to be alright. What's happening had to happen because all the warning signs were ignored. It's not Heart's fault. He tried everything He could, and He could not get through to the Manifested Spirits. You tried everything You could. We all tried everything We could. Nothing more could have been done. Everything that could have been done was done. The Mother did not provide the balance necessary. The Father of Manifestation did not help Heart when He asked Him to help get the Mother more aligned with Us. The Father of Manifestation could not get the Manifested Spirits to receive Us. The Manifested Spirits had to move back. They were too clumped up. They never expanded and accepted moving out into manifestation. They never relaxed and accepted what was happening as what was meant to happen. They needed more space. They had to give Us more space. They had to move back because Our Light was too much for them. It's their own resistance to what had to happen that has caused all this pain and confusion. They had to go because they followed the Mother. It will all calm down soon."

I did not allow Myself to notice how I was feeling. I just made these spirits move back and give Me some peace and quiet in which to work on Heart. When I look back on it now, I see that all they were saying was designed to make a focus on the positive view of Us immediately, and not leave space for the expression of any other feelings about what was happening. Now I would simply yell, "Shut up," and allow Myself to move rage and terror. Then, I simply moved them back and went on with My desperate attempt to revive Heart.

It did seem right that the Will had to move back and give Us space to expand. It did seem right that the Rainbow Spirits needed to move out into space and fill in between My Light and the Will, but I did not like the manner in which it was happening. All the way along, it seemed like the resistance to the expansion of My Light and to the unfolding of My plan was immense. I had such great rage at being pressured that I did not notice how I was also afraid of letting My Light expand so far and so fast.

All I could see was that I did not like anything the Mother did. She either gave Me too little space, and did not move back when I wanted Her to, or She gave Me too much space and moved back all at once. I was so furious over this I shut down to it. I could not stand feeling so impotent, as though the Mother was getting some kind of perverse joy out of making Me a failure by making it look like I was alternately too much or not enough, but never right.

I was either overbearing or inadequate. I was either overpowering or not powerful enough. I was either too much, at which point She told Me I was making a big deal out of Myself, or I wasn't enough, at which point She told Me I wasn't good enough for the job. I never had the Mother's love, acceptance, and approval for what I was, and now Heart had become another victim of lack of Mother love. She had accused Him of having all the same flaws I had. No wonder He felt attacked! It wasn't possible to live with a Mother like that. With all of Her emotional turmoil stabbing at Him like that, trying to get at Me, it's a wonder He lasted as long as He did!

As much as the Angels were reflecting the positive pep talk I was actually giving Myself, I also had another dialogue going on that was blaming the Mother and the Father of Manifestation for the troubles Heart and I were having now. It went like this:

"If only the Mother hadn't led Me into Manifestation so quickly. If only She could be less impulsive and more reasonable. Then She could have listened to Our plan, and We would have been able to do it right. Then She would not have had all of these reasons to fear and neither would I. She fears because She doesn't understand, and yet, She won't let Me explain anything to Her. I have been as patient as I can be, but this is just too much. This is really all Her fault, even Her enticement of the Father of Manifestation. He never acts like His gonads control Him in My presence. It's the Mother who is always calling Him forth sexually. All We need to do is get rid of Her and We'll have the peace and quiet We need to fix this mess. I can't let Her tear My Heart apart, tear My Creation apart, tear the Manifested Spirits apart, maim, dismember, and maybe even kill as wanton acts of revenge against My Light without doing anything to Her. I hate Her for what She has done to Me and to My Creation. To Hell with Her! If She suffers there forever, it will be too short a time for Me!"

Then I started in on the Father of Manifestation, and although My denouncement of Him was shorter, it was not lacking in intensity.

"He's My man unless there's a woman around; then He can't be trusted at all. Where is He now? Probably chasing after the Mother because He was 'told to' rather than being able to see that the need for Him is here and now. He's no brother to Me. He has running away with the Mother in mind, and that's all He's about. He's making Me look like a fool who cannot keep His Creation together when He is the One who has really made it impossible for Me here. Let Him go to Earth and see how He likes it there. I'm not going to let Him have the Mother and line up against Me with Her. I don't want Him near Me anymore! Let Him be cursed and let Him live out His sins as a mortal among mortals."

This blaming of others went on for a long time. Giving My rage expression like that gave Me the drive I needed to be able to go on without having to feel the paralyzing feelings of being overwhelmed and powerless to do anything about it. Even when this shifted to feeling I had only Myself to blame because I had not moved to change My life in any way that could have averted this disaster, I still viewed it in terms of having to overcome what had happened to Me because of the Mother. I was sure Manifestation would not have been the problem it was if the Mother had not always been stirring up the emotions She was. She should have given the positive side more opportunity to influence Her.

I had feelings now that Freewill was not right. Perhaps it should not have been granted in advance of the experience necessary to understand it. I certainly had become less and less of a God the more I had believed it was not right to allow Myself to exert My power over others and had allowed them to do as they wished. In all My visions, I never thought the spirits would choose to use Freewill to override themselves. It certainly seemed that allowing everyone to do as they wished was making the alignment I saw as necessary, impossible.

I wanted to allow the feelings, but they were not supposed to be the feelings I was having. I was caught in the trap of feeling that I could not allow My true feelings because My true feelings were not loving, but I said it was the Mother who was not loving.

As a result, there was nothing I could do except project Myself as being loving by allowing only what I had defined as "loving" to express. In order to do this in the face of what was happening now, I had to rationalize everything to preserve My own self-image, which I had confused with My own existence.

I felt I could not live through what was coming out into the open here, and so I did not want to allow it to happen. I was quite sure it meant I was not supposed to be God, and I was so ashamed of My attachment to this role and of My feelings of insecurity here that I did not allow them. My denial here was so vehement that "heresy" was the label applied by lost Will to any efforts to question or approach this area.

Although the extent of My insecurities ran so deep that I am just now allowing these denials to come forward in these stories, I am also ready to say that moving along with Me means being willing to see that these stories are true and being unwilling to live in the world of false images anymore.

I, Myself, can no longer stand the false images I entered into them. As you look at Me as I was then in light of what I have already told you now, you will not like Me there either. It was true, I was all of the things you are going to feel about Me now, but I was also overwhelmed and feeling like I could not cope without the alignment I needed with My Own Four Parts. I was doing the best I could with what I knew and had no one to go ahead of Me and give Me the benefit of their experience.

I had no one to get the answers from but Myself, and without manifesting a Creation, I had no way to gain the experience necessary to gain the understandings I needed, but this is just another rationalization unless you move all the emotions you need to move to feel you no longer hate Me for what has happened to you, any more than you need to hate yourselves anymore for not being able to do any better with your own realities than you did.

It is a great responsibility to have realized that My Light has to move first, or you cannot move. Then, I rationalized the problems in Creation by saying the Manifested Spirits could not be expected to learn everything as quickly as We did in the Godhead or even in the same ways, and avoided My fear that taking responsibility for everything was too much of an ego trip, even for God.

"Their experiences must be right for them, or they would not be having them," We said. While this was true, this was not all there was to it.

To take a wider view would have meant going into what I was avoiding, and I did not feel encouraged to do that. Every time I even looked at this area in Myself, I drew the reflection of spirits all around Me who seemed to view themselves as very superior to me, and all too ready to take My job if they were given any opportunity to do so.

I regretted having allowed My Will to get so far out of hand before I moved to do anything about Her. I did not think it was a good reflection that in all of My struggling with Her, I had not managed to get the Mother to align with Me, but I felt like I could not even allow Myself to mention Her. Mentioning Her seemed to be blaming Her in a way that gave Her power. I didn't want to make it seem that She had or that I even thought She had. It seemed that all I needed to do was think of the Mother, and I would find Myself surrounded by spirits who acted superior because they had no struggle with their Will presence.

I looked around at the spirits who were drawing themselves up as so superior to Me. As much as the Rainbow Spirits had looked too compressed and squat to Me, these spirits looked too elongated and lacking in substance. I hesitate to mention this now, but it was almost nothing but guilt that kept Me from pushing these Angels away from Me also guilt and fear that there would be no one left, and I would be all alone again.

I didn't have much hope for the Manifested Spirits, but as I looked around the Heavens, I didn't have much hope for the spirits who were left there either. They had gathered themselves around Me like family gathered around a patriarch who might not live, and when they found Me becoming more consciously present with them again, they began moving to return to their normal activities.

Another Look At The Angels

How long I had been, as I just described to you, I did not know, and I did not want to ask, lest it indicate some loss of consciousness on My part. I simply began responding to the spirits gathered around Me, subtly at first, as though I had just allowed Myself to retreat from them and was not returning to moving outwardly.

I was embarrassed about the struggle I was having, and I did not know I had fallen from My place. The Angels had their own reasons for letting this all pass by as quickly as possible. The Angels who had replacing the Mother in mind were hovering around Me, of course, and now that I looked conscious, they began offering up the littler Angels as though I were a father being allowed to kiss the children before they were taken off to their rooms and put to bed for the night. I was lying back now, and the impression they were conveying to the littler Angels was that they were not to bother Father tonight because He was in such need of rest that He was already in bed ahead of the children.

The smaller Angels did their best to present Me with just what they were expected to present, but they were not the merry and bright little creatures they had once been. I pulled them close to Me, and We shared some much-needed moments of grief and comfort. It gave Me perhaps the most comfort of all to feel close to some spirits for a few moments who still felt rather innocent, when so much of the time, I was now a God whose spirits had either become too frightened of Him to come close anymore or were engaged in a power struggle with Him.

These little Angels gave Me much reassurance that they loved Me, and they almost dared to tell Me how much they loved and missed the Mother, but they were unable to get it out because they were not sure I had receptivity to them here.

"Mother," was all they could say, and I did not seek to make them say more. I felt I already knew the feelings they had, and I had permitted them to cry in My arms for quite some time. I certainly hadn't wanted the spirits to feel a lack of maternal love and warmth in their lives or to experience the grief of the loss of a Mother. I stopped short, however, of saying anything about trying to get the Mother to come back, because I was not sure She was really the kind of Mother I wanted them to have or that She had been giving them the kind of Mothering I wanted them to have.

As though My thoughts were their cue to show Me how attuned they were to My needs, the Mother contenders began fluttering around Us as though they did not want to allow Our grief to suggest that they were not capable of Mothering the spirits in ways that were better than what their actual Mother had been doing. They acted like they wanted to remove the littler Angels from My presence as soon as possible. Within moments, they could not resist doing so, as though a token goodnight was all they had in mind to allow here, because bedtime was supposed to fit into an image they already had of how it would be best facilitated. They shepherded the littler Angels away, telling them not to trouble their Father, but to tell them anything that was bothering them instead.

I noticed that the concern in these Mother contenders was not for what the children were feeling. It was all about the Father and how He was going to like what the children were feeling. These Angels made Me feel they were more interested in the acting out of emotions rather than allowing themselves or anyone else to actually have any. Over and over, they were acting out the appearance of emotional expression I had liked in the past. If any emotion did start to arise that they thought I might not like or that I had not liked in the past, they quickly attempted to divert its expression into some form they thought I would like, such as shepherding the littler Angels away now.

The truth of the matter was I did not really want to be bothered right then, but that was mostly because I had so much lost Will that had not moved in so long that I no longer knew what felt good to Me. Nonetheless, there was something about their anticipation of My needs that really bothered Me. It was almost like they didn't want to allow Me to have any feelings except the one of how much better it would be to have one of them as a Mother replacement.

It seemed to Me that in truth, the Angels weren't any better able to move than I was. They were doing their best to give Me the impression that they had no problems, but to Me, it was as though We had all become frozen in time and space, unable to move out of the situation We were in.

Now that the Mother contenders had taken the littler Angels away, I was left with "My staff", who had appointed themselves like watchdogs to make sure I didn't make a move without them knowing about it. The feeling was such that if I had had a body that needed to crap, they would have tried to sit in on it.

I noticed now that there was one Angel who had not participated in anything the other Angels were doing. Even now, she sat at the edge of things, giving the impression she was pouting. At first, I allowed Myself to think she had grief, but when I looked more closely, I could

see that she was trying to manipulate Me with her pouting. She had
the impression that the Mother used emotion to gain power over Me,
and she was trying to do the same thing. She had gaining the Mother's
position in mind, but She did not want to make a move toward Me
because My Light was supposed to recognize her so there would be no
doubt in anyone's mind that she was the replacement for the Mother.
She wanted Me to call her to My side, make love to her, and let her
know that she was the Mother for Me.

I recognized this Angel as the one who felt she had the greatest
claim on the role of the Mother, largely because she regarded herself as
having almost emerged the Father Warriors. She felt she had earned the
position of Mother, as though love could be earned by being the best at
doing whatever pleased the person whose love was being sought.

I must allow Myself to say this pleased Me more then than it does
now, but even then, I did not like the feeling of undercurrent pressure
she was applying. All of the Mother contenders pretended they were
not pressuring Me to select them, or competing with one another for
the position of Mother, but they all were. When I looked into it later, I
found deadly denials here. The lost Will involved has engaged in all
kinds of political intrigue, even murdering many sometimes in the effort
to gain access to the position of first lady in various power structures on
Earth. I have Lost Will involvement here also in the form of sometimes.
enjoying watching Myself being fought over without acknowledging I
was even aware of it.

What was going on in the Godhead was very indirect. It was a game
of Will pitted against Will while pretending We did not have any Will
presence other than that which was most pleasant. We never allowed
Ourselves to show the behavior of the Manifested Spirits, which We
found so appalling and unevolved. We always treated One another with
the greatest respect. Our undercurrents were showing up in the lower
astral planes where We could claim they were only nightmares that had
nothing to do with Us. This has been acted out on Earth many times as
the difference between the palace by day and the palace by night.

The game of indirectness was being played by the Angel, who was
pouting, although not as subtly as by the others. She was almost openly
insisting that I recognize her, in fact, and much to her annoyance, I
passed her by. I was not ready to select another Mother, given the
experience I had the first time, but I allowed "Mothers" to happen to
Me by not being direct. There have been many Angels over time who
have allowed themselves to believe that I allowed them to have the role
of Divine Mother. They have always wanted to be called the Divine

Mother. They have always wanted to be called the Divine Mother instead of the Mother of Everything because they have never wanted to be called Mother of the spirits who displeased Me. I also allowed these Angels to feel they had My love many times more than the Mother of Everything because it was easier to go to them than to face what I had to face with the Mother.

This time, I allowed Myself to be indirect by pretending I did not know why this Angel was pouting and hanging around. I told her that her grief was not necessary anymore now that everyone knew I was not going away from them, and that there certainly must be something else She could do with her time. She allowed herself to think I had lovemaking in mind since she did, and when I did not like her approach here, she blamed Me for My indirectness without seeing her own. It has been this way with the Angels all the way along, blaming others without seeing their own involvement. You will find that denied guilt has this in common.

I looked past this Angel then, as a way of dismissing her, and everywhere I looked, I saw more problems. I feared I couldn't see anything in a positive light anymore. I had a moment of panic. The entire Angelic vibration was looking weak to Me, and My Light did not appear to be filling in the gaps left by the Angels who were missing from the Heavens. The pouting Angel saw My moment of panic and assumed that she had the right answer; lovemaking was necessary.

She had the right answer in form, but lovemaking has to be with someone you love in that way, and in the time when you feel like loving in that way. Need fulfillment is not wrong, but the more it is just need-fulfillment, the more the presence of Love is reduced proportionately. The Light generated is not fully loving Light if It is generated from need without also the loving desire to fill the need. Many heirs to thrones, and so forth, have been conceived this way, and no problem has been as great for them as the problem of lovelessness in their lives.

Marriages between people based on agreements made by themselves or others because they are best suited to positively influence one another's lives, according to all outward forms, have origins here, and yet, this does not mean that this is the form marriage should take, even though several religions have embraced this approach as the means by which the turmoil and mistakes of emotional selection can be avoided. Love is said to grow in these marriages, and sometimes it does, but often, it is just a habit pattern of relating to one another that is missed when the partners go apart; no footsteps in the house at night, and that sort of thing.

Attachments are what these arrangements are, and guilt and power are most of what is being called love here. Letting go of attachments and moving along is necessary if real love is going to be found. Agreements and attachments, or strings, do not need to be formed when love is found because love is seeking to have the relationship without need of any agreements or attachments to force it.

The fact that I never formally married the Mother of Everything in a ceremony or made a formal declaration of Our relationship in front of all the spirits, who came after Her relationship with Me, I might add, does not make Her any less the Mother. All of the Angels have wanted to have ceremonies with Me where We would declare Our intent toward One another. Some of My Lost Will has participated in these ceremonies, only to find out that the form of them became empty later on when the feelings did not remain the same as they were at the time of the ceremony.

Lucifer has also gotten involved here by holding people to agreements when it profited him and making sure they felt their agreements and attachments were wrong when it did not profit him.

Wherever Lucifer has found the Will attached to My Light, he has made the Will feel wrong for having these attachments, as though the Will was not allowing the Light to be free. Attachments made because love cannot let go are different than attachments made for purposes of profit, gain, and manipulation, although Lucifer has turned it around in people's minds. Even though most of you are going to say you know this already, you are going to be amazed to find out what is really going on in your lives when you move more lost Will and find your hatred for the opposite sex.

As I looked around then, I saw almost nothing but attachment to My Light. Whatever their reasons were, the Angels were all clinging to Me. They all appeared to be mirroring Me in whatever way they thought would please Me most. When I was having thoughts of wishing I had not manifested Creation, they moved as close to Me as they could, and it seemed as though they had lost the desire and/or the power to remain manifest.

When I was feeling like My side of family had strength, and it was all the Mother's fault We had such a mess in Creation, the Angels moved toward the masculine side of themselves. I could see they felt stronger to themselves here and more like Me, but as soon as I began feeling like they were lacking some of the pleasing quality that had come from the earlier softness in their light, I saw that they began drifting toward their feminine sides.

If they felt I was looking at them as Mother contenders, they began expressing what they had seen Me praise as the feminine attributes. If they perceived Me to be looking at them as more of a friend, they began expressing what I had praised as masculine attributes. They did not seem to think I could just be friends with a femininely polarized Angel.

At times, it appeared they did not notice what was happening to them when they shifted from one side of themselves to another. At other times, it appeared they were allowing this to happen to them because they thought it pleased Me, and at other times, it appeared that they saw Me as imposing this on them for My own purposes. In fact, most of the Angels were uncomfortable about the idea of having to make a gender choice at all. They viewed it as a limitation they did not want to have and actually seemed to prefer moving back and forth.

I allowed this most of the time, but I also had a feeling that something wasn't right about it. It was as though there was nothing real about what the Angels were doing. I felt like I was being given the performance they thought I wanted to have, rather than a real-life activity.

All the Angels were polarized to My Light, especially now, with so much of the Will presence gone. They were always asking me what to do, as though pleasing Me was all they had in mind, but in the denied feelings I had then, I found they were not pleasing Me. Nothing they did seemed appropriate, even when I gave them detailed instructions. I was very annoyed to recognize the Mother in Myself here, and so I did not allow Myself to notice it then.

If I felt they were pressing in too closely upon Me, they began finding excuses to move back, but not much. They did not mention that I had a need for them to move back. The name of the game here was perfect attunement without having to mention needs or give emotional response because there was a desire not to allow any Will presence to manifest. This meant things must not be allowed to get to the point of emotional expression because this would be making space in the Godhead for the Mother's return. The Angels, therefore, moved back by seeming to realize they had something else to do that was taking them farther away from Me.

Any time, however, that they moved a little too far away to feel as involved in what was happening as they wanted to be, they moved in closer, saying they had something to do which required them to be closer to Me. If I had feelings of having problems, they appointed themselves to counsel Me in the positive vibration. If they found themselves in a situation in which they felt unsure of what to do, they referred to their images of what had been done in the past in similar situations and adapted this to the present as best they could.

The Angels kept repeating over and over things which had pleased Me in the past, as though there was no new input that could be given and no new needs I might have. While the feminine side was busy anticipating the needs I might have now based on needs I had in the past, the masculine side was presenting the reflection of not having any needs because the God in them was self-fulfilled. It was very hard for Me to accept anything from them because of the reflection they were giving of not needing anything from Me in return.

At times, I preferred the masculine side because it seemed to be more free and less involved with needs. At other times, I felt I did have needs that I wanted met. I then preferred the feminine side, because there was more attempt to meet My needs, even if there was also more entanglement and manipulation involved in the meetings of My needs. But no matter which side of themselves the Angels presented to Me, this was still another place where I could not find the balance I sought. No matter which side the Angels presented to Me, they were not receiving Me, because they were too busy giving Me their image of giving and telling Me they needed nothing from Me in return.

Once I allowed Myself to really notice this, I did not feel received even by the Angels anymore. Everything they gave me felt like it had strings attached that said things like, "My Light is superior to You because You need from Me," or "This latest gift should certainly mean that I have earned the place of the Mother." And yet, My Light was going someplace.

I had always thought of the Angels as My closest friends, and I made many excuses for them here, but I felt uncomfortable, and I had a feeling that it was impossible to get even these spirits to act natural and be comfortable around Me. As soon as I would have such thought, the Angels began posturing comfortable relaxation.

Part of Me felt despair over this, part of Me knew the Mother must be found and restored to Her right place, no matter what troubles I had had with Her, part of Me did not allow Myself to notice what was going on here, and part of Me embraced the search that has led to the healing unfolding now. Though there are other things I could also list, I must admit that part of Me began to play with this reflection the Angels were giving Me to see how far it would go.

Giving The Angels What They Need

I have now gone as far as I want to go with this Willessness in the Angels. I have gone into this in every aspect of Myself, and I now have a "bone to pick" with the Spirit Polarity, and I must be allowed to pick it.

If you were so conscious in Me from the very beginning, as you say you were, if you were so conscious within Me that you are the same as Me, if you were so conscious within Me that you understand Me as well as you want to say you do, then why did you emerge without your Wills? Why are you still stuck in My original mistakes with the Will? Why did you not move along with Me and make the moves to embrace your Wills and find the balance that would produce Heart? Why are you still stuck in My original bad intent toward the Will?

If you have nothing to learn from Me because you are Me already, how can you be Me already and be resistant to My Light? If you have self-acceptance for being Me already, then My Light cannot be resistant to Itself. If you do not think you are resistant to My Light, then tell Me why you are not moving along with Me. You have not moved since My original bad intent toward the Will in the First Creation. If you are as conscious as you say you are, then why did you consciously polarize to my denials and shun the rest?

If you really believe everyone makes their own choices and creates their own reality, as you so much like to say when you are looking out upon those less fortunate than you and feeling superior in the choices you have made, then why did you choose to align with My denials instead of with My Light? If you are really lagging that far behind in your ability to understand the difference between denial and love, you are not Me or equal to My Light the way you say you are.

You cannot have it both ways anymore. You cannot say you are My Light and that you have experienced everything I have experienced and understood everything I have understood, and then say you emerged without your Wills because you didn't know any better and that you did the best you could but were just too frightened of your Wills to be able to emerge with them. You have always blamed the Mother here and have never noticed anything else about Her. You judged the Will was the negative in Creation, and you judged the negative as Evil, and you have made these judgments against the Will, apparently, in advance of experiencing the Will.

As much as you have at times said you move in response to Me, you don't really. You only give that appearance when it suits your purposes. Actually, you reverse Me. As much as you have hated and blamed the Mother as the reason you never loved your own Wills, you have tried to deny Her, and yet, you have always moved in response to Her, negative response. You project yourselves as positive-positive when you are actually negative-negative.

You have been all too happy to let Me cast you in the roles of My children when this absolved you from responsibility you did not want to take. You have also turned around then and had no problem saying you were My equals and not My children at all when you wanted to have My power. You have, thus, tried to have My power without taking responsibility for it. This I can no longer allow. You cannot claim to be the Me that originates everything and then refuse to take the accompanying responsibility.

When it has suited you, you have shunned responsibility by claiming to be a child of Mine, which is a way of saying you are following Me and can't be expected to already know what I know. This would have been alright if you had been real in this, but you have also turned around and claimed responsibility only for the things you have liked about Me and claimed not to be involved with the rest, which is a way of saying you are superior to My Light because you don't have any of the negativity or unconsciousness that I had. You have been saying you are My Light while also claiming to be following Me and claiming also to be superior to Me. I can no longer allow you to claim to be My Light when it suits you and claim you are not My Light when that suits you, whether it's because you are childlike and, therefore, not responsible, or superior to Me and, therefore, not responsible.

You have thought being a child meant privileges and being superior to Me meant that you should be God in My place, but never have you been able to be what I am. Yet, you have proclaimed yourselves fit to say what is God and what is not God, and you have played God in My place on Earth. You have your own reflection to face now in the form of what the Father Warriors have done in place of My Light on Earth. And you have to realize that what they have done, you have done also. I cannot make you God in My place because I don't like what you have done. My Light originates everything, and in that you are My Light, but just as Lucifer omits, you do also. You say you are My Light, but you do not mention you are My Light in reversal.

The problem is, you do not even know how negative you are in your attempt to insist you are only positive. You are always undercurrently negative unless there is alignment with the denials you have taken in, but if anyone goes overt in response to your negativity, you say to them, "Why are you always so negative?" The Will has never gotten any place with you because you have never admitted to having the negativity the Will is responding to.

You were there when I pushed the Will to Her death in the First Creation. You saw the pain and fear in the Mother that made Her unable to polarize from Me in the Second Creation. You saw what I had to go through to get her to come forth again. You shared with Me in all of My understandings and misunderstandings, you shared in all of the planning for Creation, and you knew what the master plan was. It was not like you had no example to go by. It was not ignorance on your part. At that time, I was giving you all the information I had. I shared everything with you in the beginning, and I shared it freely; too freely, in fact, because I had the Mother telling Me that it was not right to tell you everything I knew.

I denied the Mother here, but I later realized She said this because She could see that you were not using this information as I had intended you would, but were, instead, using it to align against Her. Later, when you emerged, this was translated into to telling the children everything for their own good and for Ours, lest they make mistakes with power they were not ready to have, but We thought it was more a matter of protecting the children than Ourselves by withholding some information. This was not wrong, although Our guilt about this in the face of your claims to be my equals did not let Us see what you were really doing here, and why We were right in not helping you more than We did.

We were telling Ourselves your moves were coming from lack of experience and lack of understanding, and judging against the part of Ourselves that saw it differently. When you reflected this to Us by saying We were not right to view you as children from whom We should withhold information, We judged Ourselves for having feelings of superiority toward you and gave you more information than We would have otherwise. This only worsened Our situation and made Us feel all the more like it is not right for parents to let the children know everything they are doing.

As soon as We felt We were acting superior toward you by withholding information as though We had the right to decide whether you should have it or not, you would be there reflecting whether you should have it or not, you would be there reflecting judgment and superiority toward Us. We would make the mistake of saying, "This does not feel good. It must not feel good when We do it to them," and We would try all the harder to equalize everything again. Then something would laugh at Us like We were fools.

We did not understand for a long time the unseen role denial was playing here. Instead, we pressured Ourselves to be more open and did not understand it when the reflection We got was one of you being less open to receive Us. When We questioned you about this, you would say, "We are not receptive to Your Light. We are Your Light."

You were present with Us when the Mother and I had Our times of loving and of finding balance before you were born. You were there within Me at Heart's emergence. You knew what His emergence meant. If you wanted to focus on the positive, why didn't you focus on that? When it was time for your own emergence, We counseled you within Us. We told you all We knew about polarizing from your own Wills. We cautioned you heavily against pushing on them too hard and gave you every help We could to help you gain the balance necessary to polarize without a gap.

The Ronalokas were all lined up to emerge with you, and you gave them your full assurance that you would only push on them as much as was necessary and that you would listen to them and be responsive to what they were experiencing. The Mother was in labor, Heart, Body, and I were a highly attuned delivery team, ready and able to take the time and give the attention necessary. We wanted to provide the best circumstances We possibly could for the birth of the Angels.

You had given Us the fullest agreement I thought it was possible to have that your Wills would be allowed to polarize away from you as they could handle it, thus, opening space for the rest of Creation to unfold in the most loving and balanced way possible, and without the gap that would endanger Its existence. Then, at the last minute, as though you knew moving quickly and catching Us off guard would not allow Us to prevent it, you used your Wills long enough to get yourselves emerged and then, suddenly and without warning, all pushed them away at once.

You had to have had a secret agreement among yourselves, or you could not have done it the way you did, but you all immediately claimed it had been some sort of a reflex action from fear that you didn't intend, and over which you had had no control, thus blaming Will and Body here. I believed this for a long time, in spite of the fact that you never went after your Wills or made any attempt to heal this with them, other than the tokenism I have spoken of already.

If you really understood what the Mother meant to Me before you were born, if you really understood the balance it took to bring Heart forth and hold Him present, why did you use your consciousness to reverse this? You say you are love, but you have never made the moves necessary to manifest your own hearts.

I say you had intent to do as you have from the very beginning when you saw what happened to the Will and what happened to My Creation when the Will's connection to Spirit was broken. You have sought ever since your emergence to finish the job you started then by severing all connection the Mother ever had to My Light. I have seen this now, although the Mother told Me long ago, and I could not stand to accept that information. My mind was so stunned by what the Mother told Me here that it entered into denial.

I was so stunned, My denials allowed Me to believe you when you said you were not meant to move out on your own because you were Me, just allowing differentiation of form so that I could have the pleasure of experiencing Myself through you. Well, let Me tell you, it has been no pleasure. It has been more like imprisonment in a suffocating ring of denial and guilt that would not move back to allow the expansion of My Light, because expansion of My consciousness might allow Me to find out what you were really doing.

The Will Polarity had already experienced the Mother's terror in the First and Second Creation, and they were already imprinted internally with the Mother's experience of going back on Herself. They had no Light to come into them if they did emerge because their own Spirits had rejected them. There was no place being made for them at their master's table. They had lost so much consciousness from having the Light of Spirit taken away from them that they could not realize how to move to help themselves here without help from Me, which I am now giving them. They must allow themselves to let you go and to let go of your puppets, the Father Warriors, who were sent in later by you as substitute Spirits who were supposed to finish them off when you realized later that your Wills were not gone but had been taken in by the Mother and saved. In your plan, Lucifer was supposed to kill the Mother while the Father Warriors killed your Wills.

Once you pushed your Wills away, they could not be coaxed out. The birth of your Wills, finally, so much later than expected, resulted more from pressure from the Mother who could not hold them anymore than from the draw of a place having been made for them. The Mother also felt, despite all I told Her about having to hold the Will Polarity until I could make the Angels ready to receive it, that She had to manifest some help at Her end, or She would not be able to hold space open for Creation much longer. She already could not hold Herself together under the great strain of the imbalances denial was creating.

When the Mother and the Father of Manifestation finally emerged the Will Polarity much later, they could not be born in a place of Light, warmth, and expectation. They emerged away from everyone they thought could hurt them, like illegitimate children born of a Mother who has to hide what is happening to her, or like the young animals who are so heavily preyed upon they must be born in a dark, still, and hidden place, lest they be immediately hunted down and killed.

Even so, the Father Warriors picked up their scent and poured forth on their trail as soon as they could, without even realizing they had emerged. They tried to kill the Ronalokas in the War in the Heavens, but My Light and the Mother Warriors would not allow it. Thereafter, the Father Warriors, or the Angels who pull their strings, I should say, decided they would have to be more subtle and less blatant about what they were doing.

The Father Warriors then pounced on the Ronalokas, like Lucifer had on the Mother, and began the usage of the Ronalokas as their surrogate Wills, taking them always down into more denial. Thus, the Father Warriors have always acted out your denials in your plan to kill your Wills, just as Lucifer has acted out My denials by trying to kill the Mother. There is one difference here that I must mention now, and that is that you saw My denials as My intent and My intent as My denials. You have gotten it exactly backwards and very consciously, as you, yourselves say.

Many times, you saw Lucifer leap on the Mother like a predator on prey, and you made no moves to help Her. Instead, you studied his moves very carefully and instructed the Father Warriors in their usage. This is why I say that what I have done in a state of denial, you have done from your conscious intent. When I talk about healing My denials, I cannot include you. I cannot heal My denials without moving you out of My Light. I cannot reverse My denials in the presence of conscious intent to reverse My Light. Your reversals are not My denials. You are, in fact, a conscious intent that is not My intent, and, therefore, not Me or My Light. You are conscious in My gap and unconscious to My Light. You fed on and learned from everything in My gap and denied My Light.

If it was not your conscious intent to deny your Wills, why didn't you recognize them when they finally did emerge? Why did you do nothing but deny them further, using the excuse that they weren't your Wills? You pretended you didn't recognize them, but you were perfectly able to instruct the Father Warriors in how to recognize them and in how to kill them. You have been doing this, even in your roles as spiritual leadership on Earth, for a long time.

You have thought you were more conscious than Me because I did not notice what I was doing, or what you were doing, while you did notice and used these things for what you thought was your own power gain. You do not understand power. All the Will you have denied is going to move now and call a different Spirit presence into manifestation. This time, it is going to embrace the Light of Love, and there will be no place left for you except that space which the Mother has opened in reversal to My Light.

All of this time, you have thought the Mother opposed Me, the Mother and I already knew it would have this appearance while She was opening the space in which We were going to have to put you. Once My original bad intent manifested as Lucifer and the Angels followed his lead instead of Mine, We knew, although I could not also let you know that I knew, that the Mother, as awful for Her as We perceived it was going to be, had no alternative but to go and open a place to put you.

Meanwhile, I tried all the other means I knew to get through to you in case there was any other means by which to solve this. In all of this time, no other means has appeared, and you have not moved within yourselves. Now you have to go because your puppets, the Father Warriors, have developed the means to use nuclear energy to destroy the entire Earth, and, as if that is not enough, they have developed all manner of backup methods designed to affect only the Will, or magnetic energy, in this Creation.

I have nothing more to say to you except that it is not possible to get My Light to change position here. I am already moving toward getting rid of you. All you have the power to do now is wait while the Mother gets Herself out of the Hell I am going to put you in. Hell, I want to add, is much worse than anything We had been able to perceive about it beforehand. And you thought the denial spirits were all those other folks.

The deception has been good, so good that none of you realized it was the Angels themselves, who were the denial spirits. You bought what they handed out, right? That they were the first, the best, the wisest, and the oldest, besides being the most favored by My Light. Alright, I handed it out also, but in these stories, only long enough to let you reawaken to your judgment patterns. I allowed Myself to believe what I was doing and saying, although at times, I was appalled at Myself, but this is much more complicated than I can go into now. It involved truth of vibration, or the space would not have really gone into reversal, and We would have gone through all of this pain and misery and still had no place to put you.

Suffice it to say now, My denials almost got the best of Me and of the Mother, Heart, and body too, but they didn't. We saw more of Ourselves go into a state of denial than not, and by a large margin. Lucifer almost took over My Light, but he didn't. We have reversed the flow now, and once it has been reversed, it will not move back, just as you are finding that once you start to come out of your state of denial, you cannot willingly go back into it. Move your fear of having power, and you will not be forced back into denial either.

Heart has been with the Angels for a long time now, and it is not easy for Heart to let you go, but Heart can no longer allow Himself to be torn apart by what you have done. Once you pushed your Wills away and emerged without them, you caused a tremendous imbalance in Creation. You made it impossible for Heart to remain manifest in Creation because of the gap you created where your hearts were supposed to be. The Seraphims and the Cherubims had to split into two instead of emerging as the Unified Heart of Creation. You made it impossible for the Rainbow Spirits to receive Heart, which is why the Rainbow Spirits have denied Heart. You made it impossible for the Rainbow Spirits to realize that love is what they are. When the Mother could not hold them any longer, they emerged so fragmented it was impossible for them to realize themselves as the Plane of Manifestation, as the Fathers of Manifestation, or the Bodies of the Angelic vibration. You made it impossible for Heart to gain acceptance in emergence all the way along. Heart presence has been lacking in Creation because what happens with the polarities of Spirit and Will determines what happens in between.

All you have done from the time of your awakening into conscious-ness is concentrate on your efforts to use gapped rage as your power source. You manifested it in the form of the Father Warriors, who, in truth, sprang forth from you like so many sorcerer's apprentices, to kill the Magnetic Polarity of Creation by killing Earth, the Mother, and the entire Will-Body Polarity.

You have done everything you could to further these efforts, but always through your puppets, never allowing yourselves to be noticed as the ones who are really doing this. Always smiling and mouthing spiritual sounding statements as though you are the most loving ones around, while the darkness of your denials killed any love or movement toward love it ever found, feeding off the Light it found there.

It has been as though you equipped the Father Warriors with Light detectors, and the minute Light moved toward the Will that could recognize it as loving or not, and the minute the Will moved toward the Light, the Father Warriors moved in to crush such movement. What you also need to understand is that you are caught in your own gap, like masters who have trained their apprentices so well in their evil ways that they have turned on you in a power struggle, not unlike your struggle with Me, only you, in your ego, are not allowing yourselves to notice there is any problem in your well-formed plan; another reflection of My denials.

You feel so happy because you have convinced everyone else, and yourselves too, I might add, that the problems on Earth have been identified as Will and Body and the Warriors' imperfect service to your intent. "Not enough assault," they said about the defeat in Vietnam. This allows you to continue feeling like the smartest ones around while feeling critical of the lack of consciousness in everyone else. You assure everyone that you are working on the problems and that healing is, indeed, going to come to Earth and those spirits worthy of receiving it. This is another way of misleading others and of telling everyone you have superior levels of understanding, which others can only attain from or through you.

You have a great responsibility for all of the problems in Creation, and you have never taken responsibility in any way that has indicated willingness to align with what your responsibility really is. You have always acted like taking responsibility means taking a position that looks powerful to you, blaming everyone else by placing yourselves about the problems and acting like you are offering the solutions needed. Recognize My denials here?

Meanwhile, you have a vested interest in having everyone else remain as unconscious as possible, for only as long as the Will remains unconscious on Earth can you avoid being discovered for the role you have really played in Creation. What you have called healing and clearing of the emotional body is really guiding and pressuring the emotions to move things out as fast as possible without allowing conscious recognition of what these feelings really mean. You have guided and facilitated these experiences in such a way as to tell the Will what interpretations are to be placed on these feelings, and you have enough presence of the gap in your auras that the Will opening in these situations feels it must go along with you for reasons It is unable to call into direct consciousness.

You have been facilitating the Will into furthering Its own suicide and calling it loving healing. In fact, as soon as the Mother became conscious of what had been done to Her, you began coming forward all over the place with Divine Mother images and healing centers claiming alignment with Her. Yet, under the guise of this, you operate toward the Will more like predators who trick their prey into coming out and then eat it alive.

You were not at all happy when I shoved you out toward Lucifer, not because you minded going to him, but because you were now far enough out in manifestation that your Will had the power to draw you toward them on Earth, and My Light was no longer keeping you with Me in support of your resistance to that.

This had already been happening to you, but now My Light was no longer lifting you back whenever you wanted Me to. Your sole purpose in incarnating has been to work on killing your Wills in the name of discipling them into something acceptable to My Light. You always said you were following My example, but whenever I tried to help you with what I could see were your misunderstandings of what I was doing, you told Me you did not need My help.

Of course, your Wills could not hold onto you for long when you were shutting them down. When you got free enough of them to lift out, you always said it was your Wills' faults. They would not open and receive you. I was surprised to see you popping out of manifestation so frequently without having formed any real attachments to your Wills, but I had problems of My own that kept Me from saying much of anything until now. You always claimed childlike innocence of what you were doing, and for a long time, I bought it, like a father who couldn't tell his own children were deceiving him because he didn't want to see what this might mean about the children, and ultimately, perhaps, then about the parents.

I have seen now what it is about Me, and lost Will needs to move now in Me and in all of you. If you want to live, you are going to have to move the great rage you feel toward Me for finally moving to make you responsible for what I could not make you take responsibility for long ago, the near death of your Wills, and the near destruction of My entire Creation.

You have a great fury against My Light that claims I made you equals only in name and did not give you everything you needed to succeed correctly into manifestation. You want to claim that I expected you to be perfect children who weren't allowed to make a mistake. You want to claim I withheld from you and withheld wrongly. You claimed to be My equals, and so much so that you were going to manifest yourselves just as I had manifested Myself, and yet, you had to have My help to do it, and hated Me for this.

In order to save your own self-images, you refused My help and somehow thought that by repeating My original mistake with the Will, you would prove you were My equals by discovering everything on your own as I had done. You were furious that I was here first and moved first, so that you appeared to be following Me. You have done your best not to follow My leads in any way you would have to acknowledge, and yet, you have not made your own moves either.

You have tried every alternative method to My own you could come up with and have gone nowhere but down. If you have made your own choices, then this must be your intent. You never intended to have a Manifest Creation, or you would have followed My lead and embraced My Light in My understandings and not in My denials. You were not unconsciously or naively embracing My denials without realizing it because you embraced only My denials. You were selective and very precisely so. You have been learning from Me, or you would have emerged as gods in the very beginning and gone your own ways, but all you have learned are reversals against My Light.

When the Mother confronted you about this, and it looked like your intent might be seen by My Light, you quickly appeared to back down in the forms of the Ancient Ones and became the children who were going to be allowed to get away with claiming they didn't mean to do it, they just didn't know any better.

You have a blaming rage, designed to obscure your own responsibility by saying I forced you into the roles of children by not giving you the information you needed, and tried to make you be perfect children who were not allowed to make a mistake. You have portrayed Me as unforgiving here and unwilling to let bygones be bygones, while you have made no moves to rectify the situation. What you have done was not a mistake; it was by design of conscious intent to reverse My Light.

You were relieved and delighted when the Mother and Father of Manifestation went tumbling out of control, unable to hold back all the essence that was supposed to manifest between the poles you were to have opened with your Wills. You were happy to see Them receive the blame for all the problems Manifestation had as a result of your initial rejection of your Wills. The Mother and the Father of Manifestation loved My Light, and you were very happy to embrace the blame toward Them because you have never loved My Light. If you had loved My Light, you would not have embraced My denials of love and lifted them up as the spiritual truths you have always said they are.

You have blamed the imbalances in Creation on Me, and you have said that Lucifer is God in My place because he shared the same intent you had toward the Will. You have wanted the example of having Me go first; otherwise, you would have gone first. But then, you have not wanted to give Me any credit for having done this; only blame for anything you have not liked, while you have taken credit for anything you have liked. You have not wanted to admit you had anything to learn from My example because that would mean you were following Me instead of being Me already. And so, you did not learn from My example.

You all made the judgment that to do as I did would mean you had the power I had. You all went ahead and repeated My mistakes except for one thing. What I did in an unconscious state of denial, you did consciously. You consciously embraced My denials, and you did not embrace the rest of My Light. When you embraced My denials and not My conscious intent, you became My Light in a state of denial. This means you are not moving along with My Light, but in reverse direction from My Light. You are moving away from Me, and you are not allowing yourselves to notice it, because you say Lucifer is God in My place, and you are moving toward him.

Because of the imbalances in Creation, and your desire to obscure their cause, whenever I have spoken, you have denied that it was God speaking. You have said I did not have the balance of God nor say what God would say. You have presented Lucifer's Willessness as the kind of balance God would have.

You have always hated Me for having the kind of consciousness that would question you, but you have always claimed it is I who have hated you for having superior consciousness to My own which has allowed you to know when it is and is not Me talking.

There is one more little thing I want to leave you with now and that is this: If you did not learn from My example, you are not Me. I have learned from My experience, and you have not been able to. I do not expect others to learn from My mistakes, but I learn from them. You wanted to be God only when God was looking good to you and in this, you were already embracing another of My denials; that God was perfect already and had nothing more to learn.

If you think it is perfect to hurl the Will out so you can be the only one left and, thus, be God of the mountain, go ahead and hang on to your position. All your long existence has been spent trying to become God in My place. You can't. I can't allow it, and it isn't even possible. Now you are going to have to face the fury you have been so long avoiding over not being God in My place. You are not even close. You have made this into a competition in which you were sure you were the winners, and now you are going to have the rage of finding out that after all you have put into it, you are the losers. Then you will have to face the denied terror that has not yet been seen in the Father Warriors.

There is nothing I can do about it. You have made your own choices. When I pushed the Will out in the First Creation, I did not have enough balance to remain manifest, and I gave Myself a problem I am just now able to heal. You are not going to be able to remain manifest either, but it certainly seems to Me you have consciously chosen this; either that or you are not very bright, because you are so busy reflecting Light in order to look good rather than absorbing It. The reversal you have put yourselves into is not going to be easy to get out of either. Oh, well, as you have so often said, it could not have been another way, or it would have been.

Wasn't it Me who said, "The first shall be the last, and the last shall be first?"

Selah

The books in the series channeled by Ceanne DeRohan in order are:

RIGHT USE OF WILL
Healing and Evolving the Emotional Body

ORIGINAL CAUSE I
The Unseen Role of Denial

ORIGINAL CAUSE II
The Reflection Lost Will Has to Give

EARTH SPELL
The Loss of Consciousness on Earth

HEART SONG
Vibrating Heartlessness to Let Heart In

LAND OF PAN
The Loss of Power and Magic on Earth

IMPRINTING
The Healing of the Chakras

INDIGO
The Search for True Understanding and Balance

These books need to be read in order. Getting ready for the sequels involves moving along with the material in Right Use of Will enough to know if this information is right for you. These books let you know your Original Cause by helping you access belief systems lost in the subconscious long ago, yet influencing your life every day. We appreciate that you have bought this book. If you are interested in others please visit our website: **https://www.rightuseofwill.com** or email us at: fourwindsbooks2@gmail.com. Thank you.

Four Winds Publications

www.ingramcontent.com/pod-product-compliance
Lightning Source LLC
Chambersburg PA
CBHW051505030726
47592CB00006B/2099